TWENTYSOMETHING

ROBIN MARANTZ HENIG is an aut[...] [Ne]w York City. She has written eight pre[...] writer to the *New York Times Magazi[ne...]*, is a journalist in her twenties. She i[...] *[Ne]w York Times Magazine* and lives in Brooklyn.

Praise for *Twentysomething*

An O, *The Oprah Magazine* "Must Read" book selection

"A helpful and handily presented corrective to the glibness of much generational writing." —*Los Angeles Review of Books*

"*Twentysomething* is massive in scope. It roams through chapters on marriage and fertility and youth psychology and sociology and midlife crises and quarter-life crises and student debt." —*The New Republic*

"Provocative information presented compellingly." —*Kirkus Reviews*

"Anyone who is twentysomething, is related to a twentysomething, or works with a twentysomething will want to read this book." —Gretchen Rubin, author of *The Happiness Project*

"Parents will love this fascinating, fact-packed, mother-daughter dialogue, and so will their 'emerging adult' sons and daughters. If you think today's young people are another species entirely, you've forgotten way too much about your own early struggles and screwups." —Katha Pollitt, author of *Learning to Drive: And Other Life Stories*

"Mixing rigorous empirical evidence, testimony from twentysomethings themselves, and the astute observations of a mother and her twentysomething daughter, this insightful and engaging book shows us that sound bites and slogans are just not up to the task of capturing life as it is being lived by young adults. Highly recommended!" —Barry Schwartz, Ph.D., author of *The Paradox of Choice* and *Practical Wisdom*

"If you want to understand young people in the decade after college graduation—their anxiety about work and relationships, intensity of friendships, and feelings of drive and dislocation—this book is the perfect guide. Robin Marantz Henig and Samantha Henig weave the relevant research into an entertaining narrative, and their mother-daughter patter is a pure delight."

—Emily Bazelon, author of *Sticks and Stones: The New Problem of Bullying and How to Solve It*

Twentysomething

Why Do
Young Adults
Seem Stuck?

Robin Marantz Henig
and
Samantha Henig

A PLUME BOOK

PLUME

Published by the Penguin Group
Penguin Group (USA) LLC
375 Hudson Street
New York, New York 10014

USA | Canada | UK | Ireland | Australia | New Zealand | India | South Africa | China
penguin.com
A Penguin Random House Company

First published in the United States of America by Hudson Street Press, a member of
Penguin Group (USA) Inc., 2012
First Plume Printing 2013

THE LIBRARY OF CONGRESS HAS CATALOGED THE HUDSON STREET PRESS EDITION AS FOLLOWS:

Henig, Robin Marantz.
  Twentysomething : why do young adults seem stuck? / Robin Marantz Henig and
Samantha Henig.
    p. cm.
  Includes bibliographical references and index.
  ISBN 978-1-59463-096-5 (hc.)
  ISBN 978-0-14-218034-1 (pbk.)
  1. Young adults—United States—Social life and customs. 2. Young adults—United
States—Attitudes. I. Henig, Samantha. II. Title.
  HQ799.7.H46 2012
  305.242—dc23
  2012018522

Printed in the United States of America
10 9 8 7 6 5 4 3 2 1

Set in Berling LT Roman
Original hardcover design by Eve L. Kirch

To the other daughter, Samantha's sister

I saw my life branching out before me like the green fig tree in the story.

From the tip of every branch, like a fat purple fig, a wonderful future beckoned and winked. One fig was a husband and a happy home and children, and another fig was a famous poet and another fig was a brilliant professor, and another fig was Ee Gee, the amazing editor, and another fig was Europe and Africa and South America, and another fig was Constantin and Socrates and Attila and a pack of other lovers with queer names and offbeat professions, and another fig was an Olympic lady crew champion, and beyond and above these figs were many more figs I couldn't quite make out.

I saw myself sitting in the crotch of this fig tree, starving to death, just because I couldn't make up my mind which of the figs I would choose. I wanted each and every one of them, but choosing one meant losing all the rest, and, as I sat there, unable to decide, the figs began to wrinkle and go black, and, one by one, they plopped to the ground at my feet.

Sylvia Plath
The Bell Jar, 1971

Contents

Introduction

Twentysomethings: They're lazy. They're aimless. They're living in their parents' basement, mooching off the good life they've gotten used to. They don't recognize the importance of hard work. They want to start at the top, they think they're too smart for this job, they've been spoiled by parents who offered praise for the most ordinary things and coaches who gave them trophies just for showing up. They think it's okay to wear flip-flops to work, or to the White House.

Or that's what you've probably heard.

The media have to take some of the blame for twentysomethings getting a bad rap. And I guess that means that this is partly my fault. In the summer of 2010, I wrote an article about twentysomethings for *The New York Times Magazine*. The piece focused on the work of Jeffrey Arnett, a psychologist at Clark University, who argues that the period between ages eighteen and twenty-nine is a distinct developmental stage, one that has arisen from the social and economic changes of the twenty-first century the way adolescence arose from the social and economic changes of the twentieth. Arnett calls this period "emerging adulthood"—which, especially compared with the other nicknames floating around (adultescents, kidults, man-children, Generation Me), speaks to his respect for kids this age and for the emotional struggles they're dealing with. According to Arnett, just as adolescence has its particular psychological profile, so does emerging adulthood: identity exploration, instability, self-focus, feeling in-between, and a rather poetic quality he describes as "a sense of possibilities."

Arnett was giving kidults a fairer shake than most. But the headline of my article—"What Is It About 20-Somethings?"—gave voice to the exasperation that nearly everyone else seems to feel about this age group. The article went viral: number one on the *Times*'s Most E-mailed list for weeks, the most-shared article on Facebook for the *Magazine* that year, the subject of lengthy analyses on *Slate, Salon, The Atlantic Wire*, and *The Huffington Post*. Tina Brown put it on her NPR list of the three "must-read" articles for the week, and the article inspired an amusing lineup of "novels about emerging adulthood" on *The New Yorker* website. And for all those shares and discussions, that headline set a tone of disapproval. I had become, through one line of text that was the choice of my editors, one of those voices of the scolding Baby Boomers. And you know twentysomethings—they're way too lazy and spoiled to read any farther than the headline. (Ha ha, just kidding.)

But Seriously, What *Is* It About Twentysomethings?

Even those who did read past the headline, and recognized my empathy toward young people just trying to figure out how to live their lives, had complaints—usually about what I had left out. And they were right; I deliberately focused on psychology and neuroscience, so I left out a lot. I didn't have space to consider the financial pressures young people are under today: student loans, credit card debt, difficulty finding entry-level jobs or affordable housing, coming to terms with the bitter realization that, for many, they'll never be as well-off as their parents. Or the role that parenting style might play in delaying adulthood, with Baby Boomers making life too easy for their children and having trouble letting go when it's time for the kids to grow up and grow away. I should have pointed out that adulthood doesn't look like much of a prize these days, full of divorces and dead-end jobs and stultifying routines that the younger generation would just as soon postpone. And

I didn't even try to grapple with one of the defining characteristics of this generation: the Facebook profiles, Twitter feeds, Foursquare mayoral races, and Tumblr posts that have transformed the way they think about themselves, their peers, and their day-to-day activities.

In other words, the stuff I left out could have filled a book. This book. And to my delight, my younger daughter, Samantha, was willing to be my co-author. (We asked Sam's older sister, Jess, to join us, but she politely pointed out that she was not crazy enough to write a book with her mother, thank you very much, and anyway she was already over thirty.) I knew Sam would give the book something the article was missing: youth cred—the kids still say "cred," right?—and the fresh perspective of someone experiencing her twenties *right now.* Sam's a Millennial, I'm a Baby Boomer, and we hoped that as a team we could keep each other in check on any grand generalizations about a particular generation, both mine and hers.

> *Hi, this is Sam. I'll jump in here, as I plan to do from time to time, to say a bit more about what it's like to be a twentysomething— or emerging adult, or whatever you want to call us—today. (For starters, yes, we still say "cred.") I'm wary of trying to speak for my generation, but I can at least give some dispatches from the front.*
>
> *Together, Mom and I have spent hours debating every word and nuance in this book, and what appears here is mostly stuff we agree on. But at times we think it's best for each of us to speak in her own voice, so you know just who you're hearing from in the places where those nuances matter.*
>
> *In terms of who I am: well, as Mom said, I'm her younger daughter. (And perhaps Jess was right about being crazy to write a book with your mother. Sit tight for the tell-all screenplay, coming in 2014.) I'm twenty-seven, and in some ways fairly grown up: I live alone in a studio apartment in Brooklyn, my eighth apartment since sophomore year. I've also lived with girl friends, with boy friends, with boyfriends, and with strangers. I pay my bills without anyone's help. I have a 401(k) and some embossed business cards that say, "The New York Times," marking my fifth job, not counting internships or part-time gigs, in the six years since I graduated college in 2006. But I'm also*

*laughably far from some of the markers of adulthood, namely, marriage
and kids. I have friends like me, friends with the reverse situation—
fast in the marriage department, slow in progressing in a career—and
friends at either extreme. I know people who have hopscotched from
one decision to another according to what sounded good at the time,
and others who have known for years exactly what they wanted and
have put themselves on a straight, sure path to get there. I'll be telling
you more about them, and about me, as we go.*

When Sam and I began researching this book, we weren't really
sure where we would end up. We knew that the most dramatic, and
sometimes troubling, characteristic of the twenties is the need to start
making choices and closing doors, and that's what we focused on for a
long time. We tried to find out everything we could about decision-
making, and how the choices of the twenties play out for the rest of
your life. How soon you decide on a career path, for instance, affects
not only how fast you advance, but how much money you ultimately
earn, and possibly even how happy you are. Choose early and you run
the risk of souring on your work, sticking with it only because you feel
you missed the chance to set off on a different path. Choose late and
you might always be a few steps behind your peers in terms of salary,
prestige, reputation, and a sense of competence and accomplishment;
you might never quite catch up.

The same can be said about choices in your personal life. If you
marry or commit to a monogamous relationship early, it means ruling
out sex with a wide range of potential, and potentially better-suited,
mates. If you forestall so you can play the field, you might find out that
all those potential mates are unsatisfying—and when you're ready to
make a commitment, they might all be off the table anyway. If you have
a baby at a young age, you close off many of the challenges and opportunities that childless co-workers, unfettered by family roles, can take
on. If you put it off until your circumstances seem perfect, you might
never get around to having kids.

*I think the need to close doors has been especially hard for my
peers and me, who grew up with the message that we could do*

anything and should keep our options open. For those of us who went to liberal arts schools, that sentiment stretched until graduation day. Choose a major, sure, but don't worry! You can take plenty of electives! Or, as many of my friends did, you can choose to double- or even triple-major, preserving that sense of possibility, that illusion that engineering and French literature will be equally relevant to your life's work, if only you put your mind to it, because you can do anything.

My best friend, Katie, who had not taken a science course in years, wondered midway through college if she should enroll in a course called Spanish for Doctors. She was taking language classes to further her study of Spanish art, and had zero interest in medicine beyond her beloved neti pot, which she was convinced was the single most effective way to stave off illness. But there was nonetheless that moment back in sophomore year when she asked herself, What if I want to become a doctor? Shouldn't I keep that option open, by learning the meaning of "estómago suelto"?

Katie's blatant disinterest in biology might have been a clue that "doctor" was one goal she could safely cross off her list when she was twenty. But it's hard to come to terms with making those choices: art historian at the expense of pediatrician; law student instead of professional golfer; involved father rather than a rock star on the road. If youth is a time of exploring all opportunities and adulthood is for honoring one's commitments, then the twenties are when those commitments get made and when some opportunities, by necessity, get lost along the way. That's a difficult thing to process—and a tempting thing to delay.

Sam and I wanted to show how it feels from the inside to flounder as a twentysomething, and how the floundering looks in hindsight to people who made it through and lived to tell. Where do these uncertainties come from? What purpose do they serve? And can you flounder your way into a functioning adulthood? As we investigated what it means to be young, we read many of the same stats and predictions you've probably read about college costs, student debt, unemployment, and later ages for first marriages and first pregnancies. We've included some of those bits of data. But mainly we looked for things you might *not* already have read, the studies and findings that relate to the subjec-tive experience of being twentysomething. We were interested in what young people feel, not just what they do. So we'll bring you details about choice overload, "satisficing," the quarterlife crisis, the reminis-cence bump, the science of regret, and lots more—including just how mature a twenty-five-year-old brain actually is and what googling might have done to it.

The more we investigated the twenties, though, the more Sam and I found ourselves asking a different question than the one we started with: whether Millennials are experiencing their twenties in a distinct, unprecedented way. The headlines suggest they are. But Sam and I wanted to figure out whether the task of decision-making is scarier and more complicated for Millennials than it was for Baby Boomers.

As Sam pointed out, Millennials have been told all their lives that they could, and deserve to, have it all. Those attitudes we associate with "kids today"—impossibly high expectations for entry-level jobs; conflicted emotions about living a self-directed life versus wanting a family; a yearning for work that's meaningful and public-spirited but that also provides a decent salary—might seem to be unique to Millen-nials. They can plausibly be laid at the feet of the current recession, or short attention spans, or helicopter parents, or MTV, or whatever else people blame for ruining today's twentysomethings.

But Sam and her cohort are not the first young people to struggle at the twenties crossroads. Much the same thing happened to me and my fellow Baby Boomers when we were young. And that has become the heart of what we'll be wrestling with in this book: the question of whether Millennials' experience of the twenties is anything new.

A Quick Word About Words

It's always hard to define a generation—is it a biological thing, a social thing, an economic thing, a thing at all? The U.S. Census Bureau tries to be eggheady and objective about this. They defined the Baby Boom as an official generation, though we're really two distinct cohorts, with older Boomers (born in 1946–1954) having different defining experiences from younger Boomers (born in 1955–1964). The first wave of Boomers—my group, now being called Alpha Boomers by some of the advertisers eager to tap into our $2 trillion in buying power—were old enough to go to Woodstock and campaign for George McGovern. The second wave—which doesn't seem to have a nickname (Beta Boomers?) and includes my kid brother Paul's cohort—never worried about the draft, and by the time they were old enough to vote, the Vietnam War was over and President Nixon had been forced to resign.

The first wave of Boomers gave birth to Generation X, defined by the Census Bureau as people born between 1965 and 1976 (although other, unofficial definitions for Gen X birth years start as late as 1970 and end as late as 1982). They were a relatively small blip; when they were in their twenties, Gen Xers made up fewer than forty million Americans, about 15 percent of the population. But they made a significant cultural impression: the dot-com bubble, *Reality Bites*, the slacker stereotype, the rise of MTV.

The slightly younger Boomers gave birth to a generation that is a little harder to define. The Census Bureau calls this group Generation Y, spanning the birth years 1977 to 1995. In 2008, according to the Census Bureau, some 80 million Americans were in this age range—compared with 73 million Baby Boomers that same year. It looked as if the famous population bulge had created its own echo.

But in 2008 those 80 million Gen Yers would have been between ages thirteen and thirty-one, with braces wearers and stroller pushers lumped together. Gen Y might be a useful designation for the Census, but this group doesn't have a commonality of experience like Gen X. The older among them grew up before Barney and *Blue's Clues*, and their musical tastes were shaped by Pearl Jam and the Dave Matthews Band. The younger worshipped Hannah Montana and Justin Bieber. For the narrower cohort whom Samantha and I plan to focus on in this book, we'll use the name Millennials—not an official Census designation, the way Baby Boomer or Gen Y is, but a group that is of disproportionate significance (and worry) in our culture today. Millennials, as we use the term, were born between 1980 and 1990—people who came of age at the turn of the millennium, and who these days are roughly in their early twenties to early thirties. They make up about a quarter of the adult population of the United States.

When we've talked to young people about our book, and then have mentioned the title, many of them have said, "But I'm in my thirties, and I don't feel like a grown-up yet, either." We hear you. And even though the book is called *Twentysomething*, we're keeping our labels a little mushy on your behalf.

Aren't Millennials a Lot Like Boomers?

Anyone who thinks Millennials have a patent on aimlessness should meet my friend Mitch. After he graduated from Cornell in 1973 (the same year I did), Mitch lived in an ashram-like commune on a farm near Ithaca, New York, putting his life savings into a big pot of money for the whole collective to use. For three years he worked in the commune-owned bakery and practiced yoga in his off-hours, and then moved to California with a woman he met on the commune. That's around the time I might have started really worrying, if I had been Mitch's mother. (I worried a little anyway.) Leaving the commune, which had taken all his $1,500 savings, meant leaving without a cent.

I rarely saw Mitch during this stretch. I was off living my own, more traditional life, having married one of Mitch's closest friends, my college sweetheart, Jeff, the month after we graduated. At our wedding, Mitch had gotten dressed up in a suit and polka-dot bow tie, his curly red hair in disarray. In those days, he was experimenting with Aldous Huxley's eye exercises, which were supposed to liberate him from wearing glasses. But Mitch was very nearsighted, and he wandered into the wrong reception, like Mr. Magoo, and was already drinking a cocktail before he realized he was among strangers.

The rest of Mitch's twenties were just as scattered. He and his girlfriend moved to Ojai, California, where he worked at a natural foods restaurant and cooked macrobiotic dinners for rich hippies. After less than a year, he broke up with the girlfriend and moved back to Ithaca, where he became part of another communal enterprise, Moosewood Restaurant. He met Martha, a Cornell librarian who was a storyteller in her spare time. Soon Mitch and Martha were a couple, and they told stories together for fun. When Mitch was thirty-two, he and Martha married, and they both quit their day jobs and began professional storytelling in earnest. Mitch had come through his twenties and out the other side—and today he still lives in Ithaca, is still married to Martha, and still makes his livelihood with her telling folk tales.

Mitch's story, which brings to mind the stories of so many of today's twentysomethings, is just one example of how the uncertainty and experimentation of the twenties is nothing new. I've got plenty more examples sitting on my bookshelf right now. One is from a book called *"Grown-Ups": A Generation in Search of Adulthood*. It's about Baby Boomers when we were young, but it reads as if it could have been written yesterday. The author, Cheryl Merser, was in her thirties when she wrote that, for her fellow Boomers, "the obvious trappings of growing up—identities, careers, marriage, children, houses, Pontiacs . . . are neither obvious nor automatic, the way they seemed to be for my parents and other adults I knew when I was growing up." Her peers had chosen a slower pace toward adulthood, she wrote. "A lot of us settle into careers, families, or houses later than men and women did a generation ago, or not at all. But why? And how does this affect the way we define adulthood?"

The media hype about her generation, Merser wrote, was that "we don't measure up [and are] in general spoiled, narcissistic yuppies who refuse to face up to the real responsibilities of adulthood."

Cheryl Merser was born in 1951, two years before I was. Which means that her "we" included Mitch and me: Baby Boomers who at the time were in our twenties and thirties. The same goes for books such as *The Postponed Generation* (1986) and *The Over-Educated American* (1976). The postponed, overeducated, underemployed generation these books are talking about, the grown-ups in search of adulthood—that was us, the Baby Boom.

And it's not just books and headlines that have stayed much the same in the past thirty years. Even some of the objective markers that seem to be unique to Millennials weren't all that different for Baby Boomers. Take those notorious laggards who refuse to launch, opting instead to live rent-free, chore-free, and job-free in their parents' basements. It's true that there has been an increase in the percentage of young people living with their parents in comparison with thirty years ago, but it's less than you might think.

In 1980, 11 percent of twenty-five- to thirty-four-year-old men were still living with their parents or other relatives. In 2008, at the start of the recession, that figure was 20 percent—an increase, but still a distinct minority. Among eighteen- to twenty-four-year-olds, the percentage still living at home in 2008 was much higher—57 percent for men and 49 percent for women. But hidden in that high proportion were college students who might have spent most of their time living on their own, returning to their childhood bedrooms only for school breaks but with no better response to offer when asked for a "permanent address." Even with that caveat, eighteen- to twenty-four-year-olds were living with their parents at only a slightly higher level in 2008 than in 1980, when the figures were 54 percent for men and 43 percent for women. And most of that increase happened between 1980 and 1990 (that is, among people born between 1956 and 1972)—which means the rate for adults under twenty-four living with their parents has been generally stable for the past twenty years.

Of course, if it's *your* twenty-four-year-old son or daughter who's sleeping down the hall again, even those relatively small figures can feel awfully significant. For this age range as a whole, though, the rise has been slight enough that some recent headlines—*Time* magazine's cover line "They Just Won't Grow Up" comes to mind—seem a bit hyperbolic.

Once we really dug into it, Sam and I found that many of the Baby Boomers currently freaking out about their twentysomething children living in the basement, or going back to school instead of getting a paying job, or sleeping around instead of marrying off, had similar, and similarly traumatic, twenties of their own. (The job crunch has affected a lot of things, but not everything.) Almost every complaint you're hearing about Millennials was made, sometimes even verbatim, about Baby Boomers—maybe even about the very person now doing the complaining. This realization can be comforting. The broke, aimless vegan baker of today could end up like Mitch: storyteller, husband, brother, uncle, homeowner, tennis player, runner, cyclist, traveler, and just about the happiest sixtysomething I know.

But Aren't Millennials Totally Unique?

Our research also turned up plenty to support the exact opposite hypothesis: that the current economic, cultural, and technological environments have converged to create a twentysomething generation unlike any other. Many arguments can be marshaled to support this point of view. In terms of economics, at least, things are harder for Millennials than they were for their parents. Young people aged twenty to twenty-four are making less today, in inflation-adjusted dollars, than people that age were making in the 1970s. And this is taking place at a time when housing, food, and college tuition are eating up a greater proportion of income than they did thirty years ago.

Graduating into a recession will have lifelong implications for today's twentysomethings. Economists say college graduates entering the workforce during a recession suffer consequences that are, as Lisa Kahn of the Yale School of Management puts it, "large, negative and persistent." This one bit of bad luck can lead to annual incomes an estimated 17 percent lower than if these twentysomethings had graduated into a better economy—an average of some $70,000 in lifetime earnings.

The technological innovations of the last thirty years have made significant impacts as well. Reproductive technology has slowed down the urgency many young people feel to grow up and settle down before it's too late; with the muffling of the biological clock thanks to in vitro fertilization (IVF) and other interventions, many young people feel free to delay marrying or thinking about babies until far into their thirties or forties. And while reproductive technology has slowed things down, web technology has sped everything up, turning some Millennials into highly distracted, highly informed, highly connected multitaskers who are constantly aware of what's going on all over the web, of what they might be missing, and of what their options are.

There are arguments to be made, then, that Millennials are going through their twenties in a whole new way—a little better than before in some respects, and in others, a little worse.

Our Questionnaire

Sam and I trawled the scientific journals for what psychologists, economists, and sociologists had to say about the transition to adulthood, now and in the past. We found some terrific experiments—such as a study in which computer gamers collect money in one virtual room while a door starts closing in another. The young players do whatever they can to keep the doors open; the metaphor is irresistible.

We also sought out another group of experts on the subject: the people who, like Sam, are struggling through it now, or who, like me, are watching their children struggle and are remembering how they themselves got through. To find these people, Sam and I put together a questionnaire with prompts such as "By what age do you think you should be ready to commit to a particular career?" and "How will you know when you're an adult?"

Sam emailed the questionnaire (a copy of which is in the appendix) to every twentysomething she knew, and asked them to forward it to everyone *they* knew. I did the same for Baby Boomers, though to a smaller circle—I don't have as many friends—and with questions that were phrased for an older crowd. We told people that our questions were deliberately open-ended, and urged them to respond with as much or as little detail as they liked.

In the end, we got 127 responses: 96 from Millennials, 31 from Baby Boomers. When we quote from the questionnaires in the pages that follow, we'll use correspondents' ages and their place of residence on the date they wrote to us, even though a few of those places, and *all* the ages, are different now. And we'll use full names when we have permission to do so and first names (the person's real first name, something close to it, or a middle name) or just an initial when people asked for anonymity.

> If we could make flashing red lights here that said "Disclaimer" (note to editor: please insert flashing red icon in enhanced e-book version) then we would, just to draw your attention to the fact that this is not a random sample. A casual survey among friends of friends is a pretty far cry from the scientific method, and the people in this group skew heavily toward white and college-educated. That's why we're counting on the academics, with more deliberate methodology, for actual research. Thanks to them, we'll have plenty of hard data; don't you worry. But the careful studies and surveys undertaken by researchers sometimes struck us as a bit lifeless. They're missing the emotions, self-doubts, and curious turns of logic that we twentysomethings

occasionally use to weave our way through decisions. Our respondents gave us more flesh-and-blood insights. It's not scientific, but it's more human.

In addition to our "snowball sample," as social scientists call it when research subjects are all linked by one or two degrees of separation, we're facing another important limitation here. We know that the freedom to have an extended transition to adulthood is a luxury. If your primary concern is paying the rent and eating, you're not able to theorize about whether Job X or Job Y is better suited to your long-term ambitions—let alone explore Potentially Enlightening Experience Z, which might not involve paid employment at all. And for young men and women who join the military, there are completely different choices to be made, with questions about education and career goals overshadowed while they're in the service, especially if they are sent to a war zone.

Young people in the military, and from disadvantaged families or racial minorities, face a constrained set of choices compared with the relatively privileged people we interviewed. And that's significant. Twentysomethings comprise more minorities than any other age group in America; in fact, one important way that Baby Boomers differ from Millennials is in their racial composition. Nearly three quarters of Baby Boomers are white, but just 59 percent of Millennials are, and the proportion of Hispanics among Millennials (20 percent) is twice what it is for Boomers. (The proportion of blacks and Asians is also higher among Millennials, but only by a little.) Young people are disproportionately disadvantaged, too; estimates are that 42 percent of people aged eighteen to twenty-nine are living in poverty or near-poverty, compared with 34 percent for the population as a whole. So Sam and I remain aware that, as long as we're focusing on a particular form of preadulthood fretting, we are for the most part looking at one piece of the population—albeit a vocal, influential one—to the exclusion of young people with less flexible paths.

Similarly, we're aware that the conundrum of the twenties crossroads is a phenomenon of the industrialized world—and even then there are idiosyncrasies particular to specific locales. In Great Britain, for instance, young people choose their educational track earlier than they do in the United States, sometimes as early as fifteen. In Italy, it's standard for young men to remain at home far into their thirties; in 2002, 70 percent of single Italian men under thirty still lived with their parents. (Such men are called *mammoni,* or mamma's boys, with a mixture of affection and annoyance.) In Israel, roughly two-thirds of eighteen-year-olds are drafted into mandatory military service for two or three years, and for them all other options are held in abeyance until age twenty or twenty-one. And in Scandinavia, young people usually are out of the house and completely independent, thanks in part to healthy government subsidies, at age eighteen, yet they rarely marry before thirty; even couples raising children together often forgo marriage completely. Global differences are even more drastic if we go beyond the industrialized world to places such as Senegal, where the average age of first childbirth is nineteen and the idea of the twenties as a time of carefree exploration is absurd.

In short, we know there are a lot of other ways to be twentysomething. We wish we had the time and the resources to engage them all more thoroughly. But whenever you write a book, you have to choose some doors to close.

The Scenic Route to Adulthood

"Emerging adulthood" or "extended adolescence"? Young people making the most of their youth, or grown-ups acting like children? Whether it's the man-children of Judd Apatow movies or the title characters of HBO's *Girls,* the existence of loafing, flitting twentysomethings—on-screen and off—elicits rousing conversations about whether the delay in achieving full-blown adulthood is good or bad, for themselves and for society.

On the one hand, as life spans stretch into the ninth decade, maybe it's better for young people to experiment in their twenties before making choices they'll have to live with for more than half a century. On the other hand, society needs them to get busy and start contributing, helping shore up Social Security and medical insurance arrangements that depend on the health and productivity of the young. So is "emerging adulthood" a rich and varied period for self-discovery? Or is it just another term for self-indulgence?

And how much of this, if any, is really something new?

In the pages that follow, we'll give you both sides of the argument about good versus bad, familiar versus new. We'll take you through important aspects of twentysomethings' lives—schooling, career, dating and marrying, childbearing, friendships, parents. I'll be doing most of the writing, with Sam chiming in periodically, with the exception of the "Love and Marriage" chapter, in which Sam will take the lead for reasons she'll explain. Each chapter will have two parts: "Now Is New" and "Same as It Ever Was." In the first part, we'll examine which aspects of young people's experience are the product of this particular moment in time, with its economic difficulties, technological wizardry, and extension of all the biological deadlines that constrained the time frames of previous generations. In the second, we'll look at which issues seem familiar, not only to me as a Baby Boomer but to the social and biological scientists who describe what it means to be young. Each chapter will end with a quick summary and a tentative conclusion about whether the weight of the evidence thus far leans in the direction of the new or the familiar. And in the last chapter, we'll put it all together.

Twentysomething

Chapter 1

The Twenties Crossroads

In an MIT lab, undergraduates are getting paid money to open and close doors: real money, virtual doors. The students are navigating between rooms on a computer screen, part of a game devised by MIT psychologists Jiwoong Shin and Dan Ariely. Players get a limited number of clicks, which they can use either to click on a door or to click inside a room. Clicking a door costs nothing but also pays nothing—all it gets you is the chance to enter a new room. Clicking inside a room pays out at a variable rate depending on which room you're in— anywhere from three to fourteen cents for every click. After a few minutes roaming the three rooms, the players figure out which one has the highest payout ratio. If they want to keep accumulating money, they'll stay in that room and keep clicking.

Here's where the game gets devious. Sometimes, while the player is happily clicking away inside the room with the best return, gathering cash, the two unused doors start to shrink. Eventually each door disappears—unless the player clicks on it in time to bring it back to full size. People get twitchy as those doors shrink; they do whatever it takes to keep them from disappearing. They'd rather rescue the door—which they have no real desire to go through, since the room it leads to doesn't pay out as much—than keep getting rewarded for staying where they are.

Shin and Ariely tested 439 twentysomethings, and the majority scrambled to restore the doors even when it meant losing the money they could have earned by staying put. Players kept clicking to save the doors even when the rules changed and the door click actually cost them something—not just the loss of a click but an additional six cents, or in some cases an additional thirty cents. The players *knew* the room they were already in gave them the best odds for accumulating pennies. But they acted as if they wanted the other doors there just in case. Just in case what?

"There is an inherent tendency to keep options open, even when doing so is costly," Shin and Ariely wrote in a report of the study in 2004. "Decision-makers overvalue their options and are willing to overinvest to keep these options from disappearing."

That's what happens in your twenties, too. You want to keep every option open, just in case.

> The best advice I ever got about decision-making in my twenties came when I was twenty-five, from a plump, wrinkled old woman in a small fishing town in England. She worked at the bed-and-breakfast where my then-boyfriend M. and I were staying for a night. On our way out in the morning, we told her we had to be back in Bath by evening, but we hoped to stop at one or two charming villages along the way. Did she have any suggestions? Boscastle, she said immediately. She explained where to park, where to walk, what we'd see. "What about Padstow?" we asked. "We heard that's a cool beachy town." She looked confused. "But that's to the south." "Right." "And you're driving north." "Yeah, but we could go south first." Her expression remained blank and bewildered. "Well, you can't do it all, can you."
>
> It was a line so perfectly crisp in its British accent, and appropriate for so many occasions, that M. and I repeated it often in the following months—about how to spend a Friday night, what to order for dinner, whether I should apply to grad school—always in that British manner of a question landing on a down note. (She had been right, of course. We drove south to Padstow first, which was fine but touristy, and we regretted not having longer at Boscastle, which was truly remarkable.) After M. and I split up, the mantra had to be stowed

away in the breakup file of inside jokes never to be repeated. But it's
a line I still say often to myself. If the motto for my early twenties was
"Never Say No"—go to that work event! accept that plus-one invite!—
then my late twenties have been defined by a recognition that you
can't do it all, can you. Saying no has become something I treasure,
an assertion of the very adult realization that my time has value. Sure,
it would be nice to stay friends with that guy I dated a few times or to
go to the birthday party of that girl from college I never particularly
liked, just as it would be nice to see that seaside village I've heard is
pretty. But it is to the south, and I am heading north.

It's true, you can't do it all. And maturity, arguably, means coming
to that realization and admitting that it's time to start making choices
and closing a few doors.

But which doors, and when do you close them? How do you find
that sweet spot between cutting off your options too soon and dither-
ing for so long that you've missed the chance to focus and become really
good at something? How do you know if you're taking too long to
grow up?

And how much of this is different now from how it used to be? If it
is different, does that mean today's twentysomethings are experiencing youth in a completely new way? That's one of the main questions un-
derlying this book: whether there are meaningful distinctions in how
Millennials, compared with previous generations, face the twenties
crossroads, in terms of both the timing and the type of decision-making.

Now Is New

Ally McBeal vs. Liz Lemon

Career deadlines, marriage deadlines, parenthood deadlines—all the
internal deadlines for adult milestones have gotten later since the Baby
Boomers' day. Traditionally, five milestones have been used to define
adulthood—completing school, leaving home, becoming financially independent, marrying, and having a first child. Millennials pass through all

the Big Five, on average, about five years later than Baby Boomers did. It's become a feedback loop: as the milestones are commonly achieved deeper into post-adolescence, cultural expectations shift even further back. Today's young people don't expect to marry until their late twenties, don't expect to start a family until their thirties, don't expect to be on an actual career track until much later than their parents were. So they make decisions about their futures that reflect this wider time frame. Many would not be ready to take on the trappings of adulthood any earlier even if the opportunity arose; they haven't braced themselves for it.

> It's surprising how cultural shifts in these age deadlines can sneak up on you. I spent a weekend recently bingeing on old episodes of Ally McBeal, which I remember watching when it started in 1997. Parts of Ally's life had seemed exciting to me as a teenager. I was especially taken with the notion of living with a best friend, in an apartment, as a grown-up. Ally and Renee sat on the couch in their pajamas, drinking red wine and eating ice cream. It looked great. But I could also see that Ally was boy-crazy, baby-fixated, and a little pathetic. Those chats with her roomie always came back to the same lament: Where were all the decent, single guys, and would Ally ever nab one in time to avoid old maidhood? Her biological clock was ticking, after all. Those visions of dancing babies weren't just an exercise in late-90s CGI.
>
> So imagine my horror, mid-marathon, when I realized that Ally, in season one, was twenty-seven—the same age as I am. It seems ridiculous to me now that a character so established in her career, with such finely tailored (though ludicrously short) skirt suits, and yet so damn desperate, could be my age. When such a character exists on TV today, she's not twenty-seven. Just look at Liz Lemon from 30 Rock: another career woman freaking out about whether she's nearing the end of her window to get married and have kids. When the series began in 2006, Liz was thirty-six, almost a decade older than Ally.

Millennials are certainly taking their time, as measured by the Big Five milestones. Of course, the whole idea of milestones is something of an anachronism; it implies a lockstep march toward adulthood that's rare these days. Kids don't shuffle along in unison. They slouch toward adulthood at an uneven, highly individual pace. Some never achieve all five milestones. (Maybe they're single or childless by choice, or maybe they want to marry but can't because their home state prohibits gay marriage.) Others reach the milestones completely out of order, advancing professionally before committing to a monogamous relationship, having children young and marrying later, leaving school to go to work, or choosing school only after becoming financially secure.

But those traditional milestones do offer some insight into how people even now typically make the transition to adulthood. And the fact that Millennials are taking so long says a lot. In 1960, 77 percent of women and 65 percent of men had passed all five by the time they'd reached thirty. Among thirty-year-olds in 2000, fewer than half of the women and one-third of the men had done so.

Why the delay? There are several reasons, according to Jeffrey Arnett, the Clark University psychologist who says young people today are going through a new life stage he calls "emerging adulthood." People need more education to survive in an information-based economy, which means staying on the student (and less grown-up) track longer. Even after all that schooling, there are fewer entry-level jobs, which means a longer wait for financial security. There is at once a sense that the years stretch out forever now that average life spans extend into the eighties, and a sense that nothing lasts given how transient some "permanent" commitments can turn out to be. And on the home front, young people may feel in less of a rush to marry and have babies because of the general acceptance of premarital sex, cohabitation, and birth control, combined with more career options for women and easier access to assisted reproductive technology for those who wait.

This is where emerging adulthood comes in. Its hallmarks, according to Arnett, are identity exploration, instability, self-focus, feeling in-between, and feeling a sense of possibilities. Much of this happens during adolescence, too, but it takes on new depth and urgency in the twenties. To the psychologists and sociologists now making a case for emerging adulthood, this new stage of life is something to celebrate—a grace period that grants young people the time they need to stretch, explore, get to know themselves, and get to know what they're doing.

From age eighteen until about twenty-nine, Arnett says, young men and women are more focused on themselves than at any other time of life. They're less certain about the future in general, but also more optimistic, no matter what their economic background. This is where that "sense of possibilities" comes in, he says; emerging adults have not yet tempered their idealistic vision of what awaits. "The dreary, dead-end jobs, the bitter divorces, the disappointing and disrespectful children . . . none of them imagine that this is what the future holds for them," he wrote in his 2004 book, *Emerging Adulthood*. Ask young people if they agree with the statement "I am very sure that someday I will get to where I want to be in life," and 96 percent will say yes.

Along with the exciting, even exhilarating elements of being this age, there is also a downside: dread, frustration, uncertainty, a sense of not quite understanding the rules of the game. More than positive or negative feelings, what Arnett hears most often is ambivalence—beginning with his finding that 60 percent of the young people he has studied told him they felt like both grown-ups and not-quite-grown-ups.

> *That pretty much sums up me and all my friends: grown-ups and not-quite-grown-ups. We can put on biz-caz clothes and swipe into our fancy office buildings, but it still feels more like dress-up, or the "identity exploration" of emerging adulthood, than like anything real. And "instability" and "feeling in-between" plague even my married friends, many of whom, despite having nailed a life partner, are nonetheless jumping from job to job and city to city as much as the rest of us—or more, since a new opportunity for one of them may uproot them both.*
>
> *Still, we're a long way from our early twenties. My friend Julian told me he recently visited a mutual friend from college and the host had laid out guest towels and a guest washcloth for him. Julian said it was strange to see an old friend, someone he'd partied with (and passed out with) just a few years before, make such a parent-like gesture. But it also would have been strange if he hadn't. We don't share beds or towels the way we used to; we tidy up before people come over; we sometimes commit to social plans weeks or even months in advance. We make casseroles. Not only that, but we make*

them in casserole dishes and bring them to friends' houses, and then our friends return the dishes to us, washed, a few days later. We complain about our aches. We complain about our commutes. We complain about our failing memories, how if we don't put something in our Outlook calendar, we completely forget about it. These are the things adults do. But we pack up our Advil and our casserole dishes and decamp to a new apartment, or even a new city, more often than our parents did; we stay out until 4:00 a.m. for no good reason; we ask ourselves and each other what it is we want to do when we grow up; we freak out when a full year goes by without any major life upheaval, because it feels like we're in a rut. Don't let the guest towels fool you; we're not our parents yet.

There are those who disagree with Arnett's view that emerging adulthood is a formal stage of development. Their main argument is that not everyone seems to have one. When I was writing about Arnett for *The New York Times Magazine*, I asked him what happens to people who skip emerging adulthood: people who marry early, teenage mothers forced to grow up fast, young men or women who go straight from school to whatever job is available or straight into the military, without a chance to dabble. Indeed, the majority of humankind—and that includes almost everyone in the developing world—would seem not to go through emerging adulthood at all. Arnett agreed that he was describing a phenomenon that's not universal. People who skip emerging adulthood might face its developmental tasks at a later time, maybe as a midlife crisis, or they might never face them at all, he said. It depends partly on why they missed it in the first place, whether it was by circumstance or by choice.

That's not the way it works, countered Richard Lerner, a psychologist at Tufts University. To qualify as a stage, he told me, emerging adulthood must be both universal and essential, meaning that "if you don't develop a skill at the right stage, you'll be working the rest of your life to develop it when you should be moving on. The rest of your development will be unfavorably altered." Lerner is friends with Arnett— they double-date with their wives, a quartet of psychologists—and he calls Arnett "one of the nicest people I ever met in my life." But he thinks the fact that Arnett can be so casual about emerging adulthood's existence in some cultures but not in others—even in some people but not in their neighbors or friends—might be enough to undermine his insistence that it's a new life stage.

As a twentysomething, I skipped "emerging adulthood" by heading straight into a marriage and a career that I stuck with—and in my case, I think it *did* come back to haunt me, in the form of a couple of bad years in my mid-forties. I'll get back to that in chapter 6, when I talk about some Millennials' experience of the quarterlife crisis.

The reason to fight over whether emerging adulthood is actually a stage is that it can change the way we think about twentysomethings. A century ago, when psychologists started thinking of adolescence as a new stage, the general view of teenagers shifted. Suddenly, people started to see adolescents not just as rebellious or lazy but engaged in the work of growing up. Only then could society recognize that the educational, medical, mental health, and social service needs of this group were unique, and that investing in them would have a payoff in the future.

Emerging adults are engaged in work, too, even if it looks as if they are aimless or failing to pull their weight, according to Arnett. And it's a reflection of our collective attitude toward this period that we devote so few resources to keeping twentysomethings solvent and granting them some measure of security.

The Paradox of Choice

Being twentysomething has always been about making commitments and closing some doors. But doing so might be especially hard for Millennials because of how many doors are out there these days. Career options, for instance, are expanded ad infinitum on the web. Not only do hundreds of websites take the place of old-fashioned want ads, making it seem that you'd find the perfect job out there if you *just kept looking*, but the web also has erected its own new frontier. It's the Wild West of entrepreneurship, where it seems possible to make a fortune inventing apps, or selling handmade arm warmers or eco-friendly party goods online. Psychologists and behavioral economists have long known that having options like this improves a person's motivation, task performance, sense of control, and overall life satisfaction. That makes it seem a lucky time to be young, when the ways to express your creativity and entrepreneurial spirit are almost limitless.

But here's the rub: while *some* choice is better than *no* choice, it doesn't necessarily follow that *more* choice is better than *some*. There is such a thing as having too many options. We'd rather have the freedom to channel-surf than be forced to watch only what the government allows, but when the channels go to a thousand, suddenly nothing seems worth watching.

Barry Schwartz, a psychologist at Swarthmore, calls it "the paradox of choice," the paradox being that something that is an overall good can make us feel so bad. "There is no denying that choice improves the quality of our lives," he wrote in his 2003 book, *The Paradox of Choice: Why More Is Less*. "It enables us to control our destinies and to come close to getting exactly what we want out of any situation." But too many options can actually make things worse. "Clinging tenaciously to all the choices available to us contributes to bad decisions, to anxiety, stress, and dissatisfaction."

Many of the twentysomethings Sam and I heard from are dealing with this paradox. "We're presented with too many choices and maybe a little too much freedom as well," wrote Justin Tackett, who is twenty-six and in graduate school at Oxford, "so that when our lives don't go perfectly or when we're not wildly successful by 24, we think we ourselves have failed in some way. It also causes us to be mildly dissatisfied with just about everything we do, not because what we do isn't great, but because we feel we could always do more."

Mike Lipka, a twenty-seven-year-old sports editor in Chicago, sees it as a generational thing. "I feel like, more so than at any previous time in history, there are just infinite possibilities for what a middle-class American can do during his/her 20s," Mike wrote. And social networking makes it worse. "With everyone constantly on Facebook keeping tabs on what everyone else is doing, there's a strange peer pressure to do something exciting/cool/ambitious with your life (or at least *appear* to be doing something exciting/cool/ambitious)." Your status update about how annoying it is to wait for the cable guy can't measure up to a Tumblr blog of your old roommate elephant-riding through Thailand.

So how many choices are too many? The maximum seems to be

about six. More than that, according to Sheena Iyengar of Columbia and Mark Lepper of Stanford, and you run up against "choice overload," which thrusts you into a vortex of sloppy, expedient decision-making. The more options there are, the more you go cross-eyed from all the factors that need to be weighed; as if in self-defense, you start making choices almost randomly.

Offer people three alternatives, according to one study, and only 21 percent will make their selections using "elimination strategy," which is not a whole lot different from eenie-meenie-miney-moe—a speedy but almost arbitrary way to choose. Offer people six options, and more of them (31 percent) will choose by elimination strategy. Give them nine options, and they essentially give up; 77 percent of them will revert to choosing whatever they land on at "moe."

Iyengar and Lepper built on the older study's finding in a different setting: a gourmet market in California. They offered shoppers the chance to taste an array of flavors of Wilkin & Sons jam, and waited to see who would taste and who would buy. When they presented shoppers with twenty-four flavors, a lot of people took samples, but only 3 percent made a decision and actually bought a jar. Among shoppers offered only six flavors to taste, 30 percent ended up choosing one to buy.

Choice overload can undermine happiness in several ways. It makes people worry about later regretting the choice they make (*If there are twelve things I could do tonight, any one of them might end up being more fun than the one I choose*); sets them up for higher expectations (*If I choose this party out of those twelve things, it had damn well better be fun*); makes them think about the road not taken (*Every party not attended could contain someone I wish I'd met*); and leads to self-blame if the outcome is bad (*This party is boring, and I'm an idiot for picking the wrong one*).

Elise, twenty-six, who works part time in a transcription office in Boston, deals with choice overload by trying to downplay the significance of any one decision. "I feel like I should be figuring out exactly the thing I want to do forever and then work toward doing that, but that's paralyzing because there are way too many choices," she told us. "I don't like closing doors and committing to one thing for my entire life; I need to convince myself that nothing is necessarily forever and that I can always change my mind."

A cousin of choice overload is a phenomenon known as "decision fatigue"—the depletion, over the course of the day, of the mental energy it takes to remain rational and prudent. It's a vicious circle, wrote John Tierney in an article in *The New York Times Magazine* based on a book about willpower he co-authored with psychologist Roy F. Baumeister. "No matter how rational and high-minded you try to be, you can't make decision after decision without paying a biological price," he wrote. "The more choices you make throughout the day, the harder each one becomes for your brain, and eventually it looks for shortcuts"—either by being reckless and impulsive, or by turning to "the ultimate energy saver: do nothing. Instead of agonizing over decisions, avoid any choice."

> Tierney's article resonated with me—and, judging from my Facebook and Twitter feeds, with a lot of my friends as well. I notice my own decision fatigue most dramatically when it comes to food. On busy workdays, which involve overwhelming demands on my time and constant choices about priorities, lunchtime often means standing in a cafeteria, walking in a daze from salad bar to sandwich station to hot buffet back to salad bar. A lot of the time I leave empty-handed, only to repeat the zombie procession at a few more establishments before I finally force myself to buy something—anything—just so the whole painful lunch ordeal can end. It's usually something safe: a turkey wrap, maybe. And it's always gross.
>
> In the 2011 book Thinking Fast and Slow, *which deals with a lot of the same topics and experiments Tierney discusses, Daniel Kahneman writes about the shortcuts we take to conserve decision-making energy, the assumptions we allow ourselves to rely on because it's just easier that way. It's a trick I remember embracing in the college application process, when I eliminated some schools from consideration without ever having laid eyes on them. (And some of my tactics, I realize, were unreasonable; a few schools were dropped because I didn't like the design of their sweatshirts at the online store.) I could have visited a few more and possibly changed my mind about them.*

*But why bother? There were already too many schools to investigate;
it seemed worth using whatever winnowing tactics I could, reasonable
or not, just to make the whole thing tolerable. The same applies to
where to live or what career to pursue. There's a chance I would be
happier managing a tech start-up in San Francisco or teaching writing
in Berlin. But if I seriously considered every job and every city, I'd be
a full-time modeler of hypothetical lives who never got around to having a real one.*

You could do worse than choosing the wrong sandwich, of course,
or going to Cornell (as Sam did) without ever having thought about
Oberlin. Many people do. But when a staggering array of options about
something significant starts to feel overwhelming, it can be all too
tempting to try to put off real decision-making indefinitely.

The Kids Are All Wired

If samples from twenty-four open jars of jam is paralyzing, try hand-
ling the 789 million results for a Google search for "jam." Technology
expands options almost endlessly: there is always another friend to text
about Friday night plans, another prospect to message on OkCupid,
another Craigslist sublet of which to take a virtual tour. The Internet
changes every metric in decision-making, which is why twentysomethings feel such a profound need to stay constantly online, forever shuffling and reshuffling their options. Ask them how important web access
is, and you might be told it's as important as the air they breathe.

And I mean that literally. In 2011 one out of three young adults told
survey researchers from the tech company Cisco that the Internet is a
fundamental resource for the human race, every bit as important as air,
water, food, and shelter. Another 48 percent said it was "pretty close"
to being as essential to life as the things biologists have always considered rock-bottom basics. More than half of the 2,800 young adults surveyed said they "couldn't live" without the Internet; two-thirds said
they'd rather have an Internet connection than a car; 40 percent said
they'd rather be online than dating, hanging out with friends, or listening to music.

The entertainment-providing screen is nothing new. Back in the 1960s, it was fashionable to wail about how TV was frying the brains of little Baby Boomers. But never has that screen been so ubiquitous. Twentysomethings today experience life in a hyperlinked way Baby Boomers never imagined, constantly tweeting and blogging and meme-generating and tagging. The twenty-first century that Boomers envisioned was about flying cars, personal robots, and steak as a health food. The hyperactive growth of interpersonal networks wasn't even on our sci-fi radar.

Having access to an infinite range of options—or feeling as if you do, just because you're aware of what else is out there—can lead to paralysis. Flakey friends who juggle dozens of possible plans every evening, occasionally ending up just going home alone; kids whose tech-driven Fear of Missing Out leads them to ignore whatever is happening right before their eyes if they'd only look up from the screen; the constant pings of something else happening elsewhere—all the fallout of living wired can be destabilizing. This frenzied feeling, this sense of possibilities that explode logarithmically, is what makes decision-making for Millennials especially fraught.

Same as It Ever Was

Thoughts of "Youth"

Forty years ago an article appeared in *The American Scholar* that declared "a new stage of life" for the period between adolescence and young adulthood. This was 1970, when the oldest members of the Baby Boom generation, the parents of today's emerging adults, were about twenty-four. Young people "can't seem to 'settle down' the way their parents did," wrote Yale psychologist Kenneth Keniston, and they "refuse to consider themselves adult." He called the new stage of life "youth."

Keniston's description of youth sounds a lot like Arnett's description of emerging adulthood a generation later. In the late sixties, Keniston wrote, there was "a growing minority of postadolescents [who] have not settled the questions whose answers once defined adulthood:

questions of relationship to the existing society, questions of vocation, questions of social role and life-style." Whereas once such aimlessness was seen only in the "unusually creative or unusually disturbed," it was becoming more common because of new social, economic, and historical conditions found in "the advanced nations of the world." Among the salient characteristics of youth, Keniston wrote, were "pervasive ambivalence toward self and society," "the feeling of absolute freedom, of living in a world of pure possibilities," and "the enormous value placed on change, transformation, and movement"—all characteristics that Arnett now ascribes to emerging adulthood.

Arnett readily acknowledges his debt to Keniston. He mentioned him right away in his *American Psychologist* paper in 2000 that declared emerging adulthood a new developmental stage. But he said the 1960s were a unique moment in time, when young people were rebellious and alienated in a way they'd never been before or since. In any case, *youth* wasn't a very convincing term, Arnett wrote, "ambiguous and confusing" and not nearly as catchy as his own *emerging adulthood*.

In 2000, it seemed that Arnett was right to say that the social forces of the 1960s were different from the forces affecting twenty-first-century youth. But the Occupy Wall Street movement that arose in 2011—with its youthful participants, guerrilla theater, and drum circles—had a clear sixties vibe. The resonance inspired nostalgia in some, contempt in others. As one Tea Party loyalist told *The New York Times*, "The parallels between Occupy Wall Street and the Berkeley Free Speech Movement are too clear to ignore—right down to the babbling incoherence of the participants." Even while dismissing the protesters' logic, though, this right-wing observer acknowledged the significance of these movements, and the timelessness of the motivations behind them. "What matters is they are tapping into a gut-level instinct that is alive, or lying dormant, in almost every human being," he told the *Times*. "And, when they unleash the power of standing up for the powerless against the powerful—David vs. Goliath—the repercussions can ripple throughout our society for decades."

For whatever reason Keniston's terminology faded away, it's a comfort to read his old article and hear echoes of what's going on with kids today. He was describing the parents of today's young people when we ourselves were young—and, despite Arnett's claims to the contrary, we weren't really all that different then from the way our own children are now. Keniston's article seems a lovely demonstration of the eternal cycle of life, the perennial conflict between the generations, the gradual resolution of those conflicts. It's reassuring, actually, to think of it as a cycle, to imagine that there will always be a cohort of twentysomethings who take their time settling down, just as there will always be a cohort of fiftysomethings who worry about it.

What Time Is It?

Although the "right age" to marry or have a baby or succeed at work is later than it used to be, the idea that there *is* a right age for these milestones persists. This shows that the twenties today are a lot like the twenties have always been: the time of life when young people are expected to start making commitments.

Some young people are incredibly specific about that "right age." Amy, a twenty-nine-year-old yoga instructor, described her fifteen-year-plan to Sylvia Ann Hewlett as part of Hewlett's research for the then-named Center for Work-Life Policy (now the Center for Talent Innovation) in 2001. "In my mid-30s, I'll go back to school, earn an MBA, and get myself a serious career," wrote Amy (a pseudonym) in an email to Hewlett. "At 40, I'll be ready for marriage and family." To my fiftysomething eye, this plan looks a bit naïve. What if Amy's life doesn't play out as expected—what if there are illnesses or financial collapses or, like Ally McBeal, she just can't find a man on her timetable? What if the babies she's counting on in her forties don't materialize? Will she be able to adjust her expectations to fit a new schedule? We'll get back to Amy and her waning fertility (of which she seems blissfully unaware) in chapter 5.

We heard the same kind of precision in the plans of the Millennials responding to the questionnaire Samantha and I sent out. Again and again, these twentysomethings tossed off the age by which they expected to marry, to have babies, to commit to a career or to buy a house—twenty-eight, thirty-one, thirty-five—with unironic specificity.

"I could definitely see myself marrying this kid," wrote Claire

Gordon, twenty-three, about the guy she's been dating for two years, "although not until I'm twenty-seven at least. I picture myself marrying more around 30." A twenty-seven-year-old man from New York told us that he was "completely, utterly single," which was okay with him because of "where I am right now and what my goals are." But when we asked about starting a family, he was quite precise that it would happen in his "early 30s"—which made us wonder how he was going to make that deadline, given that he didn't have a girlfriend and wasn't looking for one. And I remember being surprised when Sam's college boyfriend R. announced, when he was twenty-three, that he didn't want to get married until the age of twenty-eight at the earliest. Where did *that* come from, I wondered—especially since R., like Sam, had parents who had married young, straight out of college, and were still together and doing fine. Apparently the model for the "right age" can come from places other than Mom and Dad.

My own inner clock was on Daylight Savings Time, always set one hour ahead. I took pride in my twenties in racing through the milestones, being "young for" whatever next thing I happened to be doing. I graduated from Cornell at nineteen, married Jeff the following month, had a master's degree from Northwestern by twenty. My secret goal was to be famous by twenty-five (yes, yes, I know; it's embarrassing)—famous enough that I could write a check at the grocery store and have the cashier say, "Are you *the* Robin Marantz Henig?" But how would I ever get there if I kept working for obscure medical publications in the Chicago suburbs, killing time while Jeff finished up his doctoral degree?

That's why I was touched by Veronica Lee's response to the questionnaire Sam and I sent out—and took it as an indication that at least some of today's twentysomethings resemble at least some twentysomethings of the past. "I think that pretty much all my life from when I was a little kid has been a constant struggle to find my way," wrote Veronica, twenty-seven, a foreign service officer in Washington, her ninth job since college, "but when I got to my twenties that path of discovery was colored by pressure I put on myself to figure out my life before it was too late to have a family. I eventually got there, but my fiancé likes to joke about how much of a sobbing mess I was on my 24th birthday when I realized that I was so close to 25 years old (gasp!) and had not really accomplished anything yet nor had any clear path toward accomplishing anything."

I wasn't really aware of my own timeline until it was brutally disrupted. I was a few months shy of twenty-six and living with M., the man I hoped to marry. And then we broke up. (I'd say that he dumped me, but my friends object to that phrasing. I think they're just trying to be kind.) I was upset for all sorts of reasons, from the logistical (Where do I live now? Who gets the couch?) to the hypothetical (Will I ever again fall in love with such abandon?). Among my immediate woes was the fact that my timeline was now totally screwed. For the first time, I realized that I had imagined myself married by twenty-eight, and having a first kid by thirty or maybe thirty-two. I don't know where those numbers came from, but it was as if they'd emerged only once I knew they were essentially unattainable, like the numbers on a Lotto card that you continue to scratch even though you know it's now impossible to get three in a row of anything.

I have less of an internal timeline when it comes to my career, but maybe that's because my career hasn't given me as much trouble. If anything, I'm probably further along than whatever I would have said if I'd been asked, five or ten years ago, where I hoped to be professionally by age twenty-seven. And journalism isn't like corporate law or academia, where there's a clear partner track or tenure track with a transparent schedule. I suppose I have rough notions of the acclaim and stability I want by thirty-five or forty, but I think that, as with relationships, these goals will reveal themselves only when I fail to reach them.

The Twenties Bump

Twentysomethings are dramatically responsive to the world around them, perhaps more than at any other age. When older people reflect on their lives, it's the social, cultural, geographic, and historical events of their youth that they talk about. Personal events, too, affect people most profoundly when they happen in youth.

One essential truth about today's twentysomethings is that they came of age in a post-9/11 world, where it was clear that everything can change in an instant, that there are dangerous people who want America destroyed, that the world is small and events occurring on the other side of the globe can have immediate and dastardly impact here at home. These are powerful realizations, especially when they come early in life, as they did for the twentysomethings who are Sam's age and younger, too young really to know how to make sense of it all or how to put their fear in some sort of perspective. The result is that the decisions of the twenties crossroads are now being made in a distinctive swirl of anxiety and fatalism.

But this isn't just a post-9/11 burden. Go back a little in history and it becomes clear that while the specifics may be different from one generation to another, there are also a lot of similarities. My own nightmares, at age seven or eight, were about something ominous called an "Iron Curtain"—nightmares of a literal curtain made of literal iron. I remember crouching under my desk in fifth grade, the noon air-raid siren screeching, obediently facing away from the window as if that would save us during a nuclear attack—an attack that felt almost inevitable. Just a few years later, television was bringing the jungle warfare of Vietnam into the living rooms of Baby Boomers, much as YouTube and Twitter have brought the insurgent attacks in Iraq and Afghanistan into the laps of Millennials. And Baby Boomers, like Millennials, had to make important life decisions against a scary backdrop. How many of the conversations my friends and I had in our twenties about babies, for instance, began with the phrase, "I don't know if I want to bring a child into a world like this"?

Historical events become especially critical in retrospect, the collective "where were you when" that bonds a cohort. And again and again, the events of youth are the ones that loom largest, even decades later, whenever people construct a coherent narrative of their lives.

Scholars call it a "reminiscence bump." The densest stretches of older people's autobiographical memories, with the highest concentration of remembered episodes, come from adolescence through young adulthood; these memories even shape our dreams for the rest of our lives. ("Forgot to study for a college exam" is a perennial favorite.) This is a pattern that has held true in studies around the world, across generations, for research subjects whose young adulthoods were spent in either prosperity or depression, either tranquility or civil war—in studies from Turkey, Malaysia, Denmark, Austria, Japan.

The reminiscence bump makes a certain amount of logical sense, simply because young adulthood is when so many events occur that will have consequences for a lifetime. This is generally when people make the friends they will keep for the rest of their lives, meet the people they'll marry, choose the careers they'll stick with. Naturally the beginnings of these long-lived events dominate our memories.

Youth is also when people's emotions tend to be running at full throttle, more so than at any other time of adulthood. Scientists know that the brain is best at encoding, maintaining, and retrieving memories that are created at times of intense feeling. This would explain why memories from the emotion-fraught twenties are the ones called up most often when you're asked to tell the story of your life. They're right there, easily tapped.

But here's a twist: the twenties get extra attention in the life narrative even when they haven't happened yet. Not long ago, psychologists at the Center on Autobiographical Memory Research in Denmark asked 162 children aged ten to fourteen to tell the *future* story of their lives. Much like their elders, the children had the most to say about their young adulthoods—young adulthoods they hadn't yet experienced.

So maybe it's not a reminiscence bump at all; maybe it's more like a salience bump, paying increased attention to the thing that matters most. And maybe what matters most in almost anyone's autobiography is the twenties, a decade you're thinking about even as you approach it, and reflecting on for the rest of your life.

Gnaw That Bone

Way before Big Bird sang "Aren't You Glad You're You?" in 1977, or Marlo Thomas wrote *Free to Be You and Me* in 1973, or the hippies of the 1960s were telling everyone to Do Your Own Thing, Man—long before all that, there was the advice to "do what you love." Back in the nineteenth century, Henry David Thoreau talked about marching to the beat of a different drummer (a phrase Linda Ronstadt and the Stone Poneys turned into a pop anthem in 1967). "Do what you love," Thoreau wrote in *Letters to a Spiritual Seeker.* "Know your own bone; gnaw at it, bury it, unearth it, and gnaw it still." Thoreau's famous sojourn at Walden Pond was in part an attempt to uncover his own life's purpose. (Though I'd like to pause here to mention that the man so lauded for his solitary introspection also used to bring his dirty laundry home to Mama back in Concord, a short walk from his supposedly remote cabin. How Millennial!)

Abraham Maslow, who created the concept of a "hierarchy of needs," put the need to gnaw one's own bone at the very top of the ladder of human fulfillment. He laid it out in a 1943 article in *Psychological Review* that's surprisingly lyrical, full of phrases such as "Man is a perpetually wanting animal." A person's basic physiological needs (hunger, sleep, sex) dominate his consciousness until they're met, according to Maslow's hierarchy, after which they're replaced by a succession of needs that come to dominate, in order, with similar urgency: first safety, then love, then esteem, and finally what Maslow called self-actualization. "Discontent and restlessness will soon develop unless the individual is doing what he is fitted for," he wrote. "A musician must make music, an artist must paint, a poet must write, if he is to be ultimately happy. What a man *can* be, he *must* be." He called it "the desire to become more and more what one is, to become everything that one is capable of becoming."

This idea, while meant to be liberating, can be a huge burden to a young person trying to make decisions about career and purpose. How do you know what you love?

In the documentary Born Rich, *Jamie Johnson (as in Johnson & Johnson) interviewed his twentysomething peers whose surnames also tied them to vast family fortunes: a Bloomberg, a Newhouse, a Trump. He was hoping to find out how to be a proper rich person—how to spend your time when you don't need to work for a living. His father, who'd been told as a young man not to work at Johnson & Johnson—it was a bad idea to let family issues interfere with business, his elders said—took up painting to fill his days. "Like my dad,*

I'll never need to work," Jamie said in voiceover. *"And I'm not much of a painter. So I want to ask him what he thinks I should do with my life."* The father, in a smock at his easel, responds in a slow monotone, drifting off into long pauses not because he is deep in thought but because he's in no rush; there isn't anywhere he needs to be. *"You might pursue the filming a little bit . . . but you might also get interested in graduate school . . . further studies . . . building a collection of historic documents . . . papers . . . publications . . ."* *"As a career?"* interrupts Jamie, who has never shown any interest in historic documents. His father seems not to register the shock. *"Yes."*

I don't make a habit of feeling sorry for millionaires, but there's something touching about Jamie's turmoil. When you take away the moneymaking part of a job, all that's left is the self-fulfillment part. And figuring out at age twenty-two what career will make you fulfilled and engaged and feel like you're giving back to society—that's a lot for anyone to handle, even someone who grew up living in mansions, flying on private jets, and bumping into statues of his ancestors in prominent locales.

For those who want to embrace the "do what you love" mantra while also making a living, how do you figure it out early enough to be sure you're loving the right thing at the right time, but not so early that you commit to a passion before you really understand what such a commitment means? Committing too early is what happened to Jean Li, twenty-seven, a Caltech graduate student who decided in high school that she wanted to pursue a Ph.D. in chemistry and become a university research scientist. She dutifully followed that dream—keeping herself so busy that for a long time she failed to notice that she was hurtling full speed in the wrong direction.

"I went to Columbia with that goal in mind," wrote Jean in response to our questionnaire, "taking primarily chemistry and environmental science classes, forgoing the whole studying abroad or doing much of anything else but living in a research lab starting sophomore year. With that single-minded approach I was able to accomplish a lot, but I came crashing to a halt mid-grad school with the realization that, frankly, I'm good at chemistry but I don't actually like doing it that much." What followed, at age twenty-five, was what Jean called "a bit of a quarter-life crisis." She finished her doctorate—she's thorough that way—but now she isn't sure what to do next. Whatever it is, she is going to have to deal with the shift from precocious achiever to late bloomer, having lost precious time getting started on her "real" career.

"I'm still kind of in a holding pattern," Jean told us, "but I'm okay with that, having seen the evidence and fallout of what clueless, early and absolute commitment to the wrong path looks like (it ain't pretty). I know I'm pretty burned out and cynical about research and the academic world, and I'm hoping spending some time in free fall will recapture a little excitement about something out there." The definition of "free fall" is relative, of course. A lot of twentysomethings would consider the job Jean has lined up as a corporate consultant to be the basis for a pretty grounded life. But since it's not the life she originally planned, it feels scary and unsettled to her.

Just to make things complicated, it seems that the search Jean and Jamie are on to find careers they love might actually be misguided. Doing what you love might be the exact *opposite* of what's needed to live a long and happy life.

That was the finding of a longitudinal study that began in 1921, when Stanford psychologist Lewis Terman recruited nearly 1,500 eleven-year-olds who had scored extremely well on the intelligence test he helped develop. (This was the Stanford-Binet test, now the standard assessment of IQ.) He enrolled them in the so-called Terman Genius Study, designed to see how these kids turned out—what jobs they chose, how healthy they were, how long they lived. Even though this took place decades before the Millennials were born, many of the internal pressures on bright young people were the same. Which makes it especially interesting to see that the decisions that worked best for the Terman Genius Study participants (fondly known as Termites) weren't always what conventional wisdom would have predicted.

In the 1940s, when the Termites were in their early thirties, researchers kept records of every participant's interests, hobbies, and personality traits. Years later, Howard S. Friedman and Leslie R. Martin of the University of California, Riverside, went back to those early records to analyze how the subjects' personalities fit with their chosen fields. The Termites had been divided into six personality types: realistic, investigative, social, artistic, enterprising, and conventional. Each personality type was thought to fit best into a particular set of occupations. Realistic personalities, for instance, were thought best suited for jobs that involved doing things, such as engineer, firefighter, pilot, machinist, or veterinarian. Looking at the men in the study (because, in that generation, so few women, even these super-smart women, had careers) and following them to their deaths, Friedman and Martin tried to see whether there was any connection between an individual's job-personality match and his subsequent health and longevity.

"Being well-suited to one's job did not always predict a longer life," they wrote in *The Longevity Project: Surprising Discoveries for Health and Long Life from the Landmark Eight-Decade Study*. "A match could actually be a health risk factor." A good fit, they concluded, could exaggerate a person's worst traits, while a less congenial job could sometimes serve as a moderating influence. For instance, men with enterprising personalities, which meant they were aggressive and hard-driving, might seem especially suited to jobs in sales or politics—but when they chose these careers, their type-A tendencies were reinforced, and the stress, bad habits, and constant anxiety led to a shorter life expectancy. When men with this same enterprising personality found jobs that were *not* the ones for which they seemed naturally suited, they tended to live longer.

"Living one's dream was not what led to health and longevity," Friedman and Martin wrote. "It was a productive perseverance, a sense of mastery and accomplishment buoyed by one's career successes, that did that. We hope this is a comforting finding for students and young people on the brink of life-shaping career choices."

Comforting? Maybe. But it's also a little confusing. When is it better to find work that suits your essential self, and when is it better to have a job that thwarts it? It may depend partly on what kind of essential self you have—and on your definition of a good outcome. If your essential self thrives on risk, stress, and constant aggression, and if your definition of "success" is a long life, it might indeed be better to force yourself to conform to a career that tamps down your most self-destructive qualities and brings out your calmer, more health-affirming nature. But if success for you is a yacht and a country house, or the thrill of mastering a difficult challenge, then a safer, less driven job, no matter how health-affirming, might not cut it.

What Would You Change?

Regret is a bitter emotion, so painful that the urge to avoid it often drives decision-making strategies. Regret avoidance can be a reason to forestall any kind of commitment—to a job, a girlfriend, a religion, a place to live—out of fear that you'll want to revisit one of those options the instant it disappears. To many, it's worth losing the pennies to keep the door.

But we're notoriously bad at anticipating which choices we'll actually end up regretting—a glitch in the "affective forecasting" mechanism that Harvard psychologist Daniel Gilbert studies. "Anyone who has ever said 'I think I'd prefer chocolate to vanilla' or 'I'd rather be a lawyer than a banjo player' has made an affective forecast," wrote Gilbert, author of *Stumbling on Happiness* and host of the popular PBS series *This Emotional Life*. "And anyone who has made an affective forecast has found out the hard way that sometimes they are wrong." So it can be helpful to see what people actually do regret when looking back on the choices they've made.

In the 1980s, the still-surviving Termites, by then in their seventies, were asked what they would do differently if they could live their lives over. More than half (54 percent) regretted something they *had not* done that they wished they had; only 12 percent regretted something they *had* done that they wished they hadn't. (The others were mixed on the omission/commission scale.) Most often, regrets over missed opportunities involved education: 77 of the 720 subjects wished they had gone to graduate school, gone to college, worked harder in college, or been more motivated as students. This might reflect in part the uninspired teaching styles of the 1920s, especially for very bright children, who might have spent a lot of time in the classroom being bored. But a lot of it is a reflection of how much about human nature is constant, because these findings about regret have been replicated for almost every cohort since. In study after study looking at regret, people tend to feel deeper pangs about the things they didn't do than the things they did.

The second-most common regrets of omission among the Termites involved careers. Thirty subjects said they were sorry they had not pursued any real career or professional interest, not aimed higher in their professional goals, not prepared better for a career, or not gone back to work when their children were in school.

And what about the regrets over things they *had* done? The top four, named by a total of 29 respondents, were: shouldn't have married so early, shouldn't have drunk to excess or smoked, shouldn't have emphasized work so much, and—and this one must have stung for the investigators, though to me it's kind of funny—shouldn't have participated in the Terman Genius Study.

It's not surprising, when you think about it, for regrets of omission to overshadow regrets of commission. If you regret something you did, there's usually a chance to undo it—through divorce, for instance, or with tattoo-zapping lasers—so the effects of the mistake don't have to linger. (A handful of regrets of commission, such as having a child, are life-altering and impossible to undo; efforts to deal with the aftershocks of such profound remorse are of a different order of magnitude than the more ordinary regrets we're talking about here.) Even if you can't fix your regrettable action, you can often rationalize it with the thought that, yes, it was the wrong thing to do, but at least you learned a lesson from it.

But you can't really claim to have learned a lesson from the wrong thing you *didn't* do. The chance you passed up or missed could have had any number of different outcomes, and it's easy to fantasize about how much better every one of those outcomes would have been. That's why the boy who got away, the job you didn't try, the place you didn't live, will always cause more remorse than the things you did that you shouldn't have done.

> *The junior year abroad I didn't take, the traveling I didn't do—*
> *those are my regrets. Not only did I choose not to take time away from*
> *my English-speaking, all-American college experience for a semester*
> *in Buenos Aires, but I also failed to do something adventurous*

*between college and my first job, or between my first job and my
second job, or—well, ever. When I hear about some of my friends'
circuitous post-college paths, it's hard not to be envious. One of my
friends helped people farm better in Brazil; another organized an
urban hunting club in San Francisco. My six years of office work seem
pretty square in comparison.*

*When my college friend Julian, three years after graduation,
returned from a few months exploring Asia (after a summer as an
LSAT tutor in Hawaii, all living expenses paid), I asked if he felt that
his solo travels had made him, like, more enlightened, or whatever.
Julian gave a long answer that was probably interesting, but I stopped
fully listening at "no." Thank God.*

Samantha's regret about not having a sufficiently exciting youth is
echoed by other twentysomethings who are as driven and ambitious as
she is. "One issue that has plagued me in my 20s so far is a feeling that
I'm missing out," Jessica DiNapoli, twenty-four, wrote in response to
our questionnaire. Like Sam, Jessica is doing well professionally, with a
good job as a newspaper reporter on Long Island. She has a long-term
boyfriend and lives with him in the house he owns. (She pays rent.) She
looks (on paper, at least) to be settled and successful at only twenty-
four. "But I am envious when I think of college classmates who have
this time to travel, pursue their true passions and even hang out at
home," she wrote. Her hope is that if she works hard, "maybe I'll have
advanced my career far enough so that one day soon (before I'm 30?) I
could take a year off and travel, or something."

I don't know. Once you get started on the fast track toward
adulthood—which, face it, Jessica is most definitely on—it's hard to
leap off for a year of traveling "or something." I was a lot like Jessica at
twenty-four, with a job in Washington I liked, a blossoming freelance
career, a long-term relationship. (Okay, I was married, but it didn't feel
that different.) But by twenty-five I owned a house, by twenty-six I had
a baby, and taking a year off for adventuring didn't even seem possible
until I was in my fifties—and I still haven't taken one. My twentysomething pacing might have been a little fast, even by 1970s standards, but
you get the idea; life catches up with you.

Lots of things constrain the choices we make, in our twenties and at every other age, in the 2010s as much as in the 1970s. It might be fear that keeps us from choosing the best, or at least the bravest, options; it might be an earnest but misguided attempt to avoid eventual regret. We might find ourselves buckling under information overload, swamped by decision fatigue, undone by our attempt to make the best of all possible decisions, suffocated by a fear of entangling too soon. But as difficult as it is, especially for a young person just starting out, decisions must be made—decisions about where and whether to go to school, what career to pursue, whether and when to marry or have a child. That part of growing up hasn't changed.

Round One

NOW IS NEW:

- The deadline for growing up is later—so much so that we need a new name for this period of life.
- There are more choices today. Too many choices.
- The Internet changes everything.

SAME AS IT EVER WAS:

- Today's "emerging adulthood" is the Baby Boomers' "youth."
- You'll always remember your twenties.
- The ages may have changed, but the timeline is still there.
- Do what you love? Maybe not.
- Regret is timeless.

Even though we've identified so many continuities in the way decisions are made now and in the past, we'll say that this round goes to the Now Is New camp. We do think that many of the intense choices and feelings that characterize the twenties crossroads have been with us for generations, but the quantity and pacing of the choices that Millennials face set them apart from the young people who came before. The road no longer diverges; it splits into millions of Internet tubes of options. And without society demanding that a path be chosen immediately, Millennials find themselves with time for lengthier, perhaps even endless, rumination. Is that good or bad? Well, it depends on the particular decision being made—which is what we'll delve into now.

Chapter 2

Schooling

The real world can be a harsh place for a new college grad, now more than ever. In 2011, survey researchers from Rutgers University asked 571 young people, one to five years postgraduation, how they were doing. One-third said they had taken jobs beneath their educational level, and more than 20 percent had taken jobs with no health benefits, with unfavorable hours, or outside their area of interest. The youngest respondents, those from the classes of 2009 and 2010, were the most disheartened; nearly 40 percent said they were earning a lot less than they'd expected.

The Millennials raised in the most comfortable circumstances tended to be the gloomiest. In the Rutgers sample as a whole, about half said their generation would not fare as well as Baby Boomers did. But among the more privileged subset, those who had two parents with college degrees, two out of three expected to have a worse life than their parents did—a complete and troubling reversal of the American dream.

These worries and disappointments have always existed, of course, even in the relatively flush years of the Baby Boomers' youth, when Harvard economist Richard Freeman wrote *The Overeducated American*, projecting that the increasing number of college graduates would

drive down wages for an entire generation. But it's particularly oppres-
sive now. College tuition has ballooned so dramatically that it's hard for
students to take it on without going deep into debt. In 1968 a student
at a four-year public university could get a minimum-wage job and
work just 6.2 hours a week to cover the *whole bill* for tuition and fees
for a semester. Today, a student at the same public university, getting
minimum wage, would have to work 40 hours a week, a full-time job,
to pay the whole bill. That financial burden limits a lot of options for
young people: which school they can afford to attend, the way they
spend their college years, and the choices they make after graduation,
with debt often dictating their path.

"It's not like we had a great national debate about whether we
wanted to impose huge debts on young people," Patrick Callan, president of the National Center for Public Policy and Higher Education,
said recently. "We just woke up one morning and it had happened."

Many of the decisions at the twenties crossroads relate to education. Not whether to go to college necessarily—most twentysomethings
have already made that decision—but, for those who choose to continue past high school, how to do it, how fast to finish, and how far to
go. What's the right way to approach college: as a chance at intellectual
and social experimentation or as a credentialing mechanism? Is it better to pick your major with a career in mind or to think of college as one
last shot at self-development, using those years to accumulate arcane
knowledge, explore your interests, and stretch your capabilities?

And what about pacing? Do people do best when they finish school
as quickly as possible, going straight from high school to college, and
then straight from college to grad school or professional school? Or
should you meander a little, taking some time to reflect, so you're sure
about where you're heading and can avoid what some psychologists call
"premature entanglement"? Should you rack up degrees like a hare or
like a tortoise?

And do you really need to rack up degrees, plural? Is it true what
you might have heard, that the master's is the new bachelor's? If you're
going to be forced to take a job unrelated to what you studied anyway,
when is it time to cut your losses and just stop studying—especially
when more schooling sinks you deeper and deeper into debt? How do
you weigh the pros and cons of grad school, and when is the best time

to go? How do you know when to get off the education treadmill and get started on the rest of your life?

Now Is New

The Black Cloud of Debt

In the space of just ten years, 1997 to 2007, the average undergraduate debt increased by nearly 60 percent. And it keeps getting bigger, growing by about 5 percent a year: $23,200 in 2008, $24,000 in 2009, $25,500 in 2010. (In comparison, the average debt for second-wave Baby Boomers in the late 1980s, when adjusted for inflation, was just $8,700, and it grew by less than 1 percent a year.)

That debt must be repaid whether or not you get your degree, whether or not you get a job, whether or not your job is in a high-paying industry—and it haunts you even if you declare bankruptcy. (Federal student loans have been immune to bankruptcy protection since 1978, a rule that started applying to private loans as well in 2005.) For an increasing number of young people, the only recourse seems to be default—the escape route taken by 7 percent of the graduating class of 2008 in the first two years of repayment, and 8.8 percent of the class of 2009. Still, the debt eats at you; if you've defaulted on your student loan, the resulting credit carnage could affect your chances of ever getting a mortgage or a car loan.

Student debt has kept Rachel Mathews, twenty-four, from doing what she might have wanted to do (go to law school) and led her to doing a few things she might not otherwise have chosen. She paid for college at Fordham University completely on her own, she told us in response to our questionnaire: she had a scholarship that covered 75 percent of her tuition and fees, and she took out four student loans to cover the rest. When she graduated in 2009, as a political science major, she took a job with AmeriCorps. She loved the job, she wrote, but the pay was so terrible ($200 a week) and her student loans so onerous ($41,000 in total) that she had to move back in with her parents in Buffalo. Frugal living let her pay off the smallest of her loans, for $2,000, and after living in Buffalo for a year, she moved to New York and got a job as a paralegal. That means she's gone about as far as she can in a law career without a J.D., but she doesn't want to spend any more money on tuition until she's sure that law is really right for her.

Lots of young people are in Rachel's bind. Among 900 twentysomethings polled by the Gallup organization a few years ago, 90 percent had significant debt, usually a combination of student loans, car loans, and credit card debt. Of that group, 29 percent said their debt had led them to put off further education, and 19 percent had been forced to move in with their parents or other relatives.

Debt can also force twentysomethings to put personal decisions on hold. Cait Flanders, a twenty-six-year-old from Victoria, British Columbia, with a blog called *Blonde on a Budget*, says she can't even think about having a boyfriend until she finishes paying off her $28,000 in student and credit card debt. She still has about $19,000 to go. Even with a full-time job in publishing that pays $51,000 a year, even with moving back home for six months to economize, Cait can't afford to date. "When I have a boyfriend," she wrote, "I'm that much more likely to overindulge." She is taking a moratorium from all the spendy things you do with a boyfriend—movies, eating out, buying surprise gifts—until she can actually afford them. "When I finish school next summer, I will have no student debt and hopefully no credit card debt," she wrote. "Maybe then I can start working on answering some of the questions every twenty-something is faced with."

Is College a Racket?

The soaring cost of college, both public and private, and the burden of student loans have led some people to ask whether there might be a cheaper way to get an education—and whether college is even a good idea for everyone. Conventional wisdom is that everyone benefits from a college degree, as reflected in President Obama's stated goal of having the world's highest rate of college graduation by 2020. (That will take some doing; the United States is currently only number twelve, with the highest college dropout rate in the industrialized world.) But some are challenging the college-for-all ideal, and urging young people to consider other, cheaper ways to achieve a well-rounded life.

Venture capitalist Peter Thiel and hedge fund manager James Altucher are, separately but in parallel, making it their mission to promote alternative, non-college routes to success and knowledge. Thiel made headlines in 2011 by granting two dozen $100,000 fellowships to kids under age twenty with the specific instructions that they not go to college for two years. "From Facebook to SpaceX to Halcyon Molecular, some of the world's most transformational technologies were created by people who stopped out of school because they had ideas that couldn't wait until graduation," Thiel said when he announced the fellowship program. (He himself went to Stanford for undergrad and law school, graduating from both before he made his fortune as co-creator of PayPal—but, whatever.) He said he hoped the money would "encourage the most brilliant and promising young people not to wait on their ideas, either."

Altucher recommends several experiences instead of college—experiences, he says, that will teach important life lessons for zero tuition. A lot of them are pretty standard (travel, of course, as well as starting a business and writing a book). But there's one surprise item on his list: learn to do stand-up comedy. That will teach you, he wrote, "how to make people laugh." Oh yeah? I'm guessing Altucher hasn't been to many amateur stand-up shows.

My college education has done nothing but help me, financially and in every other way. (I was lucky in that I didn't have to take out any student loans.) But the college critics have some valid points. The university stint may be fun and enlightening, but how much do you learn there that you couldn't learn in other ways? If the credential itself weren't so important—and maybe it wouldn't be so important if enough smart, driven people started making their way without it—what do you actually learn on a college campus that you couldn't learn by reading independently and finding a mentor to talk to every now and then?

Financial advisors still say college is the best investment a twenty-something can make, and they recommend taking out as many student loans as you can comfortably handle—by which they mean a total combined amount of no more than your expected annual salary your first year out. (Cait's distress at having a loan that was just about *half* her salary suggests that this strategy, while it might be enough to keep your head above water, might not be enough to give you a sense of financial security.) But your postgraduation salary can be difficult to project; how many college freshmen have a clue what an insurance adjuster makes, or whether they even want to *be* insurance adjusters? The average starting salary for new college graduates these days is $33,000— but that means that a lot of new grads won't make anywhere near that. How do you know on which side of that average you'll land—especially when the economy shifts under your feet while you're still an undergrad, as it did for the classes of 2008, 2009, and 2010?

And what if your first year out of college is spent accruing *more* debt, because you decide to go to graduate school? What's the payoff for that? On the flip side, if you wait to go to grad school, will you ever be able to tear yourself away from a full-time job with benefits, and all the other obligations (spouse, house, kids) you might have started to accumulate? The people who go straight to grad school from college— 27 percent of college seniors in 2010, up from 21 percent three years earlier—might have the right idea, moving steadily forward as if on autopilot. Those who take a post-college hiatus often start second-guessing their grad school plans, a bit like Wile E. Coyote when he finally looks down after zooming off a cliff in those *Road Runner* cartoons. He was doing fine until he realized the implications of what it means to be up in the air.

The Master's as the New Bachelor's

Elise, the Boston office worker from chapter 1, was a psych major undergrad, and her original plan was to get a Ph.D., become a psychology professor, and do research. "But I was burned out after college," she wrote, "so I was going to take a couple years off, get research experience working in a lab, and then worry about applying." She moved to Cambridge and started working in a bookstore, confining her lab experience to signing on for some of the psych experiments that advertised for subjects on Craigslist or on the Boston T. She submitted herself to a series of EEGs, functional MRI brain scans, and pen-and-paper psych tests, both for the money (the pay ranged from ten to twenty-five dollars an hour) and for the chance to play a tiny role in "the further-ance of some scientific knowledge even though I wasn't doing any fur-thering of it myself."

Instead of clarifying her options, though, being out in the real world kind of unnerved her. "I'm really only becoming increasingly scared of applying," she wrote. "I don't feel like my undergrad education was ter-ribly useful (it was extremely broad and rather shallow), and I don't know how to go about discovering a narrow enough interest (that I can convince someone to admit me to study, since I presumably don't have any significant background in it) to find someone to work with."

Besides, she's worried that she no longer has what it takes to be in school. She wrote that she can feel her mental abilities slipping, and worries that she might be a bit too old for "intense school work." Talk about unnerving; at twenty-six, Elise is more than thirty years younger than I, and I would like to think my brain could rise, albeit more slug-gishly than it once did, to whatever intellectual challenge I decided to throw its way.

You think twenty-six is young? I felt my abilities slipping as soon as I graduated college! In my first year out, when I was living in Cam-bridge with my boyfriend, R., and working as a waitress, I started playing Sudoku compulsively, out of fear that my brain would atrophy. (R. used to find it really annoying when I'd curl up with my Sudoku book instead of hanging out with him, but what did he know? He was still in law school and was always using his brain.) I also loaded up my cereal with blueberries, which I'd heard stave off dementia. Despite my efforts, I think my brain's been going. In some respects, I'm more knowledgeable and competent than I've ever been: I can tell you a lot about search engine optimization or how an interactive graphic works in mobile feeds, and I can write headlines or edit prose faster than in my college days. But I don't remember a single chemical makeup or physics formula, and I rely on my computer's calculator app for even the most basic arithmetic.

Actually, most twentysomethings are at the peak of their cognitive abilities. (Sam and Elise both kind of know this; they both just *feel* a bit of encroaching stupidity in their day-to-day lives.) Studies show that cognitive function does drop off as you get older, but not until well into your thirties; overall ability, spatial ability, verbal ability, and numerical ability all peak between ages twenty-five and thirty-four, before the slow decline. But a few subsets of cognition do start slipping sooner, in the early twenties, including the ability to pick out details contained in charts and graphs.

Well, maybe it was my chart-reading ability that I felt slipping when I started reaching for the Sudoku and the blueberries. But the more noticeable slip has been in my computational skills. A few months ago, I was emailing with Mom's brother, an epidemiologist who deals with numbers as part of his job, and we stumbled upon my friend's wedding website, which featured a poll asking whether she should go to Jamaica or Europe for her honeymoon. I voted, and received the results in percentages: 50/50. Uncle Paul voted, and Jamaica pulled ahead, 60/40. So, how many people had voted alto- gether at that point? "There was a time in my life when I would have been able to do this with great ease," I emailed Uncle Paul. I had, after all, been in a math-science magnet program all through middle and high school. "This is depressing. I just ended up with $10y = -59$!" (I knew, of course, that an answer of negative 5.9 voters was nonsens- ical. But it was, frustratingly, the best I could do.) Later, I told the story to a group of fellow journalists, wordsmith-types who I figured could empathize with my growing innumeracy. Everyone else was just as clueless as I was—except for the guy who writes about Wall Street, who has to know this stuff. (Well, not this stuff, exactly, but numbers.) Apparently my journalist peers and I have lost a lot of the skills we don't use every day—which means losing the breadth of knowledge that students take for granted.

Obviously cognitive decline with age is idiosyncratic and doesn't happen in a straight downward slope. Sam's uncle is fifty-five years old, and he was able to figure out the total number of voters (five, including himself and Sam) within a few minutes, partly because he's always been good at math, partly because it's tied to what he does for a living. He's also very well-educated—bachelor's degree, medical degree, master's in public health—and studies show that the higher your educational level, the more smarts you retain as you age. According to Patricia Cohen, author of *In Our Prime: The Invention of Middle Age*, having a college degree slows the aging of the brain by up to a decade.

I suspect that what's really going on in twentysomethings who feel their minds getting mushier is that their day-to-day lives don't incorporate as wide a range of cognitive functions as they did when they were in school. Is it really a surprise that people who don't use math in their jobs, and don't have a test to pass on Monday, would get rusty on basic algebra?

Even if time away from school doesn't ruin your brain (and it doesn't), being out in the world can make you reassess the whole field you were interested in as an undergrad. That's what happened to Elise. "Now that I'm a bit more widely read and educated and am sort of living real life, I'm not entirely convinced psychology approaches things the way I really want to anymore," she wrote. "I used to value education and learning all the more when it was 'pure' and unsullied by application; now my primary motivation is to be useful."

What's next for Elise? She isn't sure. She is working as a transcriber in an office, enjoying the work because of the range of topics in the documents she types up. She is taking a college course in general chemistry, "just basically for no reason at all except that I kind of miss school" and to "keep my brain from atrophying further." The chem course probably will not lead her in any kind of professional direction, she wrote, but she loves it—and you never know. She's taking it for credit, just in case.

Some people go back to school in the belief that a master's degree is the twenty-first-century version of a bachelor's, the new ticket of admission to a better life. Just as people in my generation talked about the "college premium"—the increase in lifetime earnings for people with a bachelor's degree in comparison to those with just a high school diploma—the important premium for Millennials is the one attached to a master's. Overall, the median salary of people with a master's degree is 25 percent higher than those with only a bachelor's. And if you add in doctoral and professional degrees, grad school looks like an even better investment. In 2008, someone with a master's, professional, or doctoral degree earned an average of $83,144. That was 42 percent more than someone with a bachelor's degree alone (average salary

$58,613), and 166 percent more than someone with no more than high school (average salary $31,283).

The earnings bump is less impressive in fields already paying top dollar to people with just a bachelor's degree—say, in petroleum engineering or meteorology. And if you're already underpaid—maybe you're a studio artist—a master's won't boost your pay much, either. But in some fields, a graduate degree can make a big difference, doubling or nearly tripling your salary over what you'd get with just a bachelor's. The earnings bump for a graduate degree in biochemistry is 101 percent, and in other fields it makes an even bigger difference: biology (106 percent), public policy (107 percent), molecular biology (115 percent), zoology (123 percent), social sciences (134 percent), or health and pre-med (190 percent).

There's still debt to figure in, of course—although many programs, especially on the Ph.D. track, offer teaching or research stipends, making it more like a poorly paid but prestigious internship than a straight pay-for-credentials arrangement. Still, for someone under age thirty-five, young enough to reap the long-term salary benefits, grad school can be "the best place to ride out a recession," according to Anthony P. Carnevale of Georgetown's Center on Education and the Workforce—even though the average student leaves grad school with an additional $31,700 in debt.

In 2010, Chris Guillebeau, a writer with a master's degree in international studies from the University of Washington, leveled the same critiques at graduate school that Thiel and Altucher put forward concerning college. He paid too much for his advanced degree, Chris decided, and got too little. To save others from making the same mistake, he offered a cheaper route to knowledge, which he called "The One-Year, Self-Directed, Alternative Graduate School Experience." Among his recommendations:

- Subscribe to *The Economist* and read every issue religiously. Cost: $97 + 60 minutes each week.

- Memorize the names of every country, world capital, and current president or prime minister in the world. Cost: $0 + 3–4 hours once.

- Buy a round-the-world plane ticket or use frequent-flyer miles to travel to several major world regions, including somewhere in Africa and somewhere in Asia. Cost: variable, but plan on $4,000.

- Read the basic texts of the major world religions: the Torah, the New Testament, the Koran, and the teachings of Buddha. Visit a church, a mosque, a synagogue, and a temple. Cost: materials can be obtained free online or in the mail—or for less than $50 + 20 hours.

- Subscribe to a language-learning podcast and listen to each 20-minute episode five times a week for the entire year. Attend a local language club once a week to practice. Cost: $0 + 87 hours.

- Acquire at least three new skills during your year. Suggestions: photography, skydiving, computer programming, martial arts, flying trapeze. Cost: variable, but each skill is probably less than three credits of tuition would cost at a university.

- Read at least 30 nonfiction books and 20 classic novels. Cost: approximately $750, if you buy the actual books, less if you buy e-books or borrow the books from the library.

- Set your home page to en.wikipedia.org/wiki/Special:Random. Over the next year, every time you open your browser, you'll see a different, random Wikipedia page. Read it. Cost: $0.

The total cost, Chris promised, would be under $10,000. Bonus benefit: you don't have to wear one of those ratty rental gowns at the end of it.

For all the hand-wringing that goes into most graduate school decisions, a big chunk of new graduates expect to go. In that Rutgers poll of 571 recent college graduates, 62 percent were sure they would go to grad school, and another 18 percent thought they might. A different survey, funded by the Lilly Foundation in the late 1990s, had similar findings: of the nearly 10,000 undergraduates polled, 40 percent intended to get a master's degree and another 30 percent planned to get a medical degree, law degree, or doctorate.

My Son/Daughter the Doctor/Lawyer

Liberal arts majors with inchoate career plans—like a lot of Sam's college friends—often settle on one particular graduate program: law school. They were told by their grandmothers and other well-meaning folks that law school teaches you to think logically, opens up career paths that are otherwise off-limits, and serves as a good credential no matter what you eventually do.

One young lawyer, thirty-six-year-old Alison Monahan, takes issue with this old trope. "Law school is not a place for 'exploring your options,'" she wrote on her blog, *The Girl's Guide to Law School.* It is no more and no less than "a very expensive and time-consuming professional degree program that enables you to practice law." That's the thing about law school that so many grandmothers forget: it is, in fact, designed to turn you into a lawyer.

Alison, a 2006 graduate of Columbia Law School and a self-described "Big Law refugee," wrote that some myths about law school drive her nuts. "'A law degree is really flexible! It opens lots of doors,'" she wrote. "Do not believe this statement. Hearing it makes me want to scream." It might be true that lots of lawyers work in other professions, she wrote, but "it *does not follow* that the reason they're no longer lawyers is because their law degree opened lots of other doors. The reason they quit being lawyers is because working as a lawyer can be pretty miserable, and they decided to cut their losses and move on. Cause, meet effect."

Sam's friend Dan could have used Alison's advice. He was one of those Wile E. Coyote types who just barreled through, heading straight to law school after college. But he never stopped to think about what he really wanted—or about what it really meant to be a lawyer. He just ran off that cliff.

Dan took a job at a big New York firm straight out of law school, with a salary hefty enough to pay off his student loans fairly fast. He hoped to specialize in corporate transactions, but less than a week before he started in the fall of 2008, Lehman Brothers collapsed; there wasn't much happening on the mergers and acquisitions front. Dan was *dismayed to discover that being a lawyer meant staring at a computer all day—and, given the financial meltdown, killing a lot of time. The job quickly became nothing more than a means to an end: paying off his debt so he could do something he actually cared about. He lived with his parents to save money, and put about $3,000 of his $3,250 biweekly paycheck toward paying off his loans, counting down the days until he would be debt-free.*

After only ten months, he decided he couldn't take it anymore. Without speaking to anyone, he put an auto-response on his work email that read, essentially, "Dan no longer works here," sent his group leader a note saying, "Thanks and bye," walked out of the office, and never returned. He proposed to his girlfriend, and they drove from New York to California, where her parents live, to get married. Then they moved to Austin, where Dan tried to find work as a park ranger. His new wife, also a lawyer, got a job at a law school.

Turns out a law degree can get you a lot of free steak dinners and high-paying offers at fancy law firms, but it doesn't do much in the way of helping you get a park ranger job. No one would hire Dan without a biology degree or relevant work experience. After a year, he and his wife moved to Alabama, where Dan joined Teach for America. And they're still chipping away at the $180,000 debt he incurred for a law degree he is not sure how to use.

I guess Dan is sadder but wiser—or maybe not all that sad, since he's so relieved not to be a lawyer anymore. His message to people considering law school is "only go into debt to attend law school if you really want to practice law, and then only if you can sit in front of a computer 10–12 hours a day and still feel like a person." He is whittling down his debt over the next fifteen years, paying $525 a month. His law school also repaid $62,000 of his loans as part of its program to encourage work "in the public interest," such as TFA. Initially, owing that much money without having a law firm paycheck was "intimidating," he said. "But living with debt is just part of growing up."

Rachel, the twenty-four-year-old paralegal from New York, told us she had an "inkling" that she might like law school, but indulging an inkling to the tune of $129,000 (the average cost of a law degree) struck her as frivolous. "It's an issue of deciding what program I would like to pursue before spending all that money," she wrote. She took her paralegal job to get a better idea of what it means to be a lawyer, and was surprised that the work struck her as so dull. Does that mean that *her* work as a lawyer would be dull, too? Could be. And Rachel, still paying back undergraduate student loans, wasn't sure she could risk the investment. "I hate that so many of my decisions are influenced by the debt cloud that looms over my head."

Rachel is wise to worry. In 2010 the average law school loan was $80,000 to $100,000. (Dan's was twice that; his law school was unusually expensive—but also highly ranked, so more likely to lead to starting salaries that were unusually big.) But the average salary for a new lawyer was just $62,000, not at all in keeping with that rule of thumb about the maximum you should borrow. Between 2008 and 2011, according to a Northwestern University Law School study, about fifteen thousand legal and staff jobs at the nation's largest law firms disappeared. Many of those are the same low-level jobs that people with huge loans are often forced to take—and now they're gone.

Medical school is even more of a financial burden. The average debt of new physicians who graduated in 2010 was $158,000, according to the Association of American Medical Colleges, with almost one-third of students owing more than $200,000. That's nearly ten times the average for an undergraduate student loan—and that's a *typical* amount.

In fact, med school is so expensive that it's starting to seem that only the rich can afford to go. Today more than half of medical students are from families in the top 20 percent of household income, and people from the bottom 40 percent have all but disappeared. In 1971, when my peers were going to medical school, almost one-third were from that lowest-earning 40 percent of the population; today, just 10 percent are.

And the payoff for all that time, money, and brain-busting work? Uncertain. Back in my day—or in my brother Paul's day, which is more relevant, since he's the one with the medical degree—the status and lifestyle that went along with an M.D. made it all worth it. In 1970, physicians in private practice earned 70 percent more than lawyers did, 83 percent more than Ph.D. scientists, and 100 percent more than a typical male college grad. That's just not true anymore. Physicians still make more than other professionals, but the gap is narrowing. They earn just 25 percent more than lawyers now, and compensation has basically plateaued. And their student loans are staggering, in some cases as high as $700,000. My brother avoided monster loans by getting a scholarship from the National Health Service Corps, which covers medical school tuition plus a stipend for every year you promise to work in underserved areas after graduation. The program still exists, but only 250 such scholarships were awarded between 2009 and 2011, plus 4,000 loan repayment awards of up to $50,000 each in exchange for service. But those grants were part of the economic recovery act of 2009, a limited-time offer—and available only to doctors in primary care. Most young doctors will remain hobbled by giant debt, which might drive them into the most lucrative subspecialties rather than the specialties in which they're most interested. Debt turns medicine, theoretically a career for people who want to make a difference, into a bad bet for do-gooders.

Advancing in School, Delaying Adulthood

People who decide to go to grad school, whether for a master's, a Ph.D., or a professional degree, often have to put marriage, children, and home ownership on hold. But some young people are in too much of a rush for that—or even to stick around school long enough for a bachelor's degree. One study followed 1,410 Michigan kids from birth onward and found that educational choices set them on different pathways. When they were twenty-four years old, about 12 percent of these study subjects were already making good money in jobs they were in for the long haul. The researchers called them "fast starters," and they looked pretty grown-up compared with the other twenty-four-year-olds: 73 percent were already married, 57 percent already had children, and 55 percent owned their own homes. But the fast starters had gotten to these milestones so quickly by heading straight from high school to the workforce.

If the young people who grow up fastest are those with the least education, does it follow that those with the most education grow up slowest? Perhaps.

While researching my article about twentysomethings for *The New York Times Magazine*, I talked to a group of sociology grad students at New York University about Jeffrey Arnett's theory of emerging adulthood. According to Arnett, one of the reasons emerging adulthood has arisen as a new life stage is that school now lasts longer than ever before. I told the students this. They were unsurprised.

"How old is too old to be 'emerging'?" asked one grad student, Mike Rowan. He said he had all the emerging adult traits that Arnett described, but, at thirty-three, he thought he should be an *actual* adult by now. His wife was already a lawyer; his friends from high school back in Pennsylvania were already homeowners and parents. Mike, though, was feeling awfully in-between. Now that he was back in school, he said, "I have never in my life felt more uncertain about where I'm going to be in four years."

Others in the NYU seminar room were equally unmoored. "I feel like I've regressed by entering grad school," Anna told me. She had been a teacher through most of her twenties, with health benefits, a retirement package, the whole deal. But now, at age thirty-two, she was watching her friends start to have babies, which she said she was in no position to think about for years. Her friends becoming parents "makes a huge difference," Anna said. "It's making me a lot more aware of sometimes having the feeling that I am behind."

Of course these thirtysomething grad students still feel like emerging adults rather than full-fledged grown-ups. The protracted schooling they're living through is one of the reasons emerging adulthood was postulated in the first place. As Arnett puts it, "the spread of college education has been an important influence in creating a distinct period of emerging adulthood," and the college campus is the place where many of the period's hallmark activities—active explorations in love, work, and sensibility—typically occur. To return to campus for another round of schooling triggers another bout of the same exploration—or at least an eerie feeling of déjà vu, a sense memory of what the exploring felt like and what it meant.

It's hard to start your real life when you're still in school, doing pretty much the same thing you've been doing since kindergarten but without the Play-Doh. While you're working toward whatever higher-ed credential is around the next corner—bachelor's, master's, M.D., culinary school certificate—the road there can seem endless. Much about your life is still tenuous, an uncertain future that hinges on getting the degree, and then getting a job in a place where you can bear to live. Adult transitions will have to wait until you're finished with the journey and can finally arrive at the destination.

Same as It Ever Was

Grimly, College Grads Grimly Face Grimness

Not long ago, Kevin Carey of Education Sector, a D.C. think tank, realized he was reading a lot of articles about new college grads looking for work. All those twenty-first-century headlines about overeducated, underemployed, frustrated twentysomethings—weren't they awfully familiar? Since as far back as the 1980s, it seemed to him, scare stories had been appearing in cycles, as reliable as cicadas, about highly educated young people driving cabs or selling shoes to make ends meet.

The articles usually featured someone like Sally Cameron, thirty-one, who had a BA from Smith (where she studied French and Arabic) and an MBA from Yale. Sally was profiled in *The Washington Post* in 1982, two years after she finished her graduate degree. The economy when she entered the job market was terrible, with the unemployment rate at nearly 10 percent. So Sally started tending bar, and then moved on to a nighttime job as a proofreader, which is where the *Post* reporter found her.

Carey wondered what had happened to Sally, whose first jobs were so far below her educational level. Or to Mel Rodenstein, thirty-two, from the same *Post* article: a Peace Corps alum with a master's degree in international affairs, who at the time was stuck in a soul-sucking job as a file clerk. He tracked them down, as well as a few other young people with woeful tales, to see how their stories ended. In 2011, Carey reported in *The New Republic*, Mel was a senior research project supervisor at the Johns Hopkins School of Public Health, having worked previously at a string of management jobs at nonprofits—none of them particularly soul-sucking. And Sally was working as a senior manager at an international development consulting company, with responsibilities that included post-cyclone railroad reconstruction in Madagascar. Carey guessed that Sally's college French had probably come in handy there, something she couldn't have anticipated at Smith in the 1970s. "That's how things usually work out for people who get college degrees," Carey wrote. His point was twofold: that the things people study while becoming educated have a way of benefiting them in the real world, even if their degrees don't seem to, and that scary forecasts about the permanent effects of hard times don't necessarily come true.

Carey waggishly offered a formula for articles like the one that featured Sally and Mel, a sort of Mad Libs for Overeducated Bartender Trend Stories:

> Start with a grim headline, like "Grimly, Graduates are Finding Few Jobs" (*Times*, 1991). Build the lede around a recent college graduate in the most demeaning possible profession (janitor, meter maid, file clerk) and living circumstances (on food stamps, eating Ramen noodles, moved back home with parents). Pull back to a broader thesis, like "The payoff from a bachelor's degree is beginning to falter" (*Times*, 2005). Cite an expert asserting that this is no passing trend, e.g., "'We are going to be turning out about 200,000 to 300,000 too many college graduates a year in the '80s,' said Ronald E. Kutscher, Associate Commissioner at the Bureau of Labor Statistics" (*Times*, 1983). Finish with a rueful quote from the recent college graduate. "When I have to put my hands into trash soaked with urine or vomit, I say 'What am I doing here? This job is the bottom. Did I go to college to do this?'" (*Post*, 1981).

Carey might be a bit cavalier in his prediction that things eventually work out just fine, and in quoting him I don't mean to downplay the panic in the hearts of twentysomethings who worked hard, went to college, studied what they were told to, and are still stuck in some kind of career hell. But his detective work at tracking down the Sallys and Mels of the 1980s serves as a reminder of several things: of the cycles of the economy, of how hard it's always been to be young and just starting out, and of how important it was then (and still is now) to get some education. It would be a shame, in our view, for people to read the scare stories of the 2010s, so similar to the scare stories of the 1980s, and come away feeling that it can't possibly be worth it to get a college degree. Sally and Mel wouldn't have ended up where they did without one.

In this way, things haven't changed much. The twenties have always been the period that differentiates between the more and less educated, an either-or moment after which twentysomethings head out on different paths with distinctly different options. A twenty-four-year-old with a college degree is in a more privileged position than a twenty-four-year-old without one, and that gap will only grow. The less educated ones might actually look a lot more grown-up if you took a snapshot of their lives right now, as did the researchers with the Michigan longitudinal study. But the twenty-four-year-old who's better educated, possibly still in school, and not at all far along the road to adulthood is the one who will likely go further in the end.

What It Means to Be Educated

Education not only sets you on a different path based on credentials, but it also puts you in a different intellectual class. That alone can influence the types of connections you're likely to make in your social, romantic, and professional life.

Whether you can have a clever discourse about Keynesian economics could determine how likely you are to impress that powerful businessman you've been wanting to intern for. Being able to quote Keats at just the right moment can be enough to get the attention of that cute writer who always sits next to you at the café. Knowing something about the Russian Revolution can help you in a dinner party discussion of events in Afghanistan.

The value of education for its own sake (though not necessarily because it would help us snag cute writers in cafés) was how my mother always sold college to my brother and me, since not going to college had been the biggest regret of her life. We never really had a choice about whether to go to college; it was non-negotiable in our family, a way to live out our mother's unmet dreams. When Mom was a twentysomething in the 1940s, she lived a busy single-girl life: working as a secretary in Manhattan, taking the subway home to her parents and sisters in Brooklyn every night, in no rush to marry. But what she really wanted was to be sitting under a tree on a college campus talking about Socrates.

The great gift that my mother's generation gave to mine was the chance to go to college. Many Baby Boomers' parents never got that chance, but so many of us went to college, at least among the middle class, that being a student became one of our generation's defining features. "Today's youth is most accurately viewed through the campus window," wrote the editors of *Time*, declaring the 1967 *Time* Man of the Year to be an entire generation, "Twenty-five and Under." "Nearly 40% of all American youth go on to higher education." In my mother's day, that proportion was just 17 percent. (Today, it's almost 70 percent.)

The 1967 *Time* Man of the Year got busy transforming the college experience in the late 1960s and early 1970s, questioning the core curriculum and all its dead white Western males. He pushed to get schools to do away with distribution requirements; to offer courses pass-fail; to introduce more electives, interdisciplinary majors, and work-study opportunities; to make everything more political, less Eurocentric, more "relevant." But underneath all the reassessment, there was still an assumption that people went to college for the idealistic reasons my mother always believed in: to become better, more knowledgeable, more broad-minded citizens who could think rationally, understand complexity, and live richer interior lives.

That's still what people expect out of college, and what the idealists complain about when college doesn't deliver.

The hard-boiled view is that college is a lazy man's way of separating wheat from chaff—or, as Louis Menand of Princeton wrote, a mechanism whereby society can label its smartest members, much like a stopwatch helps a track team coach label his fastest. "Society wants to identify intelligent people early on so that it can funnel them into careers that maximize their talents," Menand wrote in *The New Yorker*, in an essay prompted by a spate of books critical of the college experience that had appeared in early 2011. From this perspective, he wrote, society's goal is "to get the most out of its human resources. College is a process that is sufficiently multifaceted and fine-grained to do this. College is, essentially, a four-year intelligence test."

But Menand and other advocates of the life of the mind see college as more than that. To them, it's the core of a civilized society, a sign that as many people as possible have read and thought about certain seminal ideas, and an assurance that we all start adulthood on the same intellectual plane. "There is stuff that every adult ought to know," he wrote, "and college is the best delivery system for getting that stuff into people's heads." (He was vague about exactly what "stuff" those adult heads should contain, other than material that "enlightens and empowers" them.) College, he wrote, exposes students to "knowledge and skills important for life as an informed citizen, or as a reflective and culturally literate human being." Or, as his *New Yorker* colleague Rebecca Mead wrote in a different essay, the goal of a college education is "to nurture critical thought" and "to expose individuals to the signal accomplishments of humankind."

Critics say that college isn't doing either job well, neither differentiating the smart from the less smart nor exposing young people to "the signal accomplishments of humankind." According to sociologists Richard Arum and Josipa Roksa, one-third of students are no better able to think or express themselves when they leave college than they were when they came in. This dismal conclusion comes from their assessment of 2,300 students at 24 colleges and universities, who were tested as incoming freshmen in the fall of 2005, again as second-semester sophomores, and finally in the spring of their senior year in 2009. Arum and Roksa used standardized tests of writing and reasoning skills, they wrote in *Academically Adrift: Limited Learning on College Campuses*. At the end of sophomore year, 45 percent did no better on the test than they had a year and a half earlier. And as graduating seniors, Arum and Roksa found in a follow-up study, 36 percent still showed no statistically significant improvement over their test performance as freshmen.

Many of them seem to have been too preoccupied to learn anything. In a typical week, according to Arum and Roksa, students spent about half their time in leisure activities including eating and socializing, one quarter of their time sleeping, and one quarter of their time on other activities: going to class, studying, working for pay, and volunteering. With all these commitments, the average amount of time spent studying was a little over twelve hours a week.

The ones who lagged furthest behind, who learned the least from the day they set foot on campus until the day they graduated, were the students who had majored in business—the most popular undergraduate major in America.

In a way, though, this is the outcome everybody is looking for. As the authors explained, students want a full college experience that focuses on social life as much as schoolwork; parents want a safe environment where their kids can mature, become independent, and get an important credential; professors want a chance to do their research; government agencies want to generate new knowledge, which comes from professors doing their research; administrators want to boost both their rankings and their bottom line. None of those goals really says anything about improving the writing and reasoning skills of eighteen- to twenty-two-year-olds. "The institutional actors implicated in the system are receiving the organization outcomes they seek," wrote Arum and Roksa. "In short, the system works." It's a cynical view, maybe, but it's probably also a realistic one.

On the plus side, Arum and Roksa found that the students in their study had high ambitions, with more than one-third aspiring to own their own business. On the minus side, even the kids who said they had goals had "no clear life plan for reaching them," and among the would-be business owners "there was little evidence that entrepreneurial skills were being developed" while they were in school.

That's the real problem with a college education, the critics say, and the real reason so many people express uncertainty about its value: it doesn't teach people what they need to know to make it in the world. The lockstep "track" of being in school is over, as Sara, twenty-five, who lives in Brooklyn and works for a fashion photographer, told us with some regret. "The big decisions before were what classes, what school, what major. Now it's all wide open." She listed all the Big Questions she's wrestling with now, which she feels not quite equal to: "Who do you want to be? Where do you want to live? What do you want your life to mean? What do you want to do? How the hell do you make a living doing it? (And, while I truly value my liberal arts education, why didn't anyone prepare me with life skills?)"

It might seem this dissatisfaction is new. But being a discombobulated young person always feels new, just as young lovers always think that no one has ever loved as deeply. Baby Boomers, too, were plagued by troubles balancing the quest for knowledge, no matter how esoteric, with the need to learn the basic facts of life. Author James S. Kunin, Columbia class of 1970, wrote that he and his friends used to joke that there should be an undergraduate course called Fundamentals of Reality. They imagined the catalogue listing, "Spring term: *Selected Problems in Living.* Emphasized are taxes, insurance, automotive legal problems, sub-leases, contracts, credit, birth control, venereal disease, zoning, local government, divorce, social behavior, job-seeking and unemployment." I could have used such a course at Cornell, and I would have signed up if I hadn't been racing to graduate in three years to save a year's tuition. Even in the Baby Boomers' day, twentysomethings felt blindsided once we left the campus cocoon and realized how much we had still to learn.

It's Still a Smart Investment

For the Baby Boomers, a bachelor's degree was a ticket onto the gravy train of the American Dream. When my class graduated in 1973, a full-time worker with a bachelor's degree earned 40 percent more than a worker the same age with only a high school diploma.

The financial benefit of college has actually doubled since my day, with college graduates today earning on average 83 percent more than people whose education stopped after high school. The average college graduate makes about $33,000 a year at age twenty-two, right out of school—which is about what the average high school graduate earns at age fifty, at the height of his or her earning potential. Over a lifetime, a typical college graduate is said to earn about $800,000 more than a typical high school graduate. In some fields, such as engineering, the difference can be as high as $1.9 million.

Even taking into account the staggering increase in the cost of a college education, it's still considered just about the wisest financial decision a twentysomething can make. Figuring in tuition, fees, and living expenses, plus the "opportunity cost" of not working during those four years, versus the return of a higher salary for the rest of a college grad's working life, economists at the Brookings Institution recently calculated the return on investment in a college education at 15.2 percent—"more than double the average return to stock market investments since 1950, and more than five times the returns to corporate bonds, gold, long-term government bonds, or home ownership." If you have $102,000 available—about the average total cost of a four-year public or private university education—this is the place to put it.

No matter how such calculations turn out, though, for a new college grad whose job offers are nothing but uninspiring, the belief that college was "worth it" can be a leap of faith. This is as true today as it was in 1982, when *The Washington Post* was running stories about the young Sally Camerons and Mel Rodensteins of the world. But now there are even snazzier labels for the overeducated, underemployed young twentysomethings—such as the one *The New York Times* came up with recently: Generation Limbo.

Generation Limbo includes Amy Klein, who graduated from Harvard in 2007 intending to work in publishing. Her timing was terrible: she applied for a job at *Gourmet* magazine just two weeks before it folded, and the rest of the industry seemed to be teetering on the brink. On a whim, she joined a friend's punk/indie band, Titus Andronicus, and went on a national tour. When she spoke to *Times* reporter Jennifer 8. Lee four years after graduation, Amy focused on Limbo's silver lining. "Plenty of people work in bookstores and work in low-end administrative jobs, even though they have a Harvard degree," she said. "They are thinking more in terms of creating their own kind of life that interests them, rather than following a conventional idea of success and job security."

But Lee talked to plenty of pissed-off Limbo-ers, too. "What was the point of working so hard for twenty-two years if there was nothing out there?" asked Stephanie Morales, twenty-three, a 2009 Dartmouth grad who had hoped to work in the arts, but instead was a waitress and a paralegal and was applying to law school. "It's horrible," said Benjamin Shore, twenty-three, who graduated from the University of Maryland in 2010—with a business degree, which you'd think would have led to a decent job somewhere—and ended up working at a call center and then as a dock hand. "I have a college education that I feel like I am wasting," he told Lee. "I am supposed to do something interesting, something with my brain."

Same Old Song

The limbo-like period being called emerging adulthood is not the first developmental stage said to arise as a result of widespread higher education. In fact, the link between schooling and a slower road to adulthood is a familiar refrain. It happened more than a century ago— back in the early 1900s, when psychology discovered adolescence.

The extra schooling in those days was high school. Mandatory schooling through the age of sixteen was to blame for a new, emotionally turbulent stage of development, wrote G. Stanley Hall in 1904 in his massive two-volume *Adolescence: Its Psychology, and Its Relation to Physiology, Anthropology, Sociology, Sex, Crimes, Religion and Education.* Hall, a prominent American psychologist, attributed adolescence to social changes at the turn of the twentieth century, among them the trend of staying in school until the late teens. Beginning in the 1880s, the child labor protection movement started demanding, and getting, state laws that prohibited children under fourteen or fifteen from holding full-time jobs. At around the same time, compulsory education laws kept kids in school until sixteen, and in some states even longer. During this new, protracted period of dependency, teens were able to address a distinct set of psychological tasks that they'd ignored when they were expected to take on adult roles straight out of childhood.

Hall saw this new stage as a time of "storm and stress," filled with emotional upheaval, mood swings, and rebelliousness. He described a "curve of despondency" that "starts at eleven, rises steadily and rapidly till fifteen, then falls steadily till twenty three." This stage of life, he wrote, also brought an increase in sensation seeking, susceptibility to media influences (which in 1904 mostly meant tawdry fiction, such as "penny dreadfuls"), and excessive reliance on peers.

Although Hall is considered the father of adolescence, he also went through emerging adulthood with a vengeance. After graduating from Williams College, he wrote home that he didn't want to be a pastor, as had been the plan, and instead headed to New York, and then to Germany to study philosophy. That's when his father wrote to him, "Just *what* are you doing?" Getting a Ph.D. in philosophy, Hall told his parents—or at least thinking about it. "Now Stanley," wrote his mother, "wherein is the great benefit of being a Ph.D.? I think a *preacher* should be a D.D. Just *what is* a Doctor of Philosophy?"

Hall did go on to get that Ph.D., but not until he ran out of money in Germany, came back to the United States to work and take classes at Antioch College, and transferred to Harvard. He was thirty-four and still unmarried, and the degree wasn't in philosophy, after all, but in psychology—the first such doctorate to be awarded to an American.

Like the teenagers in Hall's day, today's twentysomethings are staying in school for longer periods than their elders did—and their slower timetables are freaking their parents out. If emerging adulthood is in fact a new developmental stage (and, as we discussed in chapter 1, that remains an open question), it has implications not only for decisions about schooling, but for many of the other decision points at the twenties crossroads. A glass-half-full person would see this longer stretch of schooling and life prep as mostly a benefit, a chance for young people to assess their options and make the right choice about what they want to do with their lives, where they want to do it, and whom they want to do it with. A longer stretch of exploration and self-reflection might lead them to discover what truly matters to them—and might help them avoid the pitfalls that await those, like Sam's friend Dan, who hurtle too quickly into the world of work.

Round Two

NOW IS NEW:

- Higher education costs way more than it used to.
- That means more debt holding young people back.
- Advanced degrees now feel like a necessity.
- Which means even more debt—and feeling like a kid for longer.

SAME AS IT EVER WAS:

- Scare stories about how college isn't "worth it" have appeared for decades.
- College is still supposed to be all about becoming educated.

- And it's still a good investment.
- More school leads to delayed adulthood—where have we heard this one before?

We're impressed by the similarities that keep cropping up between descriptions of Millennials' higher education experiences and contemporaneous descriptions of the Baby Boomers', in terms of both the goals of education and the difficulty in finding jobs. But we're more swayed by the way overwhelming college expenses and crushing student debt, combined with the dire economic outlook, color so many decisions of today's young people. Because of that, we think that this round goes to the camp of Now Is New.

Chapter 3

Career Choices

It's not for nothing that they call it a curriculum vitae. The phrase is Latin for "the course of one's life," and "life" here is used interchangeably with "work." For many of us, that's how it feels: we are what we do, our work defines us, and switching jobs is like switching identities. Since people change jobs in their twenties more than they will in any other decade—seven times on average, two-thirds of all the job changes in a typical career—this can be, to put it mildly, an unsettling time.

"I did tons of small stuff, especially just after college," wrote Hannah Fischer-Baum, thirty-two, in response to our questionnaire. "Small writing gigs, short-term consultancy, researching for professors, nannying." Hannah moved to Paris right after graduation, to teach English in a French high school, but she felt unmoored: "It was scary having a whole life in front of me, no sense of how to fill it, and high expectations for whatever it was going to be. It was ultimately more soul searching than I could handle. I so disliked that feeling that I launched myself rather haphazardly into a career." She enrolled in graduate school in urban planning, got a master's degree, took a job with a design and landscape architecture firm, and after two years there, moved to a job at the New York City planning department. At work these days she's "happy and engaged over half the time," she wrote, which she thinks is a pretty good ratio.

Karen Robichaud, twenty-five, of Boston, has done a little bit of everything. She graduated in the spring of 2008 and moved back home with her parents, during which time she worked "as a stage manager, an office assistant for an eye doctor, an administrative assistant at a small theatre company, a babysitter, and in a box office." In the middle of all that she met a guy, and a year later they moved in together and got engaged. That's when she started full time at a nonprofit performing arts company. As staffing and company demands changed, so did her job; she began in the subscription box office and is now in the marketing department, and she hopes to learn more about graphic and web design. "I don't think I need to commit to a career path at a certain age," Karen told us. "I sort of fell into what I'm doing now and I enjoy it and it works for me."

A recitation of job-hopping is a quick way to convey the fitful feelings of one's twenties. The job-hopping itself is, in many ways, the *reason* for those feelings, turning people in their mid-twenties into "emerging adults" in the same way grad school does. If you don't know yet what you want to do, or if you don't yet do the thing you know you want, it's harder to have an accurate picture of who you are. For many people—including Sam and me and other well-educated, well-off, workaholic Americans—the "Who am I?" question boils down to the question of "What's my job description?"

That's why career decisions in the twenties are so daunting: they can have awfully long tails. Choices that seem to be about money— *what kind of career do I want? how much can I earn? how much do I* want *to earn? how should I spend it?*—are actually choices that go much deeper than that. The way we make and spend money is essentially the way we live, and decisions about career path are decisions about what kind of life that will be.

Now Is New

It's the Economy, Stupid

The recession has done a number on the job choices of Millennials. Just how much of a number can be seen in the results of a poll of 872 people commissioned by the youth advocacy groups Demos and Young

Invincibles. Participants were divided into two age groups, eighteen to twenty-four, and twenty-five to thirty-four. Among the troubling findings:

- Only 53 percent of workers aged 25 to 34 earned more in 2011 than they did four years earlier.
- Only 47 percent of workers aged 25 to 34 earned more than $30,000 a year.
- Rent for 18- to 24-year-olds took a much bigger bite of pre-tax income in 2009 (32.1 percent) than it had for their parents in 1980 (23.7 percent).
- The same was true for 25- to 34-year-olds: the proportion whose rent was more than 30 percent of their pre-tax income was much higher in 2009 (41.3 percent) than it was when their parents were young in 1980 (28 percent).
- The recession hit younger people harder than others: compared with pre-recession unemployment rates, unemployment rates in 2010 were 4.4 percent higher for workers over 35, 5.4 percent higher for workers 25 to 34, and 7.7 percent higher for workers under 24.
- A significant proportion of the young people polled—54 percent of those who had some college, 33 percent with four-year college degrees, 29 percent with graduate degrees—said they were not working in their chosen profession.
- Money woes had caused 46 percent of the survey respondents to delay purchasing a home, 30 percent to delay starting a family, and 25 percent to delay getting married.
- Iraq war veterans aged 18 to 24 (of whom there were 2.2 million that year) were doing worse than other people their age: their unemployment rate was 20.9 percent, 11 percent higher than the unemployment rate in general and 3.6 percent higher than the unemployment rate for all 18- to 24-year-olds.

Things are even worse in Europe. Youth unemployment there has reached staggering levels, the kind that can destabilize a society: 22

percent in England for sixteen- to twenty-four-year-olds, 30 percent in Italy, 30 percent in Portugal, 48 percent in Greece, 48.7 percent in Spain. (These figures were from late 2011, when the comparable rate in the United States was 18 percent, which was bad enough.) Massive unemployment was "feeding a mounting alienation and anger among young people across Europe," wrote *The New York Times*'s financial correspondent Landon Thomas Jr., and it was fueling what he called an "animus that threatens to poison the aspirations of a generation and has already served as a wellspring for a number of violent protests in European cities from Athens to London."

It's not as if today's twentysomethings will wake up in their thirties to a revived economy, either. Forecasters in 2011 expected that the unemployment rate would stay above 7 percent until 2015, and probably wouldn't drop below 6 percent for the foreseeable future. Maybe that's why, when the young people in the Demos survey were asked if they thought their generation would do better than their parents did, 88 percent said no.

This is something new for Millennials, the sad and unprecedented twisting of a basic tenet of the American Dream, that parents could always count on watching their kids grow up to surpass them.

Career Rules Turned Topsy-Turvy

Not only has the dream itself been turned upside down; so have a lot of common career tropes, such as "Start at the bottom and work your way to the top" or "Some job is better than no job." Lots of parents are using these old saws to get their twentysomething children to take what they can get and stop whining. But what worked for the parents, who were starting their careers back in the 1970s, might not work anymore. According to some economists, the rules have changed for Millennials.

"The recent evidence shows quite clearly that in today's economy starting at the bottom is a recipe for being underpaid for a long time to come," Austan Goolsbee of the University of Chicago wrote in 2006. Goolsbee, who later served on President Obama's Council of Economic Advisers, said the traditional advice for young people—work hard, pay your dues, move steadily up the corporate ladder—is bad advice. "While they may work their way up, the people who started above them do, too," he wrote. "They don't catch up." In today's tough economy, the first job sets the bar for all subsequent jobs. And there's no place for old-fashioned corporate loyalty anymore, either; the best strategy for career advancement, Goolsbee wrote, is to "forget about rising up the ladder and, instead, jump ship to other employers."

Here's a statistic to think about: two-thirds of the wage growth that happens in the course of a career occurs in the first ten years. The easiest way to cash in on that fast, early growth is to move from your first entry-level job to subsequent, better jobs in the same field. But if you are still testing out careers in your twenties, and spend those ten years bopping around from one entry-level job to another because you keep changing your mind about *which* ladder you want to climb, it's a lot harder to get as high. This doesn't mean you shouldn't switch careers if that feels right; it just means you should be aware that every decision has a cost. Choosing to try out a succession of different career options means you'll always be a few steps behind your contemporaries—something that matters a lot at the beginning.

That's what happened to Maree, who didn't settle on journalism until she was twenty-nine. "It's a little hard sometimes," she told us, to be a novice reporter when other people her age (thirty-three) are already eight or ten years into their careers. When she first graduated from college, Maree went into corporate consulting. Then she spent a few years in the foreign service, and then went to graduate school for a master's in public policy. Only then did she decide that her real calling was journalism. "I'm very glad I've had really varied professional experience," she wrote in response to our questionnaire. "I think it helps me know when I'm truly happy." But there were definite trade-offs. Four years into her journalism career, her salary and position are lower than they would have been if she had stuck with the career she began with—and lower than they would have been if she had settled on journalism from the start.

Katherine Goldstein *had* settled on journalism from the start—but when she was ready, fresh out of college in 2006, jobs were scarce. So she began working for a catering company for twenty dollars an hour—she had bills to pay and loan payments to make—and found that a crap job can be an unexpected gift. "Everyone I know had a crap job in their 20s," Katherine wrote five years later on *Slate*. "It was a frustrating, 'welcome to reality' experience for perky college grads." Her co-workers were creative types (painters, writers, actors) whose identities were not wrapped up in their day jobs. This was new for Katherine. "I had such a tunnel-vision focus on becoming a successful writer as soon as possible that it made me realize that . . . just because I wasn't writing for the *New York Times* by the time I was 23 didn't mean I was headed for failure." She found the realization comforting, but also motivation to keep moving. Within a year, she had found a better job.

My parents tend to give good career advice, especially as a team: Dad is wise about negotiation and office politics, and Mom understands the world of media. (In some ways, though, it's like getting sex tips from virgins; my father has changed jobs just once in thirty-five years as a professor, and my mother has been self-employed my entire life.) Mostly they're just there as a sounding board. But during my last job-change angst, my father said something that stuck with me. He warned me not to get too caught up in how I imagined the new job would be, since it no doubt looked shinier in my mind than the job I already had, simply because it was a fantasy.

I think this is especially useful advice for people in their twenties. We're more likely to get swept up in the allure of the unknown. In part it's because we're less risk-averse and have less to lose by starting over. In part it's because we often feel trodden-upon in our current jobs, and the courtship of a new place can be very seductive. But the thing you don't have isn't always better than the one you do, no matter how tempting—words to live by that I'll come back to in the chapter on love and marriage.

Not every young person is seduced by job offers. Take Scott Nicholson, twenty-four, the subject of a 2010 front-page article in *The New York Times* that stirred up a cyberstorm. Scott had graduated from Colgate two years earlier and had been living with his parents in a Boston suburb ever since. He'd been sending out four or five job applications a week (he was looking for work in marketing or finance), and had recently been offered a $40,000-a-year position as an insurance claims adjuster. On consideration, according to the *Times*, he decided it would be a dead-end job, and he didn't want it. He turned the offer down.

His older brother David, twenty-six, supported Scott's decision. "Once you start working, you get caught up in the work and you have bills to pay," David told the *Times*, "and you lose sight of what you really want." But most of the 1,457 commenters on the *Times* website were outraged, seeing Scott as "pathetic," a "big baby," a shameful example of a generation with artificially pumped-up self-esteem who think they deserve better than whatever entry-level drudge work comes along.

"What he is not realizing is that the best way to get a job is to already have a job," wrote Cleo of Chicago in one of the more civil online comments. "The stability of holding down a position, combined with the experience, is invaluable in getting higher positions. Furthermore, and this is harsh, but beggars can't be choosers."

Still, despite the fury he provoked, Scott might have been on to something. (And his own story seems to have ended happily; according to his LinkedIn profile, he started working a few months after the *Times* article appeared, and in 2011 became an account development manager at Forrester Research in Boston.) Maybe it's not always true that some job is better than no job. Maybe, as Austan Goolsbee says, the surest way to get to the top is to start at the top.

Smartphoning It In

In 2010 the tech company Cisco surveyed 2,800 young adults under thirty who were either college students or employed college graduates, to see how social media and smartphones affected their lives at home and at work. The study, the one from chapter 1 that found that Millennials value the Internet as much as air and water, revealed some profound differences in what young people think is important compared with what their fifty- and sixtysomething bosses value. For instance:

- Sixty percent of young employees said they don't need an office to be productive.

- Fifty-six percent said that if their job blocked access to Facebook, Twitter, and other social media sites, they wouldn't take the job—or they would do whatever they could to get around the policy and get access anyway.
- Forty percent would accept a job with lower pay if it had more flexibility in mobile device choice and social media access.
- Thirty percent said it is a worker's right to be able to work remotely on a flexible schedule.

So do these results mean Millennials are defiant, entitled, and slightly annoying? I guess that's one way of looking at it. But another way is that being plugged-in and hyperlinked is their natural style of communication, as essential to them as talking on landlines once was to their bosses, and they're just trying to integrate that natural, more-vital-than-air part of their lives into the workplace. A bit like the way Baby Boomers at their crappy entry-level jobs tried to sneak in personal telephone calls while no one was looking.

Let's parse the complaints we hear about how Millennials haven't figured out the code of proper office behavior. "All too often, the young worker shows up ten minutes late . . . [and] fidgets through her shift until things slow down enough that she can text her friends," Eric Chester, author of *Reviving the Work Ethic*, said in an interview with *Forbes*. Young people start out as "bright and ambitious recruits," he said, but soon see actual work as "something to avoid or as a necessary evil to endure prior to winning the lottery."

But it's no surprise that young people aren't always gung-ho about office culture. A lot of Millennials are tethered to jobs that are awful, making it hard to keep being all "bright and ambitious." Among the members of the class of 2000 described in *Academically Adrift*, the book we discussed in chapter 2, of those who found full-time employment, the average salary two years post-graduation was still just $34,900 a year. Give up Tumblr and T-shirts for less than twenty bucks an hour? Please.

Young workers' asynchrony with office culture might reflect something else—a matter of semiotics, those gestures, language, clothing, and hairstyles that carry a particular meaning to a particular group and a different meaning to a different group. Millennials might have a perfectly fine work ethic—but it might be one that's hard for their elders to discern.

Fiftysomething bosses see kids at their desks checking Facebook accounts or posting to Twitter from their office computers, taking breaks in the coffee room to bullshit with the other twentysomethings, back at their desks listening to music or God-knows-what through headphones—and to them, those young workers have just spent the whole day goofing off. But what the elders might not realize is that, to twentysomethings, all that chatter, both real-world and virtual, is part of the process of working. Throughout school, their teachers emphasized cooperative learning, and they've spent their youth reaping the benefits of crowd-sourcing. Chatting is how they think. G-chatting in particular is how Millennials let off steam, and it's also how they get things done, through virtual brainstorming instead of brainstorming face-to-face (which usually takes a lot more time). As for the headphones and the music at the desk: a lot of young people, Sam included, insist they do better when they multitask.

> Okay, I'll admit it, sometimes multitasking does cause problems for me. I've found myself looking at a tab on my browser—one of dozens open at any one time—with no memory of why or how I navigated to that page, the web version of walking into the kitchen and forgetting what utensil you've come to fetch. But I do like to wear headphones at my desk. And one aspect of the "entitled Millennial" work ethic I totally buy into is the desire to telecommute. The dirty secret of working from home, as anyone who's done it surely knows, is that you can do a full day's work in about four hours. The rest of the day can be spent cooking yourself lunch, going for a run, visiting the doctor, cleaning the bathroom—all the regular-life stuff that it can feel impossible to accomplish when you're in a cubicle all day.
>
> My friend Chad was laid off from Slate about six months after I was. But instead of scrambling to find a new cube on which to hang his nameplate, as I had, he decided to have a go at the freelancing life. One day, about a year into his work-from-home experiment, he and I had lunch during a little "staycation" I was taking. I told Chad how productive I'd been in my few days off: I'd taken my boots to the

*cobbler, exercised more, read a ton, bought new bras. It was fabulous!
"That's my life," Chad told me. (Except for the bras.) Those little things
that office drones can never get around to—when you work from home,
you can. Which explains why he turned down a succession of great job
offers during that freelancing stint. He just wasn't ready to return to the
ruse of the working world, the game our bosses make us play, wherein
we pretend that we all must suffer the inefficiencies of the office, lest
the truth cause the whole facade to fall away.*

"Many of the behaviors that older generations interpret as laziness
may actually enhance young people's productivity," wrote Catherine
Rampell in a *New York Times* essay called "A Generation of Slackers?
Not So Much." Millennials might be *more* industrious, she wrote, willing to work longer and harder than ever before. The fuzzy demarcation
between office life and personal life that makes it look like they're having too much fun at work is exactly what messes with the very idea of
being off duty. All that scanning of their phone screens during dinner
or before the movie starts, all the plugged-in behavior that drives their
parents crazy, is how twentysomethings stay connected to work just
about around-the-clock. And if some work emergency is announced by
email, it's often the young man or woman, constantly checking in—
even if just out of boredom or habit rather than workplace devotion—
who finds out about the problem and deals with it.

My brother-in-law, Peter, has an interesting take on twentysomethings' behavior, at work and elsewhere. Peter is a musicologist whose
specialty is Renaissance counterpoint, but when he spends time with
young people, it's the twenty-first century he wants to talk about, not
the sixteenth. He is always asking his son and nieces to introduce him to
new forms of music: indie rock, hip-hop, Auto-Tune. He doesn't always
like it, any more than Gustav Mahler liked the atonal music of Arnold
Schoenberg. But Peter says he tries to emulate Mahler's attitude. When
Mahler and his wife left the Vienna premiere in 1908 of Schoenberg's
Second String Quartet, his wife asked him what he thought of the
music. Mahler, who was forty-eight at the time, said it didn't really matter *what* he thought: "The younger generation is always right."

That they are. They're the ones who will inherit the earth, and

whether their elders disapproved of their behavior as twentysomethings, in the office or out, won't really matter in thirty years. I think
we Baby Boomers just have to get used to it.

Money Talks

Another complaint about Millennials is that they're clueless about
finances. Oldsters love to deride them for frantically texting Dad about,
say, how to fill out a W9 form for their new job, or how to get their paycheck direct-deposited. "Do you ever wonder how everyone survives?"
wrote Ryan O'Connell, twenty-four, on the group blog *Thought Catalog*.
"Like where does their money come from? . . . How do you make it?
How do you make a lot of it and not spend it all when you're wasted?"
To a person just starting out, it can all seem like a total mystery.

I, too, was mystified in my twenties about how to fill out a lease,
balance a checkbook, buy a car, and I occasionally called long distance
to ask my father for help. I never even learned how to do my own taxes;
Jeff still does them for me, and now also for Sam, Jess, and my mother,
all of us fully competent adults yet all of us undone by the 1099.

But maybe the cluelessness of Millennials really is something different
and more profound. Recently, economist Annamaria Lusardi of Dartmouth
(now at George Washington University) asked a group of 7,500 Millennials
three surprisingly easy questions to evaluate their financial literacy:

- The interest question: Suppose you had $100 in a savings
  account and the interest rate was 2 percent per year. After
  five years, how much do you think you would have in the
  account if you left the money to grow: more than $102,
  exactly $102, or less than $102?
- The inflation question: Imagine that the interest rate on your
  savings account was 1 percent per year and inflation was 2
  percent per year. After one year, would you be able to buy
  more than, exactly the same as, or less than today with the
  money in this account?
- The risk diversification question: Do you think that the following statement is true or false? "Buying a single company stock
  usually provides a safer return than a stock mutual fund."

Lusardi and her colleagues then evaluated how the subjects, aged twenty-three to twenty-eight, scored on these three basic questions. Not so good: only 27 percent got all three answers right. (They are, for the record, more than $102, less than today, and false.) When the questions are looked at separately, the rates of correct answers were 79 percent for the interest rate question, 54 percent for the inflation question, and 47 percent for the question about risk diversification.

I got them all! But that doesn't keep me from being paralyzed when faced with my own financial decisions. And that paralysis can come off looking like ignorance when it makes me do things I know are idiotic, such as delaying starting a 401(k) (which means sacrificing the free money that would come from my company's matching funds) or leaving a bunch of money in a checking account where it accrues zero interest. Just knowing what the words mean isn't enough.

The disappointing scores in the Dartmouth study varied depending on who the young people were. Men did better than women. Whites did better than blacks or Hispanics. People whose own parents had investments and retirement savings did better than those whose parents did not—a demonstration of what sociologists call "cumulative advantage," known colloquially as "them that's got, get." Psychological attributes came into play as well in marking out who would understand finance, in particular the qualities of patience and future orientation. Previous studies have shown that smokers are more impatient and live-for-today than nonsmokers—and smokers had significantly lower scores on the financial literacy test. As Lusardi and her colleagues put it, "those who discount the future more heavily may be less willing to invest resources in acquiring financial knowledge, since such an investment has a delayed payoff."

Illiteracy can lead to blunders. A 2006 Gallup poll of 900 twenty-somethings found that 15 percent had made a financial decision in the previous six months that they regretted. Most of those mistakes involved amassing credit card debt (23 percent), making an unneeded purchase (17 percent), buying a car (16 percent), or making a bad investment (10 percent).

Many had been blindsided by the real world. When they first

started living on their own, 43 percent of those Gallup poll participants said their expenses were higher than they'd expected. But only half had drawn up a budget, and 30 percent said they were living beyond their means. Of those who were working, only 45 percent were making contributions to an IRA or 401(k) retirement account. Just 60 percent managed to make regular deposits even to a plain old savings account.

> Mint.com and similar websites are designed to make twenty-somethings more financially astute, by tracking how they spend their money and helping them set goals and budgets for the future. Personally, I don't need a website to tell me where all my money goes: liquids. Not as in liquidity. As in morning coffee ($2.50), lunchtime Dr. Pepper ($1.65), afternoon mocha ($4.95), and nighttime alcohol (priceless). When I eat out I tend to spend more on drinks than on food. Does that mean that if I could limit my liquids to tap water, I'd be rich?

Delays in starting to budget wisely can have serious long-term implications, further separating the liquids from the solids and the haves from the have-nots. Let's say you want to have accumulated $1 million in your retirement account by the time you're sixty-two. Figuring an annual rate of return of 8 percent, that means you can get there by investing $4,000 a year if you start your contributions at age twenty-two. But if you don't start contributing until age thirty-two, you'll need to invest more than *twice* that amount *every year*—$8,800 a year instead of $4,000—to get to your $1 million by sixty-two. Twice the money in to get the same money out—and all because you delayed getting started by just ten years.

People in serious debt don't usually think about long-term investments or retirement funds. And for Millennials, debt is the new normal, as we saw in the last chapter. Of the 90 percent of young people in the Gallup poll we mentioned who had significant debt, some of them made career decisions they wouldn't otherwise have made had they not had such money struggles, by either taking a job they wouldn't otherwise have taken (22 percent) or failing to take a job they wanted (12 percent). A perfect setup for getting started on the wrong career track—which is, in turn, a perfect setup for always being just a little bit behind where you expected to be.

Same as It Ever Was

Recession's Shadow

We know that the impact of the high unemployment rates of the early 2010s will probably last a long time, as young people try to claw their way up a career ladder that keeps slipping further into the muck. But we know this partly because we've been here before—back when the Baby Boomers were young.

In 1972, the year before Jeff and I graduated from college, young people with bachelor's degrees were so often considered "overqualified" that they were more likely to be unemployed than were people their age without bachelor's degrees. In October 1972, as the re-election campaign of Richard Nixon was drawing to a close and the national unemployment rate was a respectable 5.1 percent, new college grads were already in trouble. Among those who had graduated the previous spring, the unemployment rate was more than twice the national average (11.7 percent), and in some fields it was especially brutal (15.4 percent for humanities majors like me, 16 percent for social scientists like Jeff). For twentysomethings of the same age who had only a high school diploma, the unemployment rate was just 7.7 percent.

Slight variations in the economy can make a huge difference. Back in the introduction, we mentioned the research of Lisa Kahn, the Yale economist who found that graduating into a recession means a lifetime of lagging behind. It was the careers of second-wave Baby Boomers that led to this conclusion, young men who were a little younger than Jeff and I. Kahn's study included men born between 1957 and 1967 who graduated from college between 1979 and 1989, when the overall unemployment rate ranged from 7 to 11 percent. (In decent economies, it's more like 4 or 5 percent; in the early 2010s, it hovered at around 8 to 10 percent.) She found that the men who graduated into a 10.8 percent unemployment rate in December 1982 earned on average 23 percent less in their first year out of college than men who graduated with the same credentials just a year and a half earlier, in May 1981, when the unemployment rate was 7.5 percent. For each percentage point rise in the unemployment rate when they entered the job market, she found, young men earned 7 to 8 percent less in their first jobs out of school.

And the gap persisted for years. Even eighteen years out of college, the late-1982 graduates were earning 6.6 percent less than the men who had graduated in mid-1981. Their professional confidence had been shaken, too. Those who'd had trouble finding decent first jobs tended to be skittish, even years later, about letting go of what they already had. They stayed at the same jobs for much longer than did men who started out in boomier times. This had long-term consequences, because the surest way to move up, in terms of both wages and status, is by changing jobs often in the early years of work.

A rocky start can affect not just subsequent job patterns, but also subsequent mental health. People who go through long bouts of unemployment in their twenties have higher rates of depression in middle age, and higher rates later in life of problem drinking (defined as five or more drinks in one sitting). This is true even for people who do find work eventually; it's the hard knocks of that early stretch that can haunt them for years.

Everybody Hops

Flitting from job to job might seem to be typically Millennial, but in truth it's probably just part of being young. Not long ago, the Bureau of Labor Statistics analyzed the early careers of second-wave Baby Boomers, born between 1957 and 1964. They might love to lecture their kids about the importance of working one's way up the corporate ladder, but when Baby Boomers were young, they were just as prone to job-hopping as their children are today. For those coming of age in the 1980s, it was rare to stick with an early job for long. Of the jobs they took when they were aged twenty-three to twenty-eight, just 4 percent were at the same job fifteen years later. Instead, the trend even then was to move around, to an average of *eleven jobs* before age forty-four, with most of the changes occurring before twenty-seven. (A job was defined as an uninterrupted period of work with a particular employer; a promotion or lateral move within the same company wasn't counted as a job hop.) This was true for all races and all levels of educational attainment, except for some racial disparities in the youngest group, eighteen to twenty-two, when whites moved around more often than minorities, possibly because they had more opportunities to do so. In those four years, whites had an average of 4.6 jobs, compared with 4.0 jobs for Hispanics and 3.5 jobs for African Americans.

Job mobility for Baby Boomers steadily declined as they got older. When the people in the Bureau of Labor Statistics study were eighteen to twenty-two, 70 percent were at jobs where they'd been working for less than one year; when they were twenty-three to twenty-seven, that proportion had dropped to 60 percent. But there was still a significant subset who kept moving around even into their forties: the proportion of men who'd been at their current jobs for less than one year was 50 percent among twenty-eight- to thirty-two-year-olds, and 33 percent for those aged thirty-nine to forty-four.

"I was originally going to school to be an art teacher," one such meandering Baby Boomer, Fayanne Kanner, wrote in response to our questionnaire, "then switched to architecture, then eventually to Mass Communication (Television)." Fayanne, sixty, lives in Los Angeles, and said she's glad she didn't stick with her original plan. "I am a totally different person than I was in my 20s," she told us. "In my 20s I didn't have the passion for things as I do now."

Mona, fifty-nine, moved around a lot in her twenties, too. "Babysitting, waitressing, sales girl in a neighborhood bakery, sales girl in a children's shoe store (in Israel); an unpaid apprenticeship with an art conservator and [another with] a sculptor to explore these fields, a freelance job with 3-D animation production," she told us. All this was followed by three full-time jobs, still in her twenties, "with (1) an American-Israeli investment corporation, (2) CETA (a federally funded program) at Lehman College, CUNY, and (3) an international organization."

I have a lot of friends whose résumés are as kinetic as Mona's and Fayanne's, and usually I think they're having more fun than I am in my deliberate slog from one journalism job to another. I visited one such friend, Julian, during the two-week break I took to catch my breath between my fourth and fifth post-college jobs. Julian had just moved to San Francisco, and he thought two weeks was an awfully short respite.

"I'm a defer-er," he reminded me, as we spent a day exploring the beachy, bourgie outskirts of the city. "I deferred college for a year, I deferred law school for a year, and now I'm deferring my law firm offer for a year." He considered it a weakness. Why did he have trouble just saying yes to the next thing? But I saw it as a sort of strength. Because of all those deferrals, in the eleven years since high school Julian had worked for AmeriCorps in the Adirondacks, done tutoring in Hawaii, traveled in Southeast Asia—and gotten himself a bachelor's degree and a J.D. along the way. And now he was living in San Francisco, trying to start a tech business.

Julian's deferrals have let him plop down somewhere new and make a life for himself from scratch, even if it's temporary. And when he goes into each next phase post-deferral, he does so with a greater sense of what else is out there and, as a result, greater confidence in the choice he's making. If he ends up as a corporate lawyer in New York next year, which is looking likely (he has a lot of student loans), he won't have that nagging curiosity about whether, if only he'd had the guts to try, he could have made it as a tech entrepreneur instead. He'll have tried and will know that, at least in the year he gave himself, he couldn't.

Julian's deferring is a way to avoid closing doors, a way to keep all options open for just one more year. But as much as people might hate it, doors do eventually close—sometimes because of things you did, sometimes because of things you didn't do. Then you reach what Ben, twenty-nine, called "a point of no return in your late 20s," when your future feels constrained by the decisions you made five or ten years earlier. "If I really wanted to be an urban planner," wrote Ben, a writer in Brooklyn, in response to our questionnaire, "I think I'm a little too far beyond the curve at this point."

Social scientists have a term for this phenomenon: path dependence. It means that choices made now determine the choices that are possible later. To understand how it works, think of the QWERTY keyboard. When the first English-language typewriters were designed in the 1870s, hitting a letter activated a particular rod in the inner workings, which struck the paper like a hammer on a piano. If too many rods were activated and struck too close together, they jammed. So the keyboard was rearranged to avoid jams, keeping the rods that were likely to get struck in sequence, such as *T* and *H*, as far from each other as possible. That first manual typewriter keyboard was transferred to the electric typewriter keyboard, and from there to the first computer keyboard and to every other English-language computer, laptop, and tablet keyboard ever since. We're long past the point where we have physical levers to keep from jamming. But even though studies show that there are much more efficient ways to arrange keys if the goal is speed, QWERTY has become so enshrined in English-language typists' fingertips that it seems to be with us for the duration.

In terms of careers, path dependence is what tripped up Samantha's friend Dan, the one who so abruptly quit his law firm job—and found that the choice he had thought would keep his options open had inadvertently closed them. Law school sent him down one path constrained by his particular credentials plus the $180,000 debt he'd accrued, instead of the path he might have preferred, being a park ranger. As Sam described in the last chapter, Dan did manage to get out of the rut of a life dictated by debt. But he still hasn't become a park ranger.

At some point—usually in the late twenties or early thirties—George Costanza realizes he will never be a marine biologist, Tim Riggins admits he doesn't have the chops to make it in the NFL (or even college football), and Jack Black's *School of Rock* character has to settle for teaching music instead of playing it.

Closing doors has always been part of growing up. That's what Susan Littwin wrote in *The Postponed Generation*, a book published in 1986 about why Baby Boomers were taking so long to reach adulthood. "The hardest lesson for this generation," she wrote about the Baby Boomers, "seems to be this: Choice is limited. You cannot do everything and be everything in one life."

Weighing Opportunity Costs

When trying to figure out if some job is better than no job, what really complicates everything are the opportunity costs. These are the hard-to-identify costs you incur by not choosing whatever it was you could have chosen instead of what you chose. There are opportunity costs to going to this movie and not that movie, going to that party and not this seminar, choosing to sunbathe while others swim. There are opportunity costs to marrying, taking a vacation, forgoing a vacation, deciding to stay home when you have a baby, deciding to hire a nanny and go back to work.

Economist Dan Ariely (he of the ingenious shrinking-doors computer game from chapter 1) went to a Toyota dealership and asked people, "What will you have to give up if you buy this car?" A few people said, "If I buy this Toyota, I can't buy a Honda." But Ariely wanted something more. He was looking for some real weighing of opportunity costs: the amount spent now on this Camry means, as he put it, that "in the future I will have to give up two weeks of vacation and 70 lattes and 1500 books." This is a hard thing to quantify, and Ariely has since created an iPhone app to do it for you, which he calls Oranges2Apples. You tap in your fondness for trips to the Bahamas, lattes, and books, and the app calculates the trade-offs. Sam and I downloaded the free app and gave it a try. Turns out it's not quite as helpful as we had hoped. You indicate your favorite things at various price points, from $1 to $100, and then you tell the app the cost of the item you're thinking of buying. A fancy dress for $300? Okay, says the app, but for that money you could have had ten cocktails *plus* two professional massages. Maybe if the app had better graphics, or if it knew that half a ticket to a Broadway show doesn't mean much in the real world, it would have been a more powerful way of our finding out something we already sort of knew.

What would really help is an app for the imponderables of a major life choice such as the job search. Some trade-offs are clear: a better salary at job A, say, compared with more responsibility at job B. Some are less obvious but still intuitive: that job X will provide so much gratification that it's worth taking the lower pay you'd get than at job Y, which you consider smarmy and demeaning. All these trade-offs are easier to spot than the opportunity costs—costs such as what might happen if you take a job you hate and therefore aren't free to take a job you might love.

I faced such a decision myself when I got my journalism master's degree from Northwestern in the spring of 1974, one year after Watergate turned every other English major into a Woodward or Bernstein wannabe. My job hunt was restricted to Chicago, since Jeff was still in grad school. I was offered a public relations job with the gas company at a salary of $14,500 (about $65,000 today), way more than I'd been aiming for. But even though I hadn't been swept up in the trendy aspiration of investigative reporting, I hadn't quite pictured myself writing throwaway inserts for gas bills. So I did what a lot of young people did in those days, and what 40 percent of new grads do even today when they get an unappealing first job offer: I turned it down. Maybe I was being the same kind of self-centered brat that Millennials are accused of being, acting as if I deserved better. But I thought I *did* deserve better—and I figured something better *had* to materialize soon.

Nothing did. After a few weeks of coming up empty, my job hunt took an unexpected detour: in late June we were burned out of our apartment, and Jeff and I spent the summer back in Queens, in my parents' basement, until we found another place to live. (Yes, we were out of work and living in my parents' basement, and we weren't even Millennials.) The next offer didn't come until the fall, and it, too, was not my dream job: associate editor of a start-up medical journal produced out of the back room of a crazy ophthalmologist's office in the Chicago Loop. This time, I took it.

I hated working there. The ophthalmologist—part Mr. Smithers, part that guy who played Grandpa on *The Munsters*—would storm in at 7:30 every morning and turn on the water full force in the office kitchen, letting it run loudly for an hour to get out the carcinogens (or so he insisted) before his assistant, Ginny, was allowed to make coffee. He barked constantly at Ginny, and in between glaucoma patients, he would come into the back room and bark at me.

But the commute was easy, and I didn't have to stress about impressing anyone. Most days, I wore my best pants, a pair of gray corduroy jeans, along with a rotation of sweaters. (Gray goes with everything, right?) I knew I didn't look stylish, but I assumed I looked presentable. Until one day in December, when I was saying good night to the crazy ophthalmologist, about to leave for a long weekend to visit my in-laws. He pulled out his wallet, grabbed a handful of twenty-dollar bills, and threw them on the table. "Here, take this and buy yourself something to wear," he shouted. "I'm tired of looking at those pants."

Maximizers and Satisficers

When I took that job with the crazy ophthalmologist, I used the decision-making strategy known as satisficing, a combination of *satisfy* and *suffice* coined in the 1950s by Nobel Prize–winning economist Herbert Simon of Carnegie Mellon. To a satisficer, whatever suffices is satisfactory, and whatever is satisfactory will suffice.

There are two types of decision makers: satisficers and maximizers. Maximizers want to explore every possible option before buying a camera, settling on a television show, ordering takeout, choosing a job. They gather every stick of information in the hope of making the best possible decision, even if they exhaust themselves in the process—and drive themselves mad when they realize, inevitably, that there's more information out there that they missed. If you're a satisficer, however, you make decisions based on the evidence at hand, not on all the evidence that might possibly exist anywhere ever.

You can see why satisficers have an easier time of it. They don't sweat the small stuff. They avoid the "decision fatigue" we mentioned in chapter 1—the phenomenon of the depletion, over the course of a day, of the mental energy it takes to keep making the prudent, rational choice—by taking the first good-enough camera, entree, or job offer that comes along.

For twentysomethings, this dichotomy plays out most dramatically in decisions about work. One recent study of young people on the job market found that maximizers and satisficers get different kinds of job offers, and feel different about the offers they accept. The study involved 548 members of the Class of 2002, who were followed as their job search unfolded over the course of senior year. The investigators, Sheena Iyengar and Rachael Wells of Columbia University, and Barry Schwartz of Skidmore, began by determining whether these young people were maximizers or satisficers in other aspects of their lives. Do you agree or disagree, they asked their subjects, with the statement "When I am in the car listening to the radio, I often check other stations to see if something better is playing, even if I am relatively satisfied with what I'm listening to." How about "When shopping, I have a hard time finding clothes that I really love." A maximizer will tend to agree with both statements, while a satisficer will tend to disagree, figuring that if what's on the radio is okay, there's no point station-surfing for something better. The investigators also asked how much the students relied on outside sources of information—parents, peers, career counselors at their school, experts in their field of interest—during the job search.

In November of senior year, the students estimated how many jobs they expected to apply for. In February they had to agree or disagree with the statement "I often fantasize about jobs that are quite different from the actual jobs that I am pursuing." In May, as graduation approached, they had to agree or disagree with "I wish I had pursued more options in my job search process." The February and May questions were intended to tap into how much the students ruminated on the might-have-been.

The maximizers put themselves through more contortions in the job hunt. They applied to twenty jobs, on average, while satisficers applied to only ten, and they were significantly more likely to make use of outside sources of information and support. But it turned out to be worth it: the job offers they got were significantly better, in terms of salary, than what the satisficers got. Satisficers were offered jobs with an average starting salary of $37,085; the average starting salary offered to maximizers was $44,515, more than 20 percent higher.

The surprise was that the maximizers looked at those sweet job offers and were miserable.

I am a maximizer—at least when making inconsequential decisions, which I constantly overthink and then instantly regret. It's worst when I'm hungry or stressed out. On May 5, 2009, about a week before the Slate *website I was working on was set to launch, I was both. That was the day of the Great Cookie Meltdown, which I described to my friend Jonah on G-chat.*

> **me**: omg i just went on a cookie mission that made me cry
> i am freaking out right now
> **Jonah**: why?
> haha i have no idea what that sentence means

me: everything's fucked so i wanted a cookie
but then every place i went for a cookie something was wrong
like they didn't have cookies, or it had closed down
and i wanted to go to this place with $3 cookies that are
awesome but i was like no that's too much money for a cookie
so i went to this other place with gross packaged cookies
and i bought one
and it was $3
and i said "i don't want this if it's $3, that's ridiculous"
and she said "i can't cancel it"
so i just left
and started to cry
and now i just started to eat it and it's gross!!!!!!!
Jonah: ha awww sammy!
me: but the whole point was to make myself feel BETTER!
Jonah: and it did the opposite!
me: yes!
Jonah: motherfucking cookies!
me: gaaaaaaaaaaaa

At that point Jonah, trying to be supportive, sent me a link to a delicious-looking cookie. Exasperated, I replied "that just makes me hate my cookie even more!" That's the problem with maximizers. Our belief that there exists some perfect cookie out there like the one in Jonah's link, one that not only is fresh and gooey but also will ease anxiety and make the website launch go smoothly, just turns all real-world cookies into disappointments.

In the study by Iyengar and her colleagues, the maximizers were significantly more likely than satisficers to be unhappy with the job offers they accepted—even though, remember, the offers came with salaries that were 20 percent higher than the ones the satisficers got. Maximizers were also more likely to have spent the search process fretting about the options they didn't pursue, more likely to wish they had applied for more jobs, and more likely to have gone through the whole process feeling stressed-out and sure that things would end badly. Despite having worked so hard to come up with exactly what they wanted, they were always thinking about whatever else they might have wanted more.

Maybe part of the problem is that the very notion of a perfect job is an illusion, and that a cold, hard truth about growing up is recognizing that life is a series of compromises.

Sam's childhood friend Jesse McIntosh, twenty-six, is not yet ready to compromise—even though, five years out of college, he's still waiting for his lucky break. He has always wanted to be an actor—in middle school, he had a swagger onstage that was striking, even when he was playing a Shakespearean fairy—and he went to the University of Southern California to study theater. He's had the same job as a waiter in L.A. for more than five years, Jesse wrote in response to our questionnaire, "but it feels temporary. I'm not working in the field I want to be in." He's still awaiting a big acting gig. "I have no real concept of living for the future," he wrote. "I have no investments, no retirement plan; I'm dealing with finances on a week to week basis, and in that way, I feel the same way I felt when I was 15."

Jesse has always been financially responsible: he used his own money to buy his first car at seventeen and his second car at twenty, and when he chose USC over a free ride at a state school, he did so with the understanding that he would shoulder as much of the cost as he could on his own. But financial responsibility isn't the same thing as financial planning. That's the piece of Econ 101 that lots of twentysomethings have still to learn.

Not Quite What I Expected

Young people tend to have great expectations. As we mentioned in the intro, when pollsters asked a group of twentysomethings a few years back if they agreed with the statement "I am very sure that one day I will get to where I want to be in life," 96 percent of them said yes. But this isn't Lake Wobegon, and not everyone can have his or her dreams come true.

Unmet expectations carry a special sting. It can be worse, according to psychologists, to anticipate one kind of life and wake up in another than it would have been to wake up in that life in the first place, without having envisioned anything different. The experts call it "goal-striving stress."

In 1979, investigators with the National Longitudinal Survey of Youth were curious about the psychic cost of goal-striving stress. The study has followed 12,686 second-wave Baby Boomers, born between 1957 and 1964, from adolescence all the way through midlife. The survey's still going on, with the subjects now in their forties and fifties and coming back for interviews every two years. At the first round of interviews, when the subjects were aged fourteen to twenty-two, the investigators included a simple question: What do you expect to be doing in five years? Five years later, it was possible to compare expectations to reality.

At the original interview, 94 percent of the adolescents said they expected to be working in five years, 50 percent expected to be married, and 54 percent expected to be a parent. But five years later, when they were aged nineteen to twenty-seven, just 67 percent of those who expected to be working actually had jobs, just 65 percent of those who expected to be married actually had spouses, and just 64 percent of those who expected to be parents actually had a child.

That's a lot of unmet dreams. And those who had unmet dreams in their twenties, one researcher subsequently found, were more likely in their thirties to experience symptoms of depression. It was the expectations that made the difference, not the objective achievement.

"Achieving a lower level of education than expected and being unexpectedly out of the labor force predict subsequent symptoms of depression" ten years later, wrote Krysia Mossakowski, a sociologist at the University of Hawaii, who did the analysis of the NLSY data in 2011. This held true even after she corrected for possible confounding influences such as being poor, being nonwhite, or being someone whose preexisting mental health problems got in the way of employment. The results, she wrote, "are not explained by being selected out of the labor force for long durations because of mental or physical illness, attending school, keeping house, or other reasons." Thwarted dreams turned out to be their own risk factor.

Having one's youthful dreams dashed or deferred is, sadly, an old story. Back in 1986, journalist Susan Littwin wrote in *The Postponed*

Generation about twentysomething Baby Boomers who expected too much too soon. She criticized young people who "feel entitled to good times, expensive equipment, and the kind of homes they grew up in" and who believed they deserved "instant status, important, meaningful work, and an unspoiled environment." They started out with "limitless choices, arrayed like cereals on the market shelves," she wrote, and then grew up "only to find that scarcity was back" and that "society had changed its promises. It wasn't just a matter of a bad economy or even a lean economy. It was a changed economy with different values and different priorities."

Scarcity, changed promises, different values—these phrases from the 1980s could easily be applied to the dreams deferred among young people today. But Littwin wasn't writing about Millennials; she was writing about their parents. In both cases, being forced to let go of some expectations is a bitter reality.

Yet even stuck in low-paying jobs and grappling with astronomical expenses, these members of Generation Limbo are still cockeyed optimists, surprisingly and almost maniacally upbeat. When asked in one survey, "Is the American Dream achievable?" seven out of ten young people said yes.

In a different study, researchers from Notre Dame conducted in-depth interviews with 230 Millennials aged eighteen to twenty-three, asking questions about values, goals, and lifestyle. As psychologist Christian Smith and his colleagues wrote in *Lost in Transition: The Dark Side of Emerging Adulthood*, the young people expected to achieve the financial success they longed for. They were fans of consumption, Smith wrote, with two out of three saying "that their well-being can be measured by what they own, that buying more things would make them happier, and that they get a lot of pleasure simply from shopping and buying things."

Smith pressed for details. He wanted to know what *really* mattered to them; he was sure it must go beyond the simple accumulation of *stuff.* "What is your idea of a 'good life' when it comes to the ideal kind of lifestyle you might have?" he asked his subjects. "What are your goals when it comes to buying, owning, and consuming in your life—or maybe living modestly and simply?" Even though he'd put the notion of modest simplicity right out there, only a few took him up on it. Almost all Smith's interviewees were specific about their material needs. They wanted the basics, and occasionally the frills, mentioning second homes, frequent vacations, boats, fancy cars. The young person's race, sex, and social class didn't seem to matter; almost everyone expressed some variant of the desire for comfort and financial security. One Millennial rattled off a typical list: "Have a nice house that belongs to me. Have a nice, reliable, dependable vehicle. Have something to play with on the weekends, maybe a boat, a four-wheeler, or a bike or whatever. And be able to provide for the family, and, basically, the best way to put it is, I'm comfortable. I'm not struggling."

The same theme (accumulating stuff and becoming financially secure) emerged in responses to the bigger question Smith posed: "What, ultimately, do you want to get out of life?" To Smith himself, the good life means "progressing on some kind of journey to become something more than what we already are . . . realizing some higher purpose or value, often of a personal and perhaps even spiritual nature." Some of the young people in his study mentioned such things, he said. But in 57 percent of the replies, the Meaning of Life was expressed in terms of career success and material comfort. To Smith, this is a sign of the cramped horizons of today's youth. Having a nice family, being happy, being financially secure—this seemed to be as far as most of his respondents were able to go in imagining their futures, with just a handful mentioning goals involving serving the community, creating art, protecting the environment, or growing spiritually. He was disappointed and dismayed, he wrote, not to see more "existential wrestling."

I understand Smith's dismay. But maybe these responses are variations on the theme of the hierarchy of needs that I've played before (and will play again before this book ends). Abraham Maslow's theory states that the most basic needs (food, clothing, shelter) must be dealt with before the higher needs can be addressed. For young people today, worried about whether they'll ever be able to make a living, raise a family, buy a home, travel, partake in all the pleasures they once thought almost their birthright, it's understandable that when they're asked about their fondest wishes, they'll focus on stuff. Possessions represent a kind of ease and security that too many Millennials are afraid might forever remain just beyond their reach.

Round Three

NOW IS NEW:

- The economy is unusually bad and unemployment is unusually high.
- Climbing the corporate ladder isn't the only way up.
- The Internet makes it easier to work from home, but smartphones make it harder to clock out.
- What's a mutual fund?

SAME AS IT EVER WAS:

- Baby Boomers graduated into a recession, too.
- Youth has always been the best time for job hopping.
- Every choice has a cost.
- People choose in two distinct ways.
- Both styles of decision-making can lead to disappointment.
- But young people still remain surprisingly upbeat.

The argument that Millennials are the first-ever generation confronting the prospect of downward mobility is a powerful one, given the high rates of unemployment they face. But the similarity to previous generations, who also confronted these troubles and recovered—albeit with a kind of financial limp that persisted for decades—strikes us as more compelling, and we're going to give this round to the camp of Same as It Ever Was.

Chapter 4

Love and Marriage

This is Sam writing now. Up to this point I've been happy to let my mother tell the bulk of the story about what the statistics, the studies, and our respondents say about being young. But for this chapter, I'm taking the reins—in part because, although Mom knows far more about marriage than I, she doesn't know much about spending your twenties dating, sleeping together without being committed, living together without being married, going through a dry spell, or trying out (and failing at) any of the other forms of romantic relationships lying somewhere between celibacy and monogamy. She got married when she was nineteen (*and a half*, she was always quick to add, *and* with a college degree, as though those two details would prevent my sister and me from dropping out of high school to marry our boyfriends). During her twenties, Mom didn't face any of the decisions about when and with whom to settle down that most twentysomethings do; she had already found and chosen my father.

The other reason I'm calling dibs on this chapter is that I know that whatever Mom wrote would seem to me to be weighted with subtext. Her "the happiest marriages are between people who married at age twenty-two to twenty-five" would read to me as "You already missed your window, Sam." So, for the sake of my own peace of mind and our mother-daughter relations, I'll be the one summarizing the studies. I'd rather feel that my singledom is being silently judged by some distant scholar than by my mother.

In my early to mid-twenties I was a serial monogamist, and I struggled with the questions many coupled-off twentysomethings do: How do I know if the problems with this person, with this relationship, are problems that I can (should?) spend the rest of my life dealing with, or whether these are deal breakers? Where's the line between being discerning versus being picky, between seizing something worthwhile and salvageable versus settling for something less than you deserve?

These days I'm single, and my concern is more a stereotypical woman-nearing-her-thirties one: Will I find someone great with whom to spend my life, and will I do it in time to have the family I've always pictured?

Because I'm still so enmeshed in these questions, the scientific studies on love and marriage carry an extra charge for me. It's hard for me not to read them all as endorsements of (or tsk-tsks against) the decisions I've already made, and guidelines for what I should be doing next. But I will do my best not to take it all too personally.

Now Is New

I Do. Well, I Will. Eventually.

When people talk about how much longer twentysomethings are taking to grow up, it's often code for how much longer we're taking to marry. And it's true; the median age of first marriage has increased dramatically in the past fifty years, from 20.3 for women and 22.8 for men in 1960 to 26.5 and 28.7 in 2010. In 1960, 59 percent of adults between eighteen and twenty-nine were married; in 2010, that figure had dropped to 20 percent. The timeline is even slower in Europe, particularly in Scandinavia, where people wait much longer to marry, if they marry at all. The average age of first marriage in 2010 in Finland, for example, was 30.3 for women and 32.6 for men.

Still, the slower marriage pacing today is less of an anomaly than it might seem. In fact, as we mentioned in chapter 1, what's weird isn't how old people are when they get married now; it's how *young* they were when they got married in the 1950s, the *Ozzie and Harriet* "good old days" we insist on comparing ourselves to. Back in 1890, for instance, the median age for men at first marriage was 26.1—not a whole lot different from what it is today.

But I'm guessing that being a not-yet-married twenty-five-year-old in 1890 wasn't nearly as much fun as it is now. And that fun—yes, I am using *fun* partly but not entirely as a euphemism for *sex*—isn't something young people are eager to give up. In a national survey of 1,010 heterosexual men, 81 percent of the unmarried respondents in their late twenties said that "at this stage in life, you want to have fun and freedom," and 62 percent said they were "not interested in getting married anytime soon." Why kill the buzz?

I get it. Thanks to shows such as *Friends* and *Sex and the City*, I've always had a fairly glamorous notion of dating in one's twenties. It would involve a rotating cast of men, each with something to teach me, plus plenty of "me" time—although I might not choose to spend it shopping for thousand-dollar shoes. In a lot of ways, that's what it's been like. Not only has the dating life exposed me to a variety of people (a guy who grew up home-schooled and without running water or electricity), places (the Village Vanguard), foods (pit beef adorned with horseradish), and activities (Wii bowling) I might not have come across otherwise, but being unattached has also meant that I go out as often or as rarely as I want without someone making me feel guilty for not pacing my activities according to his wishes. When my cell phone dies, I don't fret about a significant other wanting to get in touch with me and worrying when I don't respond. And during my nights off (frankly, one of my favorite things about "dating"), I can come home and eat chickpeas out of the can for dinner and not have to explain myself.

"I have been single for the majority of my 20s—for the most part on purpose," Annie Karni, a twenty-eight-year-old journalist from Brooklyn (and friend of mine), wrote in response to our questionnaire. "I would say this has been a selfish decade—I basically do what I want to, when I want to, with nobody to report to." That's the great thing about being unattached in your twenties: you get all the carefree opportunities of the college years, with more disposable income and fewer roommates.

Because of that lack of accountability and sense of possibility, the single life can be a little addictive. It's easy enough to put off marriage for some future self, someone who looks the way you imagine a married person looks. One young woman quoted in the 2011 book *Premarital Sex in America* pictured herself in her late twenties ready to marry because, as she put it, "I would be completely done with school, my spouse would be done with school, and we would both be in stable jobs and both know where we're at in life." She was only twenty-two when she said that—and I think even she might find her expectations charming and laughable when she gets to her late twenties and finds herself like a lot of us, who very much *don't* know where we're at in life, don't have stable jobs, and may actually be back in school as a result.

It's Robin here. In this chapter I'll be the one to jump in occasionally to comment on Sam's observations, the way she's been doing about mine up until now. I had a warped view of dating when I was in my twenties because, as Sam said, I was married the whole time. Whenever I went out with a single twentysomething friend, I'd go home to Jeff, hug him, and say, "Thank you for saving me from that life." By "that life," I meant spending humiliating evenings at singles bars and then going home alone to cry. I had no idea if that's actually what dating was like for my friends, but I was pretty sure that's what it would have been like for me. Whatever kind of single twentysomething I might have been, I know at least that it would not have been an adventurous scenester à la Sex and the City. The more realistic TV role model was probably The Mary Tyler Moore Show. Mary Richards was a revolutionary sitcom character for the 1970s, a single career woman—thirty years old in the first season; practically a spinster!—with a failed engagement in her past and no apparent marriage in her future. She was feisty and independent, which I admired, but she also didn't seem to be getting any. I might have liked to have a cool apartment and a perky wardrobe like Mary's, but to me she seemed kind of lonely. It wasn't a life I wanted.

What's crucial in the twenties is sequencing. You can't suddenly be an adult on all fronts at once; something always lags. Either you find the person you want to spend the rest of your life with and then focus on your career, it seems, or you figure out your career first and get around to the marriage and family bit once you're more professionally settled. In a national survey of 1,003 people in their twenties, the vast majority chose the second sequence. Eighty percent of unmarried respondents said that they valued educational pursuits and career development over marriage, and 86 percent said a person "must be economically set" before marrying.

Jamie Currier, an animal science major in Rhode Island, told us that she has a "formula" for when to get married, which she has dubbed "2-2-2." It goes like this: "You'd meet your significant other at age 20–22, when you've had a chance to settle down and figure yourself out after high school and be finished/almost finished with school, plan in place. You date for two years so that you get to really know each other and have some fun. You get engaged somewhere around this point." After that, Jamie wrote, come two years of engagement (to give you time to plan the wedding—and, if needed, call it off), followed by marriage at 24–26 and two years of a "honeymoon period" before you complicate the whole thing with a baby. Then you have kids "around 26–28 years of age; you're old enough to have settled down and grown up some but young enough that when they grow up and get out of the house you should still be in good enough shape to go out and do things, to enjoy your newfound freedom." Is it surprising or predictable that Jamie, charting a course that takes her all the way from high school through empty-nestdom, is only twenty years old? And that she is following the formula? Though, actually, she has stepped up the pace some: she's engaged already, to someone she met when she was eighteen.

This track seems awfully fast in a generation where the median age of first marriage is in the late twenties. But according to some studies, Jamie's schedule is better attuned to the timing that ends up working best. According to Norval Glenn, a sociologist at the University of Texas who died in 2011, Millennials might think they're being grown-up and responsible by focusing on their careers and delaying marriage, but the truth is, later marriages are not necessarily happier marriages. In 2009, Glenn analyzed marital happiness in about 10,000 couples from four national data sets from the early 2000s. The couples who did best, he found, were those who married between ages twenty-two and twenty-five—right in Jamie's sweet spot. The association might not mean much of anything—social scientists often find correlations that prove nothing about cause and effect—but one thing is clear, Glenn reported at the American Sociological Association conference that year: "most persons have little or nothing to gain in the way of marital success by deliberately postponing marriage beyond the mid-twenties." Presumably that argument went over better with a roomful of sociologists than it would with a boyfriend who can't commit.

Because it aims for marrying so young, Jamie's 2-2-2 model doesn't allow much time for dating different people before choosing the lucky one. Is that a loss? Rachel Mathews, a twenty-four-year-old paralegal in Manhattan, thinks it would be. "Maybe it's just because I've never been one of those people who knows what they want to do their whole life," she told us, "but for those of us who don't know that, I think the best route to take is exploration." Rachel's recommendation: "Date all types of people until you know what qualities you prefer and what you can work with."

That's something my friend Brian never got to do. He met his wife when he was twenty-two and married at twenty-seven; two daughters and eight years of marriage later, he and his wife separated. That was two years ago, and Brian, now thirty-six, blames the split on Grass Is Greener Syndrome, combined with the notorious Fear of Missing Out. "I think the way to get that feeling out of your system is to experience a wider swath and know that no, there is nothing better," he told me over wine one night in his Brooklyn home, after he had put the girls to sleep.

Woody Allen's 2011 film *Midnight in Paris* resonated with Brian, not because Gil (Owen Wilson) was engaged to the wrong woman— although, dear Lord, was that woman *annoying*—but because of the endless loop of insatiable longing it portrayed. Gil thinks everything would be perfect if only he lived in Paris in the 1920s and could hobnob with F. Scott Fitzgerald and Picasso. But when he gets to 1920s Paris and meets a woman who is living the life he wants, he finds that *she* wishes she were living in the Belle Époque, with Henri Matisse and Henri de Toulouse-Lautrec. And the two Henris—well, *they* would give anything to be alive during the Renaissance. Brian quoted Gil's glum conclusion: "That's what the present is. It's a little unsatisfying because life is unsatisfying."

For Brian, then, playing the field and sowing one's oats—and whatever other agricultural metaphors apply—is the less fanciful version of Gil's time-tripping: a way to come to terms with the sad truth that the grass everywhere is a little bit brown.

Love at First Algorithm

The way we meet and begin to date is very rooted in a particular era. My father's parents met in a candy shop in New Jersey; my mother's parents, at a dance hall in New York. Many studies throughout the 1930s, '40s, and '50s found that "the chance of marriage between people declined sharply with the distance between their addresses," according to Stanford sociologist Michael J. Rosenfeld, author of *The Age of Independence: Interracial Unions, Same-Sex Unions, and the Changing American Family.* Back then, he wrote, "the typical finding was that 30 percent of marriage licenses were granted to couples who lived within roughly 5 blocks of each other." He quoted sociologist James H. S. Bossard's comment from 1932: "Cupid may have wings, but apparently they are not adapted for long flights."

Not anymore. There's no way to say this without sounding obvious, so I'll just say it: the Internet has changed the way we meet and fall in love. In a lot of ways, those changes are for the best. We have more choices. More ways to find the people who complete us, or attract us, or will cater to our fringe fantasies, such as the adorably tame fetish mentioned in a *New York Times Magazine* article about sex columnist Dan Savage's controversial stance on infidelity. (He's okay with it.) If a man gets off on having birthday cake smashed in his face, as did a college student Savage met, why, then, the Internet will help him find just the cake thrower he needs, and will save him from having to ask awkward, hedging questions in real life to suss out a potential partner's willingness to go there. (As it turns out, the cake lover in question did tell Savage about his predilection in person, not online; Savage "took the young man up to his hotel room and smashed a cake in his face.")

The web can simplify the dating process by pulling out people who should be of interest to you and running down their key stats, the way a White House staffer does before a big state dinner. Some of those stats are deal breakers that can be hard to ascertain in more natural social settings (such as religion, desire to have children, or thoughts on the best use of birthday cake). Given the convenience, it's not a big surprise that online dating is now the third-most common way for people to meet, according to a study commissioned by Match.com, and accounts for one in six new marriages.

Years ago, my friend Rishi told me he'd rather let a dating site choose his girlfriend than do it on his own. "They have algorithms," he explained. "Really good algorithms." His thinking was that he was but a man, an irrational actor who, left unchecked, would pick women by such traits as hair color (blond) or breast size (big). He didn't trust himself to choose based on things that mattered—values, intelligence, compatibility, whatever—or even to know what those other traits should be or how to discover those things in the course of a conversation screamed over bad karaoke. (Does loving horror movies count as a meaningful "shared value"?) He'd rather let the algorithm make that call, saving him from his own bad impulses—Odysseus strapped to a laptop. At the time, I wondered if his faith in some third-party judge was partly cultural. He's Indian, and his parents had had an arranged marriage—the modern kind, where they had full veto power of their prescreened marriage options, making it all the more like a dating site.

My grandmother's algorithms are a bit more idiosyncratic than OkCupid's. She has only a few criteria for a potential suitor for me: that he be single, that he be roughly my age, and that he have a grandmother who has lived either in her Florida development or anywhere in New Jersey. Grandma Bobbi's attempts at matchmaking come via emails, typed by my grandfather, who likes to put the names of the lucky lad in all-caps, as though he's writing a gossip column. In one email, dated just two weeks after M. and I broke up, my grandfather advertised a young man, ANDREW SILVERSTEIN, whose grandmother "says he's an A+." I agreed to have my info passed along to him—it seemed easier than resisting—even though I was still living in the apartment M. and I had shared, cooking with M.'s pots, watching M.'s television. Andrew never called. A week later, Grandpa followed up. "It appears that Andrew has developed a relationship with another woman," he told me by email. "That probably explains his not following thru on the lead to SAMANTHA HENIG." I had been dumped a second time in two months—and this time, via my grandfather.

Grandma Bobbi's pool of eligible bachelors might be small and dubious, but my own pool, like that of many people my age, still feels plenty big. And that's the trouble. "We want all the options, bigger and better and faster and shinier, or taller or sexier or stronger or smarter, and yet somehow also different and completely our own," Jen Doll wrote in a piece in *The Village Voice* about being single in New York. "We want the tippy-top of what we can get—why shouldn't we? And we want to push those boundaries."

Online dating only expands the options, and the sense of how high the tippy-top goes. Marina Adshade, an economist at Dalhousie University in Nova Scotia, calls it "beauty inflation." Because online dating profiles are carefully curated presentations of one's most flattering photos and witty reflections, people browsing them have an inflated sense of what's out there, and of what they can get. It's like a mating bubble. "Given that we are depreciating assets, i.e., our value on the market falls as we age, the more accurately we can determine where we sit on the market early on, the better off we will be in the long run," Adshade wrote on the group blog *Big Think*. "Over-estimating our place in the market may result in our having to exit the market"—that is, get married—"later (after a period of honest self-reflection), likely making us worse off than we would have [been] had we priced ourselves accurately in the first place."

Even those who do assess their value and exit the market early can be burned by Internet inflation; the lure of a carefully curated online persona. In a survey of 1,000 Americans in early 2012, 69 percent said that the Internet has made it easier for people to cheat on their partners, and 35 percent stated that relationships online can prove too much of a distraction to offline relationships.

So the same system that's theoretically winnowing the pool, based on those algorithms Rishi trusts, is also making us think that pool is infinitely expandable. And that's what makes so many of us so resistant to just picking and sticking with someone; it means letting go of all those might-have-beens, who might have been better.

Sliding Down the Aisle

Mom and I have talked in previous chapters about the way people make decisions: maximizers versus satisficers; paralysis in the face of too many options; an illogical compulsion to keep all doors open. All that plays out a little differently when it comes to love. Mates are not jams, arrayed before you ready to be tasted, selected, and brought to the register. Nor are they like jobs, to be won with a solid résumé, glowing references, and relevant experience in the field. You could apply the label "maximizer" to someone who tries out all possible mates the way he would laptops or curtain rods. Or you could call him a player.

There's an additional style of decision-making often used in matters of the heart, one that social scientists call "sliding." Sliding is basically what it sounds like: navigating a path by going with the flow rather than making deliberate choices. It's how a lot of people end up married without ever really meaning to be.

The beginning of a relationship is all about making choices: to call, to go out, to kiss, to call again, to sleep together, to sleep together exclusively, to hop in a cab to the airport twenty minutes before she's scheduled to fly across the country never to return so that you can tell her, no, stay, I love you. (That really happens, right?)

But then you're together. And after a certain point, sheer inertia would have you stay together. The real choice, then, the one that requires contemplation and action, is to break up. And who wants to do that? Breaking up sucks.

This is where the slide begins. You start hosting parties as a duo, and coming up with cute ways to co-sign emails from the two of you. And you spend enough nights together that, actually, now that you think about it, doesn't it seem silly that you're paying two rents and constantly leaving the shoes you need at the wrong apartment?

The slide continues. Living together has its hardships, but it's also sort of fun, like playing house. You experiment with cooking braised short ribs and bicker about throw pillows, just the way you always imagined you would one day. The things that concern you about the relationship are still there, but however hard it would have been to break up before, now there's the shared couch to consider, and the fact that you could never afford such a big living room on your own. (And yes, this "you" here applies to "me," the veteran of two live-in relationships that ended in breakups and couch custody battles.) Pretty soon you start to look like a married couple anyway, so maybe it makes sense just to make it official. Suddenly you have a wedding website and you've posted a poll asking if the honeymoon should be in Europe or Jamaica, without ever fully facing the very real question of whether you actually want to spend the rest of your life with this person.

In 2005 there were five million cohabiting couples in the United States—nine times the number in 1970 (around which time my parents were unmarried, living together, and hiding it from Mom's parents). So how do you get from there to marriage? The movies would have you believe it's a big dramatic choice, one that starts with the man having a late-night heart-to-heart with his dad or older brother, and ends with him on one knee, in the mud, delivering a speech about how he can't imagine his life without the woman who is standing, shocked and teary-eyed, before him.

In fact, proposals these days tend to be more mutual—and often less of a leap than a coast down a slope you started on years before. Michael, a thirty-eight-year-old engineer, described his proposal, such as it was, to Ellen Lamont, a graduate student at NYU, who was doing her doctoral research on gender norms in courtship. "She finally brought up, hey, where is this going?" Michael said. "Are you going to shit or get off the pot kind of thing. It was that sort of ultimatum. I thought about it and decided, yeah, I like my relationship, I don't want it to end, so I proposed sometime later."

That's pretty much how Brian, my now-separated friend, ended up married. He had moved to Boston with his then-girlfriend so she could go to graduate school, and she was ready for the next step. "When she said 'why haven't you proposed yet,' I said, 'because you feel like my sister.' And then we fought. And I didn't want to fight." As he saw it, the choice was straightforward: "Either we get married or we break up. There was no third way. And I didn't want to break up. So we got married."

The momentum-based "slide" into marriage is pretty common; two out of three first-time brides, after all, are already living with the groom on their wedding day. And it accounts for what researchers call the "cohabitation effect": the finding, in study after study, that couples who lived together before marriage ended up less happy in their marriages, and with a higher risk of divorce, than the ones who didn't. Even when controlling for things such as religion, education, and ethnicity, the couples who lived together beforehand consistently reported lower levels of marital satisfaction, worse communication, and less commitment to the relationship.

Since variables such as religion don't seem to change the findings, the cohabitation effect probably can't be ascribed to the type of people who choose to live together in the first place. It's more likely, researchers say, that the very act of living together triggers a slide toward marriage that wouldn't otherwise have occurred. It's simpler than detangling. Because the couples never really, fully chose that path, the cohabitators' marriages aren't as strong as those of couples who get engaged from the perch of separate apartments. To lend credence to this interpretation, there's also the fact that couples seem to be insulated from the cohabitation effect if they decided before they moved in together that they wanted to get married eventually. In other words, it's not having a marriage license before a shared lease that improves the marriage chances; it's the plan for marriage—a plan formed before commingled bookshelves can cloud the decision—that does the trick.

When I mentioned the idea of sliding to my friend Brian, he laughed. "That's totally me," he said. "One hundred percent. You know that Talking Heads song 'Once in a Lifetime'?" He quoted the end of the first stanza—"You may ask yourself, well, how did I get here?"—and chuckled. "That's my fucking life."

Same as It Ever Was

What's in It for Me?

One compelling explanation for why Millennials have been dragging their feet down the aisle is that there's less of a clear case for the

immediate benefits of marriage—and that shift began decades ago. In
the old days, marriage was a simple exchange: man provides economic
stability, woman cares for children and home. With their financial
security on the line, women had reason to rush. Now they have more to
gain from staying single (time and space to focus on career advancement) and less to gain from coupling. And in the modern era,
intelligence—something women were once advised against feeding or
expressing, for fear it would turn men off—ranks high on men's lists of
desirable qualities in a mate, just after mutual attraction, dependable
character, and emotional stability. Changing sexual mores and birth
control have also modified the equation, since you don't need to be
married to have plenty of sex.

This is new if you're comparing modern day to *Downton Abbey*, but
not if you're thinking about Millennials in the context of the last half-
century. Back in 1988, as women flooded the workforce, sociologist
Valerie Kincade Oppenheimer of UCLA developed the "search theory"
of marriage, likening a young woman's search for a mate to the search
for a job. In each case, she wrote, the seekers recognize that some
matches will be closer to "perfect" than others, and they accept that
they will incur certain costs along the way (missed wages, new suits,
nerves, or rejection in the case of jobs; in the case of true love: dinners
out, sexy underwear, nerves, rejection). But people also have a limit as
to how long they're willing to look, which Oppenheimer called the
"reservation wage," the point at which they decide that the costs of the
search outweigh the benefits. Another few weeks of looking might
bring a better job prospect, or a better romantic interest, but it will be
such an incremental improvement that it makes more sense just to take
the current offer. (In the last chapter, we called this method "satisficing.") In the search for a companion, according to Oppenheimer, the
reservation wage is higher in the modern era of greater gender equality.
Less is lost from staying single longer, and less is gained from coupling
sooner, when a woman's financial security and sexual satisfaction don't
hang on a marriage proposal.

Making the comparison between searching for jobs and searching
for mates comes naturally to those of us who are in the midst of one or
both—which, like many twentysomethings, I seem perpetually to be.

That's why the questions Mom posed earlier about careers are also germane to love and marriage. Is it wiser, she asked, to take whatever you can get, or hold out for something more? Is some job better than no job? Or are you hurting your chances of finding something great if you take yourself off the market for the sake of whatever ignominious job comes along first? It's easy to reframe those questions for dating. If you care about having constant companionship or getting sex on the regular, then any relationship—even one that's not all that great—may be better than none. But if you spend every night at home cooking dinner with a partner you're only half into, you don't have much of a chance of meeting someone else who could be a better match.

At the other end of the spectrum, bouncing too quickly, and too many times, from one brief fling to another is no more appealing to a would-be mate than a flurry of short-term jobs is to a potential employer. The search theory says a woman with more relationships should be more likely to get married, because the odds are higher that she will find an ideal match. (Oppenheimer didn't carry out tests of her theory so much as use existing data to argue on its behalf.) Monica Gaughan, a grad student in sociology at the University of North Carolina, thought that didn't sound like her own or her friends' experience, so she set out to challenge the search theory. Using data collected in 1990 of 341 Bay Area women in their late twenties (which means they were second-wave Baby Boomers), she found that "the more extensive a woman's involvement with non-marital romantic relationships, the lower is her propensity to marry. Hence, more information about romantic opportunities does not lead to greater certainty in the marriage market." In 2002, while she was teaching at the Georgia Institute of Technology, Gaughan published these results in support of her "substitution theory" of marriage. Women are too busy to marry young, she wrote. They're focusing their attention elsewhere—on their education and careers and the establishment of their "human capital."

Ain't that the truth. At twenty-seven, and with an ever-increasing string of "non-marital romantic relationships" in my wake—I'll leave the exact number vague, as one does when one's mother is present—I am finding that each one contributes only to a sense of sameness, actually making me feel more distant from that ideal match that, according to search theory, I should be circling in on.

> *Why is it that I married my college boyfriend and Sam didn't marry hers, when they were both such smart, devoted, wonderful guys? I think it reflects what's so distinctly different about Millennials—their sense of the elasticity of time. I was in a rush to get going with my real life, and Sam, a child of her generation, wasn't—or at least she didn't think that a "real life" needed to include being settled and married at such a young age. She had other options, other dreams, and saw her twentysomething years as fluid and ever-evolving. That was the model of the twenties everywhere she looked.*

Michelle Paster, a thirty-one-year-old filmmaker in L.A., is a poster child for the substitution theory. At twenty-five, she followed her long-term boyfriend to Arizona so he could pursue his real-estate dreams. She lasted one year. "I lost my sense of self during that time," she told me on the phone. With the breakup, she gave up thoughts of marriage and substituted two things: career exploration and an exploration of her own identity. "I'm a lot more confident in who I am now than I was when I was twenty-six. That whole journey from twenty-six to now has been fabulous. So now I'm confident with who I am and what I do for a living." That confidence, she said, has given her the necessary foundation for a serious relationship. "I need to feel strong and secure with myself before I can be vulnerable with someone else."

My separated friend Brian says his marriage broke down partly because of his failure to spend his twenties getting that strong sense of self. His wife is a year and a half older, and was always the more driven (and higher-paid) of the two. They got married, bought a house, and had two daughters, all on her timetable, he told me, which was faster than he thinks it should have been. "We never had room to figure out how to be grown-ups. She was settled in her own skin. I wasn't. I'm still not." From the vantage point of thirty-six, Brian said his mistake was to pin too many expectations on his wife. "I was depending on her for my happiness and life fulfillment," he said. "But I should have taken care of that first."

Settling versus Settling Down

Another thing that hasn't changed for Millennials is that the search for a partner can get harder with age. It's not that there are no great guys out there. There are plenty. Most of the ones I've dated, whether we met through mutual friends or an online dating site, have all the basic requirements. They're smart, good-looking, and funny enough that you can tell yourself they're funny. They value time with friends, care about their jobs, love their mothers. But they all have flaws. Nothing major, but little things: this one interrupts a conversation to make you sit in front of his sound system so you can really *feel* the music; that one posts too many black-and-white glamour shots on Facebook of himself wearing old-fashioned hats.

If all these guys I've dated seem roughly equal, does that mean it's in my power to decide *which* quirk is the one I'll spend the rest of my life gently chiding someone about—whether to resign myself to a life of turntables or fedoras? How does one choose such a thing?

Five years ago it would have been easy: I'd have picked the quirks of R., the one I was with, the one who cleaned up after me without complaint when I threw up in his bed on my twenty-first birthday, who watched me transform from a nineteen-year-old tomboy into someone vaguely more urbane and ladylike at twenty-three. He had an obvious advantage: he was there first, and knew me best. But for a variety of reasons, R. and I went our separate ways. And once you open the field to all players, it gets tough to handicap them.

When Sam followed R. to Cambridge when she was twenty-two, I half-hoped it was the prelude to marriage, just as my first cohabitation had been the prelude to mine. But I realize now that their arrangement, and even their apartment, looked like my dream of being twenty-two, not hers. Such a pretty apartment, with its French doors and eat-in kitchen—it fit my picture of young-couple domesticity perfectly, even more perfectly than the actual apartment Jeff and I moved into, which had a kitchen so cramped we couldn't both stand in it at the same time. It's not that I wanted to be a wife and mother only—I always intended to have a career, as did all the twentysomething

women I knew—but I wanted to be a wife and mother also. In a way,
marrying early made my life easier; I chose a husband, which imposed
enough constraints on my subsequent decisions to offer a kind of clar-
ity. Sam has no such clarity. I feel for her (while at the same time
admiring and even envying her independence). I've read enough stud-
ies about the paradox of choice to know how tough that wide open
field can be.

Renee Autumn Ray, a thirty-three-year-old urban planner in Tupelo, Mississippi, has also been having trouble finding the right person for long-term commitment. "I spent my 20s exploring my own needs and my career while everyone else was partnering up, and now I'm left with few options for a relationship," she wrote in response to our questionnaire. She was married briefly in her early twenties, to a transgender man, and then decided she had to "spend some time being single and thinking about why I 'needed' to be in a relationship." She dated casually for six years, mostly men, and then had an eighteen-month relationship with a woman, which ended. "I now feel as though I'm 33 [and] I can't get the one thing I want, a lifelong partnership." She's proud of being an independent, driven woman, she wrote, "but I'm not sure how to form a partnership with somebody else who might not be as ambitious or focused on a relationship as an important life goal."

So what's an aging girl to do? I know what Lori Gottlieb would say. She's the psychologist and single mother who made a splash in 2008 with a story in *The Atlantic* called "Marry Him!"—the first in a string of Lori Gottlieb articles about modern life that drove me batshit crazy. Gottlieb would probably tell Renee to expand her concept of marriage material to include people who aren't so obsessed with their own careers. It doesn't take a bachelor's degree to inseminate an egg or do the dishes, she would say, and any income, even a modest one, is better than nothing, and nothing is what you'll have IF YOU WAIT SO LONG THAT YOU END UP ALONE. (It doesn't matter what size typeface Gottlieb actually uses; I have trouble reading her words in anything but an all-caps, scoldy voice.) "Marriage ultimately isn't about cosmic connection," she wrote. "It's about how having a teammate, even if he's not the love of your life, is better than not having one."

What does that mean for the young and the teammateless? Here's what Gottlieb suggested: "Settle! That's right. Don't worry about passion or intense connection. Don't nix a guy based on his annoying habit of yelling 'Bravo!' in movie theaters. Overlook his halitosis or abysmal sense of aesthetics. Because if you want to have the infrastructure in place to have a family, settling is the way to go." And by "settling," Gottlieb means something different from "sliding." She means an intentional kind of sliding: deciding you want to marry someone, finding a willing someone, and, even if that person is not the love of your life, marrying.

This is a classic story, as familiar to people in my grandmother's generation as to people in mine. It seems there will always be older folks who urge the young'uns to avoid the mistakes they themselves made—and the mistakes they obsess about often seem to be related either to marrying the wrong person or to not marrying at all, a crowdsourcing of regrets so varied and contradictory that there's not much collective wisdom you can take away.

Still, there's obviously *something* to the settling case, at least if you want kids. The longer you wait, the cobwebbier your reproductive system becomes. (For men, the need to settle isn't quite as severe, since the pool of eligible single ladies expands with every passing year, and older sperm can still get the job done.) But the advice to settle is also appalling, especially for the high-achieving women who spend their most fertile years advancing their careers, then find themselves competing for partners with younger, more fertile prospects. (Sylvia Ann Hewlett of the Center for Talent Innovation found some sobering marriage statistics about high-powered women; more on that in the next chapter.) After all, the whole thing about being high-achieving is that you don't *want* to settle, for *anything*.

I was horrified to hear a Gottlieb-like "case for settling" come out of my own mouth one evening with Sam not long ago—especially since I knew how infuriated she'd been reading that Atlantic *article. Jeff and I were having an early dinner with her at a restaurant downtown before she rushed off to some party, and I asked casually about her date a few nights before. I didn't know much about the guy—I can't even remember his name—but I thought they'd had a charming meet-cute, and I was curious. She replied that he was a very nice guy, they'd had a very nice date, but he didn't make her feel "glowy."*

"Well, you know, Sam," I began, already hearing from my tone of voice that I was about to say something I'd regret. "You're almost twenty-seven years old. Maybe you shouldn't really be expecting 'glowy' anymore." Oh shit, I thought instantly, what did I just SAY? That wasn't what I meant, WAS it? I knew Sam deserved to be with someone who made her insides quiver. I knew that twenty-seven was too young for her to be thinking about settling for the next nice guy who came along. I knew it was none of my business anyway. But there was a tiny part of me that worried that Sam was on track to talk herself out of ever finding someone good enough for her. I'd seen it happen to my own friends, who ended up fifty and single and surprised to be living lives they hadn't really intended. A few days later, still smarting at the memory of what I'd said, I apologized to Sam for being so thoughtless, and asked if I had hurt her feelings. "Not really," she said, ever the diplomat. "But I did tell my friends about it."

Gottlieb relied more on anecdotes and theorizing than on data, but she did mention a few numbers: specifically the numbers ten, eight, and occasionally six. She described a woman who said she's not looking for a perfect ten; she'd be satisfied with an eight—which is how she'd rate the guy she was already with. But what if she'd be happier with a *different* eight, a guy who loses points for being bald and too into his fantasy league, perhaps, instead of for being pudgy and a bit of a braggart? "The thing she has to remember is that every eight becomes a six over time," Barry Schwartz, the psychologist who wrote *The Paradox of Choice*, told Gottlieb. "You can trade your six for a new eight, but eventually that eight will become a six, and you'll be trading him in for another eight, too."

I'd like to go on record here as questioning Barry Schwartz's suggestion that every eight becomes a six over time. I don't dare give a score to Jeff's desirability, in his twenties or in his sixties, in private or in print. But I can say unequivocally that he's only gotten better with age. He spent his twenties unsure of whether he'd be any good at all the things he wanted to do well, as a husband, a father, a provider, and a political scientist (not necessarily in that order). As he gradually became more sure of himself in all those roles, he became better in all of them, too, especially the ones I care about the most, husband and father. My direct experience of other men is limited, as Sam would be the first to point out. But I don't think Jeff is all that unusual in this regard.

Even without the eights and sixes, the whole settling thing can start to feel like a trick question on a Game Theory exam. Marry too early and you might always wonder what else is out there; wait too long and there might be nothing left. It's a microcosm of that same confusion that characterizes the overall transition to adulthood. As the blogger Jessie Rosen, twenty-eight, wrote on the old Lemondrop site (now a part of *Huffington Post*): "What am I gaining by taking my time versus what I'm losing by just getting to it already? With every year I wait to be ready to get married, am I letting all the people there are to marry pass me by? Will I be a better, more mature mother at 35 or would I have been just as adept and instinctual at 25? . . . Does being an adult mean having the maturity to know you're not ready for adult things, or having the maturity to dive in and just figure it out? Won't I be a better, happier, healthier adult if I take my time getting there?"

My childhood friend Peter Cirincione feels like he's in a spot a lot like Jessie's. I used to call him "the steady boyfriend"; in middle school he'd ride his bike home in the rain to fetch an umbrella for a girl he liked, and he agonized for weeks about how to get his girlfriend to hold his hand. In his twenties, he's still "the steady boyfriend"—a serial monogamist, moving from one long-term relationship to another. Responding to our questionnaire Peter, twenty-six and a teacher in San Francisco, wrote that he still prefers "deep, meaningful connections" over hookups, but he sometimes thinks these familiar, comfortable relationships might be working to his detriment. He wonders, he told us, if he's "walling myself off from (a) finding something even better" and "(b) discovering important things about myself as an individual."

There's also, of course, a less existential, angsty reason to be cautious about getting too serious too quickly: divorce. As many children of broken homes can attest, divorce can be painful, and fear of its inevitability can make young people skittish about marriage. But maybe that fear is misplaced. The common meme that half of all marriages end in divorce is actually outdated. It was marriages from the 1970s that failed at that rate, marriages from our *parents'* era. But the divorce rate per thousand people peaked in 1981, and has been falling ever since.

That's the remarkable and often-overlooked fact: the divorce rate is going *down*. In 2005 the divorce rate of 3.6 per thousand people was at its lowest level since 1970, and it hovered at that level through 2010. A partial explanation is that fewer people are "at risk" for divorce because the proportion of the population marrying in the first place has also been falling. Even as a measurement of divorce among married couples, though, there's been a decline, from a peak of 22.8 divorces per thousand married couples in 1979 to just 16.7 divorces per thousand in 2005.

But it's not as if people sit down with divorce statistics, or any other statistics, before they decide to get married. Decisions about love and marriage are usually way less logical than that.

Soul and Spit Mates

Despite marriage's spotty reputation, young people hold on to some surprisingly romantic notions. In a Gallup poll of a representative sample of twentysomethings commissioned by the National Marriage Project at Rutgers, 94 percent of the 612 respondents who had never been married agreed with the statement "When you marry you want your spouse to be your soul mate, first and foremost." And 88 percent also agreed that "There is a special person, a soul mate, waiting for you somewhere out there." There is of course the small matter of locating said soul mate. But not to worry. Of that same sample of never-married twentysomethings, 87 percent said that they would find that person when they were ready. Convenient.

If you think these respondents sound like dreamy idealists, how's this: even though about 20 percent of Americans were divorced when the poll was taken, only 6 percent of the respondents expected that they themselves would ever divorce. In other words, 94 percent had no doubt that their own marriage would last a lifetime. And why shouldn't it? It's a union of *soul mates*.

But rather than trying to plumb the depths of our partners' souls, maybe we should be trying to plumb the depths of their saliva. Wait, I'm not being junior high-ish—or not *only* being junior high-ish. This is actually something scientists study. It turns out that one (gross) way of looking at perfect matches starts in the salivary glands. There's evidence that our bodily fluids contain proteins that advertise our immune function genes and, according to Helen Fisher at Rutgers, kissing might be a good way to sample them. A kiss in this view is just taste-testing the genome, to find the one that will best match our own. This theory has the same problem as much of evolutionary psychology—it's easy to dismiss it as a "just-so story" instead of real science—but the tale being spun here is still fun to mull. It goes like this: what we think of as sexual chemistry might be nothing more romantic than the adaptive advantage of two well-matched immune systems, just different enough from each other to lead to more successful pregnancies and more robust offspring. According to this theory, evolution has favored people who are able to pick up on these immune differences in their potential mates' saliva when they kiss. (By the way, these proteins appear in sweat, too, and we can also assess those potential mates' genes by sniffing their pits. This was tested in just the way you'd expect. Ew.)

Sexual chemistry is important to many young people, even if they don't couch it in "soul mate" or salivary terms. A lot of us are waiting for that knee-weakening kiss or holding out, much to our mothers' chagrin, for the person who makes us feel glowy. We're tossing out people with whom sex feels awkward or unsatisfying—but we might be doing this too quickly. "Sustained sexual chemistry actually takes time and requires conversation," Mark Regnerus and Jeremy Uecker wrote in a forlorn footnote in *Premarital Sex in America*, drawing attention to the gap between that reality and the belief among many young people "that good sex should emerge rapidly and silently with the commencement of a sexual relationship. (It seldom does.)"

There's no doubt that certain relationships, should you choose to accept them, are statistically more likely to work out than others. So if you can convince yourself to ditch the concept of perfection or instant chemistry, what should you aim for instead? Surely not all eights are created equal.

Researchers at the Kinsey Institute recently looked into what works and what doesn't work for older couples. The Kinsey Institute is the place that shocked the world in the late 1940s and early 1950s with its findings about homosexuality, infidelity, and the female orgasm. Its new study, published in 2011, analyzed 1,009 couples in committed relationships (either marriage or cohabitation) where the men were aged forty to seventy. They came from Brazil, Germany, Japan, Spain, and the United States. Some had been together only a year, some more than fifty; the median relationship duration was twenty-five years. So what worked for them? What can long-lasting relationships tell us about when and with whom to settle down?

A pithy summary of the findings, from William Saletan on *Slate*: "promiscuity makes you sad, commitment makes you happy, and men prefer love and cuddling." Indeed, men like cuddling more than you might think. Of all the factors that the Kinsey researchers took into account—health, education, age at the start of the relationship, relationship duration, sexual functioning—the ones that predicted the best odds of a happy relationship for men were the degree to which they kiss and cuddle with their partner and how much their partner touches or caresses them. That mattered for women, too, but barely more than any of the other factors. For men, it was major.

> *I'm surprised to hear that cuddling matters so much to men. One of the hardest things for me in my twenties was getting used to the fact that I was married to a guy who just wasn't into caressing, at least not at his own instigation. He could barely do hugs, even as a recipient: if I hugged him while his hands happened to be in his pockets, I had to physically remove his hands and wrap them around my waist. I tried to laugh about it with an old Marx Brothers line, which I'd repeat in Chico's accent: "Don't you know what a hog is?" But it wasn't actually that funny.*
>
> *Not only was it not funny, but for a while it became a pretty big deal. It got all tied up in a midlife crisis I had in my mid-forties, one that sent me to a therapist to try to figure out what about my life was*

bothering me and what I wanted to change. I hadn't thought the hugging was all that important until my therapist expressed shock at how withholding it seemed. Well, maybe. But what if Jeff not knowing how to hug me was just one of those "quirks" Sam alluded to earlier, one that I had just decided to put up with? Everyone has such quirks, annoying only if you choose to define them that way. And I wouldn't be surprised if the Kinsey researchers found that long-married people often made a deliberate decision to reframe a partner's quirks as funny instead of deal breakers. That's pretty much what I decided to do with the hugging thing, no matter what my therapist said.

Sex matters, too. Among the couples in the Kinsey study who were in long-term relationships, sexual satisfaction was a common predictor of relationship satisfaction. (Another important predictor, for both men and women: valuing their partner's orgasm.) But sexual satisfaction often takes time. It's not that instant chemistry sort of thing like in the movies. Using the data they collected, the Kinsey researchers predicted the probability of sexual satisfaction for men and women over time. Men's satisfaction was predicted to increase gradually over the course of forty years with one woman, while women charted a more complex course. "During the first 15 years of the relationship, women had significantly lower probabilities of reporting satisfaction than men. From year 30 on in the relationship, however, women had a significantly higher probability of reporting satisfaction."

The same patterns emerge with overall relationship (as opposed to sexual) satisfaction. The length of time together had a significant and positive effect on men's satisfaction with the relationship. For women, it's again more complicated: for the first fifteen years of a relationship, their satisfaction decreases with each passing year; after twenty years, that turns around.

There's no mystery here, at least to this long-married woman: for the wives and long-term girlfriends, sexual and relationship satisfaction tracked almost perfectly with external demands on the couple's time—in particular, with how old the kids were. Women's satisfaction declines during the first fifteen years of a relationship? Of course it does; that's when women are dealing with children most intensely, and their husbands and marriages are always going to come second. Women at that stage are too tired and distracted for sex, or even for the long, intimate conversations that are part of "relationship satisfaction." I don't want to make Sam and her sister feel bad, but I don't think their father and I even thought of our marriage as a "relationship" until we'd been in it for twenty-five years and the girls were less of a day-to-day distraction.

If Mom is worried about shielding my sister and me from the fact that her marriage flourishes in our absence, she's a little late; she wrote as much in a *New York Times* essay in 1991, when Jess and I were eleven and seven. "Our kids were away last summer, and it was heavenly," she began. "For the whole blissful month of August, my husband, Jeff, and I had only each other to worry about." Well, now we're away again, as grown-ups living our own lives, so I'm glad that the marital bliss can return.

Uh-oh, looks like my mother was right. She told me that essay would one day come back to bite me. In my defense, I ended the piece with how delighted we were when the girls came home from camp, and I also wrote about (and I quote, since Sam is quoting) "what it means for a child to give shape to your life, what it means to enfold your own little girl, to breathe in her puppy-dog scent and believe she is totally and forever a part of you." Still, I guess overall it sounded a bit harsh, and if I remember right, Jess was pretty miffed about it even then; she was a very astute eleven. Sorry, girls.

But kids aren't the only thing to blame for lower marital satisfaction. (And before I drop it entirely, *smells like a puppy dog?* Not helping!) Having a lot of sexual experience before marriage could also be a factor—but probably not in the way you'd expect. The Kinsey researchers found that for the men they studied, a greater lifetime number of sexual partners predicted *less* sexual satisfaction in their current long-term relationships. It's hard to tease out cause and effect on this one. The same thing that drives you to sleep around might also keep you from being satisfied in a monogamous relationship. Or, on the flip side, being unsatisfied in a monogamous relationship might be what drives you to sleep around.

But what about the fun of playing the field, the high of sexual conquest? A study from 2004 by David G. Blanchflower of Dartmouth and Andrew J. Oswald of Warwick University in England surveyed 16,000 American adults about the relationship among money, sex, and happiness. "The more sex," they found, "the happier the person." But money does not buy either more happiness or more sex. And although more sex may make you happier, sex with more people probably won't. "How many sexual partners in the last year will maximize a person's happiness?" asked Blanchflower and Oswald. "The simple answer according to these data is one."

So one monogamous partner is the route to happiness? Well, not for everyone. With all the talk about how people choose this lifelong mate over that one (or choose to wait for the one they haven't met yet), it's important to note that there have always been people who choose none of the above. For lots of people, the ideal marital state is single.

"I am happy," wrote psychologist Bella DePaulo, who never married, in *Singled Out: How Singles Are Stereotyped, Stigmatized, and Ignored, and Still Live Happily Ever After.* "I have a life, and there is no way I will grow old alone (a matter that has little to do with having a serious coupled relationship or even living by yourself). That's just for starters. But it is also exactly the point: The conventional wisdom about people who are single is a mythology, a gloss. It is not an accurate description of the textured and varied lives of real people who are single."

According to DePaulo, pop culture, book authors, advertisers, and even scientific researchers skew facts about single people to play into the stereotype that they're all sad, isolated, and would prefer to be coupled off. "At a time when marriage is so inessential," she wrote, "mental blanketing aims to instill in an entire populace the unshakable belief that marriage is exactly what it is not: utterly and uniquely transformative."

Franklin Schneider isn't falling for that marriage-is-transformative thing. "Think about the difference between meeting someone and deciding that your life will be positively enhanced by their continued

presence (rare) and meeting someone and deciding they meet the minimum requirements for your urgently vacant 'significant other' position
(depressingly common)," he wrote in 2011 in the Washington, D.C.,
City Paper. Franklin, thirty-three, has basically made a career out of
rejecting adulthood. (Although he certainly wouldn't call it a "career";
careers are things adults have.) "This, my friends, is marriage in a nut-
shell," he wrote; "a shit product that only exists to fill a need created by
clever social marketing ('marriage = adulthood,' 'sex is bad/dirty/dan-
gerous')."

That "clever social marketing," or, to use DePaulo's term, "mental
blanketing," can take many forms. Tax breaks. Legal rights such as hospital visitation or Social Security benefits, which have come to the fore
in the context of debates over gay marriage. Different expectations from
your bosses about your ability to work nights and weekends, or from
your friends about your willingness to go along with someone else's
plans. There are a lot of ways that it pays to be married, and a lot of ways
the normalization of coupledom seeps in. But as I mentioned earlier, in
2010 nearly half of all American adults were *not* married. Some of them
were divorced, some widowed, some on the prowl, and some, such as
Bella DePaulo and Franklin Schneider, happily on their own.

Round Four

NOW IS NEW:

- People are getting married later.
- The web makes it seem as if the options are limitless.
- Therefore, many young people slide rather than decide.
- And they just marry the person they're living with, because
  it's easier than moving out.

SAME AS IT EVER WAS:

- Women with careers needn't rush to settle down.
- There's no such thing as the perfect mate.

- And if you want kids, there is such a thing as waiting too long.
- Still, some matches are better than others.
- And some people would rather stay single.

Ultimately, love is timeless, and there hasn't been any seismic shift in the expectations surrounding marriage. The pacing may be different from how it was in the 1950s, as are the make-ups of marriages (more interracial marriages today, same-sex marriages legal for the first time) and the way people find one another. But the major things that people fret about—Is this the right person? Am I ready for this sort of commitment? Am I better off being with someone imperfect than being alone?—are old hat. So we're calling this for the camp of Same as It Ever Was.

Chapter 5

Baby Carriage

Samantha handed the writing over to me again. I'll start with a story: think of it as "A Tale of Two Magazine Covers." The first is *Newsweek*'s from 1986. It's a huge line graph with a plunge steeper than Splash Mountain's, accompanied by the ominous headline "The Marriage Crunch: If You're a Single Woman, Here Are Your Chances of Getting Married." By the time the sloping line gets to age thirty-five, it has practically disappeared into the X axis. In other words, chances at thirty-five = almost zero. This is the article that famously announced that a forty-year-old woman had as much chance of getting married as she had of dying in a terrorist attack. My single friends, mostly about thirty-five at the time, really took it to heart: if they didn't marry soon, how would they ever have kids? Cultural trend-setters took it to heart, too, repeating the analogy as gospel even seven years later, when Meg Ryan's character used it to make a point in *Sleepless in Seattle*. It didn't matter that the demographers whose work was the basis for the article insisted they had made no such analogy. Nor did it matter that other social scientists who looked again at the raw data said the original calculations had been wrong. It was too late; the "killed by terrorists" line had struck a chord.

The second magazine cover is from 2011, from *New York*. This one is a photograph of a naked, aging woman in profile. She has drooping breasts, wrinkled skin, gray hair, tired eyes—and a hugely pregnant belly. The cover line asks, "Is She Just Too Old for This?" (Both of these covers are about women, since women are the most frantic when it comes to baby-making, but these decisions affect men in their twenties, too.) The article is about women who are having their first babies at fifty—*fifty!*—after having been brought artificially out of menopause and getting pregnant through IVF using donated eggs. It is still a rare event, according to *New York*, but becoming less so: the 541 babies born in the United States to women over fifty in 2008 was more than three times the number in 1998.

What a difference a quarter century makes. When the *Newsweek* story came out, if you didn't have a baby by forty, you assumed you never would. It was less than five years after the birth of the first American test tube baby, and IVF was still controversial, slightly embarrassing, and hugely expensive, with a success rate of just 5 percent and an out-of-pocket cost of about $5,000 per cycle (equivalent to almost $10,000 in today's dollars). And it was rationed back then: most clinics wouldn't even perform the procedure on women over thirty-five—or, for that matter, on women who weren't married. The notion that forty- or fiftysomething women could or *should* get pregnant was . . . well, it was unimaginable, even for science fiction. In Margaret Atwood's *The Handmaid's Tale*, published the same year as the *Newsweek* story, the Handmaids were forced to become breeders specifically because the Wives (exact age unspecified) were too old to have babies of their own.

All that had changed by the time of the *New York* magazine cover. By then, an estimated 600,000 babies were born each year to women over thirty-five. IVF was common and was often covered by insurance, and a range of more sophisticated assisted reproduction techniques (ICSI, ZIFT, assisted hatching, embryo freezing) had brought the success rate to as high as 70 percent overall, though the odds were worse the older you got. While most first-time mothers in the United States were still between twenty and thirty-four, the birth rate had grown most dramatically for older women: a 47 percent increase in first births to women in their late thirties between 1990 and 2008, and an 80 percent increase to women in their early forties. American motherhood, as the Pew Research Center noted, had a new demography. And that demographic change has shaped the way men and women alike think about the timing, probability, and desirability of having babies.

Now Is New

Note to Self: Schedule IVF at Forty-three

In the same way that there's no shame these days in going high-tech to find love, there's no shame in going high-tech for a baby. In fact, some young women now *count on* using assisted reproductive technology at some future date, making it a central pillar of their lifetime to-do lists.

When Sylvia Ann Hewlett, a researcher at what was then called the Center for Work-Life Policy, interviewed 1,647 high-achieving women in 2001 about their career and childbearing decisions, she divided them into two age groups: younger (aged twenty-eight to forty, considered to be in the childbearing range) and older (aged forty-one to fifty-five, thought to be past childbearing—which might have been true for the Baby Boomers in her study, but now . . . not necessarily). Many of them, aware of the hit that their careers would take if they stopped to have babies, had kept nose to grindstone and put plans for a husband and children on hold until a date TBD. As a result, they had entered their forties or fifties childless, not because of any choice they'd made but because of what one of them called "creeping non-choice." The higher up the career ladder her subject was, Hewlett found, the less likely she was to be a mother; she'd just gotten too busy with her career, and before she knew it, it was too late for a child. "An accomplished woman who delays commitment and marriage," Hewlett wrote in *Creating a Life: Professional Women and the Quest for Children*, "can turn around and discover that she has inadvertently squandered her fertility."

Among high achievers in Hewlett's sample—which she defined as women who made more than $55,000 a year in the younger group, more than $65,000 in the older ($70,000 and $83,000 in today's dollars)—42 percent had never had children; among ultra-achievers, who made more than $100,000 a year ($127,000 today), that figure was 49 percent. But 86 percent of the women told her that back when they were in their early twenties, they had wanted to have kids someday. Hewlett's conclusion, then, was that among these highly successful women, careers had gotten in the way of their maternal ambition. The iconic Roy Lichtenstein print leaps to mind so immediately that I'm surprised it wasn't reproduced on the book's cover: the distraught cartoon blonde with the speech bubble reading, "I can't believe it . . . I forgot to have children."

"What gnaws at me is that I always assumed I would," Lisa Polsky, a Baby Boomer and successful banker, told Hewlett. She was in her mid-forties at the time and wasn't assuming this anymore. "Somehow I imagined that having a child was something I would get to in a year or so, after the next promotion, when I was more established."

Another Baby Boomer told Hewlett that "Looking back, I can't think why I allowed my career to obliterate my thirties." And a third mused that "I just didn't get it together in time." Classic cases all of creeping non-choice, all exhibiting what Hewlett called a "palpable" sense of loss.

"For many women," Hewlett wrote, "the brutal demands of ambitious careers, the asymmetries of male-female relationships, and the difficulties of bearing children late in life conspire to crowd out the possibility of having children." The cruel twist to all this, she wrote, is that the prime years of career-building overlap "almost perfectly" with the prime years of childbearing—that is, the twenties. "It's very hard to throttle back during that stage of a career and expect to catch up later"; and it's just as hard to "catch up later" when the thing you skip is the baby.

But Hewlett found, possibly inadvertently, an attitude in the younger women in her study that made it clear how different today's twentysomethings are from earlier generations. These young women had mapped out a wholly new timetable for the famous work-life balance. Among Hewlett's respondents was a twenty-nine-year-old yoga instructor she called Amy, whom we met back in chapter 1. Amy seemed to have it all figured out—and a trip to the fertility clinic was most definitely part of the overall plan. She knew that the only way to fit in everything she wanted—a few more years teaching yoga, travel to Bali and other exotic locales, a return to school for an MBA, and at last embarkation on a "serious career"—was to put motherhood on hold almost indefinitely. Amy was born in 1972, which makes her officially a part of Generation X, but the timeline she laid out was typically Millennial. "I've got fourteen, fifteen years before I need to worry about making babies," she told Hewlett. (That would put her at forty-three or forty-four, and that's just when she plans to *start* worrying.) She could take this leisurely approach, she said, thanks to the miracles of modern medicine: "I can't tell you how glad I am that this new reproductive technology virtually guarantees that you can have a baby until 45. Or maybe it's even later. It seems that every time I pick up the paper there's another medical breakthrough. Go, doctors!"

Millennials feel much the same way as Gen Xer Amy did in her twenties, according to a poll called Fertility IQ 2011 conducted by the National Infertility Association. Among the 1,000 women surveyed, who were aged twenty-five to thirty-five and had already talked with their doctors about their plans to get pregnant, the typical Fertility IQ was distressingly low. Only about half of them even scored a passing grade. Most of these women thought, for instance, that the chances for a thirty-year-old to conceive in any given month of trying were 70 percent, and that the chances for a forty-year-old were nearly 60 percent. The true stats, according to the pollsters, are 20 percent at age thirty, and 5 percent at age forty.

Accurate or not, though, for twentysomething women such as Amy, the possibility of late-life babies is a reprieve, permission to work harder on their careers and their relationships before committing to a child. This possibility is at the heart of the difference between my youth in the twentieth century and Sam's youth in the twenty-first. As the upper limit of childbearing expands far beyond what my cohort ever thought possible (or even desirable), the rate at which twentysomethings expect their lives to unspool has changed, too. More than any other decision point we've considered in this book so far, the lengthening of the now-or-never moment about babies strikes me as the single most important reason why Millennials—males as well as females—are taking their time growing up. They're stretching it out because they can, and they can because of this new timetable for reproduction. "Waiting to have kids is much better because you'll have a level of maturity (hopefully) you wouldn't have earlier on," wrote Peter

Fritch, twenty-three, who told us he doesn't expect to have children until his late thirties or early forties. By waiting until then, he wrote, it might be possible to avoid "an element of resentment towards your spouse or partner at the fact that you've sacrificed your youth for your family."

There are still hazards to waiting so long to get pregnant. Women over thirty-five or forty have higher rates of pregnancy-related hypertension, eclampsia, gestational diabetes, placenta previa, breach presentation, postpartum hemorrhage, birth asphyxia, prematurity, low birth weight, and stillbirth, and greater use of labor-inducing drugs and Cesareans. (Recent studies have associated health risks in babies with older fathers, too, suggesting that sperm are not quite as eternally youthful as people used to think, and that the biological clock also ticks for guys.) But these complications in older mothers are "not at prohibitive levels," according to infertility specialists Anne Steiner and Richard Paulson of the University of Southern California, who looked at the long-term effect of maternal age in patients at their fertility clinic. And the risks might be outweighed by the benefits that older parents bring: more disposable income to spend on the child, fewer competing obligations, and an overall more enriched atmosphere for the babies they do have.

In 2007, Steiner and Paulson mailed questionnaires to all the women who had given birth after IVF at the USC clinic between 1992 and 2004, and got back 64 responses that they could analyze: 22 from women who had given birth in their thirties, 22 in their forties, and 18 in their fifties. (*Their fifties!* Sorry, it still amazes me.) Years later, the mothers over fifty did just as well as the others in terms of physical and mental health, and actually exhibited lower signs of parenting stress than the younger mothers. This is in line with other research that found that women who conceived using donor eggs—which by definition includes all IVF patients over fifty—were happier mothers. In those other studies, women of any age who had used donor eggs showed more positive parent-child relationships and greater emotional involvement when their babies were infants, and greater pleasure in their children when the babies were aged two.

Steiner and Paulson said the USC study brought into question the position of the American Society for Reproductive Medicine, whose ethics committee was at the time considering opposing fertility treatments for women over fifty. The committee wrote that "because parenting is both an emotionally stressful and physically demanding experience, older women and their partners may be unable to meet the needs of a growing child and maintain a long parental relationship." Steiner and Paulson said such a position needed to be reassessed.

Money Talks

One thing that hasn't changed for Millennial women is that if they want to have children, they're still forced to make the same kind of career trade-offs Baby Boomers had to make. The difference, though, is that women's contribution to the family income tends to be larger now than ever before—so those trade-offs have become even more consequential. About 23 percent of wives now out-earn their husbands, and that number will grow as Millennials continue to marry and have babies. In all but three of the 150 largest cities in the United States, twentysomething women who are single and childless make more money than men their age. In some cities (such as Atlanta and Memphis), they make 20 percent more, on average, than young men; in Sam's city, New York, they make 17 percent more. What will happen to the household incomes that these young couples have come to count on if the women's lucrative careers go into an artificial stall for the sake of their having kids?

For the women themselves, it's clear what will happen—they'll never earn as much as they could have if they hadn't had kids, or had had them later. A recent analysis of Census data found that among women with advanced degrees, those who waited until age thirty-five to get pregnant had annual salaries $50,000 higher than those who had a first child at twenty. In a different study, economist Amalia Miller of the University of Virginia found that for college-educated women in professional and managerial jobs, every year of delaying pregnancy means a significant bump in wages, hours worked, and total lifetime earnings.

Miller made an "opportunity cost" evaluation of choosing motherhood over career that would have made Dan Ariely proud (though it wouldn't have fit too well into his Oranges2Apples app). She imagined a hypothetical woman who steps out of an upwardly mobile career for one year to have a baby. This woman's "wage profile," the slope by which wages increase over time, will flatten even after she returns to a comparable job following that year at home. If the flattening begins when this hypothetical woman is thirty, it starts from a higher wage than if it begins when she's twenty-three. "Women can achieve higher earnings by delaying motherhood during their twenties and early thirties," Miller concluded. For every year a woman puts off having a baby, she wrote, her wages increase by 3 percent and her lifetime earnings increase by 9 percent. In other words, a woman who has her first baby at thirty-four will, on average, have lifetime earnings 72 percent higher than a woman who has her first baby at twenty-six.

That opportunity cost seemed so high that I contacted Miller by email to make sure I had gotten the numbers right. Yes, she assured me, waiting eight years yields, on average, 72 percent more in lifetime earnings. Another way of looking at it, she wrote, is that a delay of ten years in having your first child will *double* your lifetime earnings. Then I asked if her findings had affected her own personal decisions about childbearing. She is thirty-five years old and doesn't have children yet. "I think that my career is in better shape now than it would have been if I'd had a child in my twenties or even early thirties, though, of course, I can't prove that or even know for sure," she wrote. "This may not be true for everyone, but my personal experience does seem to fit the general pattern in the data that I found in my study that there is a trade-off between early motherhood and career outcomes."

There was a woman at Newsweek, *where I worked when I first moved to New York, who specialized in talking to younger co-workers as often as she could about careers and parenting. The young women in the newsroom used to exchange stories about the first time we had each been taken aside by her so she could tell us her cautionary tale. She had taken a decade off from her reporting career to raise her two daughters, she'd tell whichever young woman she had sequestered during a late night at the office, and when she finally returned, it was at a dramatically lower pay grade. "Don't get me wrong," she'd say. "I love my daughters and the time I got to spend with them." But her career had suffered, she told us again and again. I never knew quite what to make of it. Was she telling us not to make the same mistake? Or just lamenting that the choices are so tough if you want to be a successful woman and a mother?*

I'm angry that my co-worker's story is so typical, and that women's salaries are so often slashed after they take time off to be with their kids. But what freaks me out just as much is another salary: that of a nanny. While still at Newsweek, I heard from another colleague that he paid his nanny $25,000 a year. I repeated that number often to my friends, and we were all struck by a horrible realization: our jobs didn't pay us enough to justify working once we had kids. It feels almost selfish to plan to stay in my career just because I love it, if my salary will barely cover the cost of day care. But when the hypothetical nanny calculations get too depressing, I make a different calculation: Mom is flexibly self-employed and lives just a subway ride away. So . . . maybe granny day care? I hope she's down for that arrangement. If it's good enough for the Obamas, it's good enough for me.

For women on a traditional corporate track, the fallout from babies can be dramatic. (And yes, Sam, I'll theoretically watch your hypothetical children.) This is especially the case for what psychiatrist Anna Fels calls "front-loaded" careers such as medicine, law, academia, and business, which require a lot of schooling during the same years that are often also traditionally devoted to childbearing. It can be a "miserable bargain," Fels wrote in *Necessary Dreams: Ambition in Women's Changing Lives*, being forced to choose between career and childbearing. Young adulthood presents the starkest choices for women, she wrote, and they feel the full force of social and institutional discrimination. They "have left the educational system and started pursuing their ambitions. At the age when women most frequently marry and have children, they must decide whether to try to hold on to their own ambitions, or downsize or abandon them."

The Best Age to Have a Baby

In the past, reproductive biology and societal roles lined up more evenly than they do today; people generally were ready, emotionally and financially, to start their families by their mid-twenties, while the reproductive system was in its prime. I certainly felt ready when I was twenty-five—and with only a little convincing, Jeff said he felt ready, too. He was twenty-seven, had finished grad school, and had a tenure-track job at George Washington University; I had a new reporting job I liked at a small monthly magazine called *BioScience*, with good health insurance and a retirement plan; and we owned a house on a street so suburban and child-friendly that every neighborhood gathering made us feel like we were on *The Dick Van Dyke Show*. Three bedrooms, a crabapple tree in the backyard, young mothers down the block with kids in elementary school who spent their days *actually cleaning the house*—it was time for babies now, right?

But for young people today, according to sociologist John Mirowsky of the University of Texas at Austin, there's a troubling disconnect in timing when it comes to *being* ready versus *feeling* ready. "Humans mature reproductively about a decade before Americans mature socially," he wrote.

How, then, do you figure out the "best age" to have your baby? Well, how do you define "best"? The late teens or early twenties are best biologically, according to Mirowsky, since that's when "oocytes are fresh and the body's reproductive and other systems are at a youthful peak," and when women are least likely to have developed chronic health problems that would put them or their babies at risk. This is the age with the lowest rates of miscarriage, ectopic pregnancy, stillbirth, and infertility. But early pregnancy doesn't work well in today's society, which is organized around smaller families and more full-time employment for women. If pregnancy occurs too early, social difficulties often follow. At age twenty or younger, Mirowsky wrote, pregnancy is "more likely to happen out of wedlock, more likely to interfere with educational attainment, and more likely to crystallize a disadvantaged status."

Even the early twenties seems too young, in some circles, to have a baby—including when the mother is married and has a college degree. Michelle Horton, for instance, gave birth to her son, Noah, when she was twenty-one, an age that seemed reasonable enough a generation ago. She started a blog called *Early Mama* to document her sense of isolation when she took Noah out and nosy strangers asked incredulously how old she was. She usually said twenty-five or twenty-seven, just to shut them up. "But while I can lie to strangers, the fact remains that I am still a very young mother," she wrote on her blog. "Most of my friends are in grad school, cheating on their boyfriends, getting wasted. I'll have to face future play dates where other moms are 10, even 15 years older than I am. But for me, for us, we're ready and we're happy, despite your upturned nose."

The biological "best age" for a baby is clearly out of step, then—at least for the well-off, well-educated twentysomethings who go through emerging adulthood and consider themselves *way* too scattered and irresponsible to have a child.

"Best age" can be defined in other ways, too. It can mean the best chance for the health of the infant, rather than the social needs of the mother or the health of the pregnancy itself. With that definition, according to Mirowsky, one California study concluded that the "best age" for first birth, in terms of lowest rates of birth defects, is twenty-six. Nice to know, I guess; that's how old I was when Jess was born—and she *was* pretty perfect. A different study, based on national data, looked at a different measure of a baby's health—rates of overall infant mortality rather than birth defects—and pinned the "best age" even older, at thirty-two.

You could also define "best age" as the best outcome for the mother's long-term health—which puts the ideal age older still. Using data from a phone survey involving women aged forty-five to ninety-five, Mirowsky found that those who reported feeling most fit and energetic in middle or old age, and with the fewest self-reported physical ailments, had had their first babies on average at age twenty-nine. Those who reported the best health overall in middle or old age had had their first babies on average at thirty; those with the fewest aches and pains and the fewest chronic diseases had had them on average at thirty-four. Put it all together, he said, and the optimum age at first birth in terms of the mother's long-term physical well-being was thirty-one years old.

And if you define "best age" in terms of the longest life expectancy for the mother, the optimum age is oldest of all. Mirowsky conducted interviews with 1,890 mothers, asking about their current health, including chronic illnesses, mobility problems, and self-assessments of malaise and other problems. Then he looked at mortality data, made some adjustments for educational attainment, and concluded that the overall "best age" for a first child, in terms of long-term health and mortality for the mother, was thirty-four. Social pressure that delays the beginning of parenthood, he wrote, "greatly outweighs the biodevelopmental advantages of youthful organs." For twentysomethings thinking about how to time their schooling, career advancement, and family building, he offered this advice: they can "reasonably expect optimal health outcomes from delaying motherhood into their thirties."

Mirowsky put it bluntly in a comment to a reporter for the *Daily Mail*: "A woman who had her first child at 34 is likely to be, in health terms, 14 years younger than a woman who gave birth at 18." The reporter then went on, oddly, to draw the reader's attention to the gorgeous Sophia Loren, who had her first baby at thirty-four. At the time the article was written (2005), Loren was seventy years old and still received "as much praise for her health and beauty as she did as a young screen siren."

A different assessment of the long-term health of older mothers presents a slight complication, at least for women who want to have more than one child. While having a first baby at age thirty-four might be fine, this other study suggests, what's even more fine is to have a *last* baby before age thirty-five.

That was the conclusion made by Angelo Alonzo, a sociologist at Ohio State, who in 2002 conducted a study similar to Mirowsky's using a different data set, the large National Health and Nutrition Examination Survey (N-HANES). After adjusting for social factors that affect health (race, age, income, health insurance coverage, smoking), he compared the health status of two groups of mid- and late-life women: those who had *any* births after age thirty-five, and those who had finished having babies by then. So this wasn't looking at age of first birth; it was looking at thirty-five as a cutoff for age of *last* birth. Women who had had babies after age thirty-five, Alonzo found, had higher systolic blood pressure, higher blood glucose, poorer health as assessed by a physician, and poorer mobility later in life than women who had had all their babies before thirty-five. This doesn't contradict Mirowsky's findings, exactly. It just means that two different studies came to two slightly different conclusions: for the sake of a woman's long-term health, it would seem, the best timing of pregnancy would be to start at thirty-four and stop before thirty-five.

Same as It Ever Was

"I Forgot to Have Children"

Biology is biology, no matter what the dramatic magazine covers say, and the most sophisticated technology in the world won't make it routine for us to have babies at fifty. That's why, even though the ticking might be drowned out by people insisting that assisted reproduction changes everything, Millennials are up against the same biological clock that has bedeviled young men and women for generations.

Fertility inexorably declines with age: at age thirty it's 20 percent lower than it was in the early twenties; at age thirty-five it's 50 percent lower; at age forty, a distressing 95 percent lower than it was at its peak. Here's another way of looking at it: say a group of couples have been spending their time trying to get pregnant (the fun, old-fashioned way, with no syringes or Petri dishes). If the women in that group are twenty-eight years old, 72 percent will get pregnant after trying for a year; if they're thirty-eight, only 24 percent will.

It's all about the ovaries. A woman's eggs are manufactured once, in utero, and that's all she'll ever get. (This dogma was upended slightly in early 2012, when a team of Harvard researchers reported that they found that ovaries also contain stem cells that can be extracted and grown in the lab into mature human eggs. The lead scientist, Jonathan Tilly, said if this finding is confirmed it could revolutionize assisted reproductive technology. But while Tilly's work is interesting and potentially exciting, fertility doctors proceed under the old assumption that women cannot manufacture new eggs.) Baby girls are born with two ovaries fully loaded, usually about a million or so immature eggs in all. The majority of those immature eggs get reabsorbed during childhood, leaving about 300,000 to 400,000 egg follicles at puberty. During most menstrual cycles, one of those egg follicles matures and is released from the ovary to be fertilized, but not every menstrual cycle is "ovulatory" (accompanied by the release mid-cycle of a mature egg); when the woman menstruates that month, all that comes out is the uterine lining. The proportion of cycles that are ovulatory is at its lowest before age twenty, reaches a high of about 80 percent between twenty-six and thirty-five, and then starts a steady decline—to about 70 percent after age forty and about 50 percent after forty-five. That's one reason that women over forty can have unprotected sex for so long without a pregnancy—you get a shot at fertilizing an egg only if there's an egg to be fertilized.

Fertility problems might also be caused by age-associated changes in the reproductive system, such as endometriosis, when the uterine lining dislodges and turns up throughout the pelvic cavity, causing painful periods and scarring; and fibroids, non-cancerous growths in the uterus that can interfere with implantation of a fertilized egg, much the way an IUD does.

It takes two to make a baby, and males also can encounter some age-related problems. Folks used to think that since sperm are made afresh with every ejaculation, there is no such thing as old sperm, and no added risk of chromosomal damage the way there is with older eggs. Wouldn't that be convenient for men? But something must go awry, because studies indicate that fathers over age forty increase their babies' risk of a variety of problems, in particular childhood cancer, autoimmune disease, schizophrenia, and autism. It's not yet an accepted medical consensus, nor does it seem to have seeped into the consciousness of young men, who apparently think the biological clock is a woman's thing.

It's almost as hard for fortysomething women to *stay* pregnant as it is for them to *get* pregnant. According to the American Society of Reproductive Medicine, the miscarriage rate in women goes up dramatically with age: 10 percent for women younger than twenty-nine, 12 percent in the early thirties, 18 percent in the late thirties, 34 percent in the early forties. By the time a woman is over forty-five, her chance of having a miscarriage is 53 percent.

Despite Amy's heartfelt cheer of "Go, doctors!" in gratitude for her babies-whenever options, fertility doctors aren't magicians, and most fortysomethings won't go home from the clinic with a baby. In 2009, doctors at Boston IVF reviewed their records for 2000–2005, during which time 6,164 women went through in vitro fertilization. The overall success rate after six IVF cycles (the maximum that most insurance companies in Massachusetts covered at the time) ranged from 51 to 72 percent. The range reflects two different ways of counting the women who didn't return after one or more failed cycles; the lower number is the "conservative" estimate that assumes *none* of those women went on to have babies, and the higher is the "optimistic" estimate that assumes they had babies, possibly after treatment elsewhere, at the same rate as the women who stayed. There was a clear age stratification for this success rate. For women under thirty-five, 65 to 86 percent ("conservative" to "optimistic") ended up with a live birth; for women over forty, just 23 to 42 percent did. These were rounds of IVF using the patient's own eggs, I should point out; treatment using donor eggs tends to boost the success rates for fortysomethings. "We can't take an infertile patient at 43 and give her the fertility of a 33-year-old," one of the Boston IVF doctors told *Newsweek* reporter Claudia Kalb. "We can't reverse the biological clock."

More recently, infertility specialists have tried a little tough love with Millennials who seem to think that somehow doctors *have* reversed the biological clock. The American Fertility Society, for instance, mounted an educational campaign aimed at young women to let them know that no matter how much they ate right and exercised, their eggs were still getting old. Throughout 2009 the organization sponsored a series of events at chic nail salons in a dozen cities, calling them "Manicures and Martinis"—free manicures, free lectures, and booze-free "fertilitinis." These soirees were aimed at twenty- and thirtysomethings as a not-so-subtle reminder that they might want to think about having babies sooner rather than later. Not everyone appreciated the effort—including doctors. "This is not a secret," Owen Montgomery of the University of Pennsylvania told Kalb. Young women, he assured her, "hear the ticking as loud as anybody else."

Wow. Non-alcoholic martinis and people scolding you. This sounds like the worst night ever. I'm not sure I agree with Dr. Montgomery that young women have all that firm a grasp on their shriveling odds of getting pregnant. But I do agree with him that talking at us probably isn't going to make a difference. Young women feel invincible about babies because young people feel invincible in general— and that has nothing to do with a shortage of lectures at nail salons.

Maybe they should have invited Sylvia Ann Hewlett to be a guest speaker at one of the Manicures and Martinis evenings. That's been her party line for years. "Figure out what you want your life to look like at 45," she wrote in 2002 in *Creating a Life*, addressing her younger readers. "If you want children (and between 86 percent and 89 percent of high-achieving women do), you need to become highly intentional— and take action now." By "action," she meant giving "urgent priority" to finding a partner, and having a first child "before 35." Despite the "occasional" miracle, she wrote, "late-in-life childbearing is fraught with risk and failure."

Remember how furious Sam and her friends were when they read Lori Gottlieb's "Marry Him!" polemic in 2008? That's how furious their older sisters were about Hewlett's argument six years earlier, and for much the same reason: she was telling them to make different choices, choices midlife women (including Gottlieb and Hewlett themselves) wished they had made when they'd had the chance.

"There's no room in Hewlett's view for modest regret, moving on or simple acceptance of childlessness, much less indifference, relief or looking on the bright side," wrote Katha Pollitt in *The Nation* shortly after *Creating a Life* was published. Yet, Pollitt pointed out, those are the sentiments Hewlett wanted women to cultivate in terms of their careers: lower your career expectations and just get on with the baby-making.

Pollitt is right; there should be room for other family models, including childlessness. I've seen how the lives of people without children can be enviable—they have more disposable income, more freedom to travel or relocate, more time to spend as a loving couple instead of as harried co-parents, more chances to perfect their crafts, whether career-oriented or just for fun. And they can still get some of the benefits of parenthood, without the costs. "I've been wondering if we might be witnessing the rise of the aunt," Kate Bolick wrote in a much-discussed Atlantic *article from 2011 about being thirty-eight and single, "based on the simple fact that my brother's two small daughters have brought me emotional rewards I never could have anticipated." And Mitch and Martha, the storytelling friends Mom mentioned earlier, not only have their nieces and nephews, but also hundreds of schoolchildren they work with each year in storytelling workshops, to mentor and shape and from whom to reap those emotional rewards.*

For me, though, childlessness has never been a future I'm willing to consider. I don't think it's time yet for me to start freaking out about whether I'll be able to put into action decades of planning how to be a parent, starting from back when I identified with the Danny Tanners and Patty Chases of Television Land, rather than with the children who were pushing their buttons. Nor do I plan to scale back my career ambitions anytime soon. But I have already let go of my previous notions of how long I should be dating someone before we get married, how long we should be blissful newlyweds before we have kids, or how financially secure we need to be to pull it off. There might not be time for all that.

I understand the fury at Hewlett and Gottlieb's retro, patronizing advice. But I see the reasoning behind it, too. Young women still want to have it all, the great career, the fascinating husband, the adorable kids. And they *can* have it all, or a lot of it. They *should* have it all. But they should go into their decisions about careers, marriage, and babies with their eyes open. Women do indeed have babies after forty-five—in fact, 8,000 American women did in 2008 (the most recent official government figure), and the number keeps growing. But that doesn't mean getting those babies was easy. And it doesn't mean that when any one particular Millennial decides, in 2030 or so, that she's ready for her baby at last, her body will cooperate.

Age Thirty Still Feels Like a Deadline

Despite the background hum of late-life babies as an option, the median age at first birth for women in the 2010s is almost as young as it was for their mothers and grandmothers. Reading press accounts of the spurt of late-life babies, or walking through upscale urban neighborhoods crowded with fortysomethings pushing twin strollers, might give a different impression. So might an over-reliance on statistics about the average, or mean, age of first birth, which is about twenty-six today—a number made artificially high by a relatively small group of outliers. That's just how averages work, giving extra weight to people at either end. Medians, the point at which 50 percent of *individuals* come out above and 50 percent come out below, are a better measure of how most people behave. And according to the CDC, the median age for first pregnancy in 2000 was twenty-four and a half. That's only a little older than the median age of twenty-three in 1980, when I was pregnant for the first time—which in turn is only a little older than the median age of twenty-two and a half in 1953, when my mother was pregnant with me.

In Sylvia Ann Hewlett's study, at least some women expected to put off childbearing practically forever. And 89 percent of her younger sample believed they'd be able to get pregnant into their forties. But among the people Sam and I heard from, it was unusual to find anyone who expected to wait that long. In the "snowball sample" of people responding to our questionnaire, 75 of the 96 Millennials specifically mentioned whether they wanted to have children and when they expected that to be. Their answers skewed surprisingly young. Eight people wrote that the ideal age for starting a family was the late twenties (including three young women who already had had their babies by then). Another 30 said they planned to start having babies by their early thirties. Only four people, three of them male, even mentioned the number 40 in response to our question about the best age to have kids—three young men who tossed it out without much apparent thought, and one young woman who seemed to have thought about it a great deal. "I am actually making a phone call today about freezing my eggs," Michelle Paster, thirty-one, told us. (What she'll find out, most likely, is that egg freezing has been used on a few thousand women in the United States, with about a fifty-fifty success rate, it costs about $15,000 per cycle for the hormone injections and egg harvesting, and the American Society of Reproductive Medicine still considers it experimental.) She wanted to put off having children until about age forty, Michelle wrote, because "I want to be more financially secure. However, my mom would love for me to have them earlier." Speaking as the mother of someone the same age as Michelle, I can only say that I'm sure she would.

Other than Michelle, most of our questionnaire respondents seemed to feel they needed to make a decision about babies relatively soon—which is difficult to do when there are still so many unknowns to deal with: where they might end up living, what job they might end up with, or even who their parenting partner might be.

Anne, twenty-two, knew she was in no position to have children yet; she was going for a master's in social work, living with her parents, and was just three months into her first real relationship with a guy she'd met on OkCupid. She said she wasn't sure she even *wanted* kids. But for someone who wasn't sure, she certainly had a long list of worries—worries not much different from those of any introspective young person, no matter what the generation. "I'm concerned about having another American mouth to overfeed," she wrote. "I'm concerned about the political and environmental effects of having kids. I'm also just concerned that I might never be financially stable enough to support kids as kids should be supported. I worry how my life might change as a career-focused woman if I have kids. I worry about being overstressed, and the sheer mechanics of childbirth scare me a bit. I worry about all the kids without homes and wonder if it's selfish to have kids. I worry how my parents will be able to forgive me if I never give them grandkids. And all of this before we even hear from my future spouse? What are his concerns and feelings? What if I never have a spouse? Could kids fit in my life then?"

This list sounds a lot like the one Jeff and I drew up back when I was twenty-five and felt the age-thirty deadline looming. I assumed that if we were going to have children, we needed to get started soon, but neither of us was 100 percent sure we even wanted them. We didn't want to stumble into the decision without really turning it over in our minds; we might have sort of stumbled into our marriage, but children are forever.

So we sat down at the dining room table one night and wrote up a list of pros and cons for kids. The list of cons was long, filled with all the things we'd never be able to do if we were tied down to babies at home and if all our disposable income went to piano lessons and sleepaway camp. On strictly rational, cost-benefit terms, having kids is hard to justify. It costs a ton of money, not only to have them (especially if that includes tens of thousands of dollars in fertility treatments or adoption), but also to raise them. Estimates are that a baby born in 2010 will cost his or her parents $226,920 to get to age eighteen—and that's not even counting college. The estimate, from the Department of Agriculture, increased nearly 40 percent over the previous decade—at a time when the median income in the United States was declining by 7 percent. The biggest chunk of the expense was housing—unless there's more than one young child in day care, at which point day care costs more than rent.

More cons: kids would probably mean a setback in the trajectory of my career. And they might undermine our marriage, introducing a set of stressors that can sometimes be enough to tear a couple apart.

On the pro side of the pros-and-cons list, there was only one entry. But that entry was all it took: "If we don't have children, we'll regret it when we're forty." We chose forty because, in those days, it was *obviously* the point at which all doors to babyland would be closed.

Young people are still drawing up pros-and-cons lists—not necessarily with a spouse, as I did, but as a hypothetical exercise with friends. Sara, the twenty-five-year-old woman living in Brooklyn and working for a fashion photographer, told us that she and her crowd talk about baby-making more than they did in their early twenties. "I had many conversations with my amazing female friends over the past year about how to work families into our lives," she wrote, "and thinking about factoring motherhood into our futures and careers. We're excited by it, I think." But they're also a little irritated that this seems to be a girls-only preoccupation. "As much as we feel on par with men in every part of our lives," she wrote, "it doesn't seem like this is something they think about as much."

I'm not sure that guys don't think about it as much—at least if you ask them directly. A lot of the guys who responded to our questionnaire took our query about babies quite seriously. I thought it was interesting what we heard from Phil, a twenty-seven-year-old New Yorker and someone I've known for a while—but not in a talk-about-your-plans-for-babies kind of way. "I don't know if I want them," he wrote. "I do, but I don't want them to die or become sick. I haven't fully lived out my own dreams, and would fear being either too pushy or unavailable." But who knows, he went on. "Down the line, I may feel very different. I do love kids." The truth is, not only might Phil feel very different down the line, but so might the person who ends up being the hypothetical co-parent to his hypothetical kids. And that partner might have some ideas of ways for Phil to be a father that involve his being neither "pushy" nor "unavailable."

Then there was Dan from New York, who's thirty-two and wrote that "I don't have kids, I would have expected to have them by now, now I'm not sure I ever will though I still would like to." And Ruben Galbraith, twenty-seven, from Portland (the one in Oregon, not Maine), who wrote that "I worry about waiting too long and never having my kids see me 'in my prime,' whatever that means." And my friend Jonah—who has taken to pulling out his iPhone every time we hang out and thrusting videos of his adorable niece in my face—who told me that being an uncle has made him think a lot about having children, and how decidedly unready for it he is. "You have to have a hand on them at all times!" he marveled.

Well, duh. I, like many of my female peers, learned all about that by babysitting and watching my relatives care for their young ones. I don't think it's that twentysomething men aren't thinking about babies; it's just that they're thinking about them with a sort of "gee, babies are adorable but also hard work" naïveté that many women our age got over fifteen years ago.

Sometimes the best-laid plans have to be revised, of course, even when some of the playing pieces, such as spouses, have already been put into place. Vivian St.George told us that she and her husband "had tentatively discussed having children before I turn 30 (32 for him), but that was before he started graduate school and I got a better paying, more demanding job." She is twenty-six, has been married for one year, and works in magazine production in New York. "Before these things happened, I would have said that I expected to have children by age 28, but now it will probably be more like 29 or 30," she wrote. "I think 28–30 is a good time to have kids. There is much lower risk of complications, and you're still young enough to keep up with small children." Vivian is listening to an older cousin, thirty-nine now and struggling with infertility, who urges her not to wait too long. The realization that fertility wanes, Vivian told us, is "a message that I think a lot of women my age take to heart."

The Parenting Animal

The desire to have your ducks in a row before you get pregnant is not only the modern outgrowth of reproductive technology and emerging adulthood; it also makes evolutionary sense. In 2010, nearly seventy years after Maslow, a group of psychologists led by Douglas Kenrick of Arizona State did a major tweaking of the pyramid in Maslow's hierarchy of needs—or, as they put it, they "buttressed" the pyramid "with a few architectural extensions" that led to a more "contemporary design." The modernization was in response to the trendy science of evolutionary psychology—which, as we already suggested in the last chapter in our description of the split-compatibility quotient in love, is a science that has its critics. Kenrick's most significant, and most controversial, buttress was at the top of the pyramid, where he replaced Maslow's "self-actualization" with three "reproductive goals," in ascending order: "mate acquisition," "mate retention," and, at the apex, "parenting."

"No human need can be meaningfully separated from biology," the authors wrote in explaining why they had knocked Maslow's self-actualization off its perch. It's hard to see what is adaptive about self-actualization, they wrote. They suggested that self-actualization might be just a by-product of other mechanisms that do lead to greater reproductive success. Or, they wrote, maybe it offers an advantage indirectly, yielding beautiful symphonies or Nobel prizes that attract mates in the manner of a peacock's tail.

In a way, as Kenrick and his colleagues recognize, parenting is almost the exact opposite of self-actualization. Having children "is not ultimately about self-gratification," they wrote, "but involves a considerable diversion of resources away from selfish goals and toward other human beings."

Kenrick insisted that he wasn't saying that parenting is necessarily "more important than any of the things below it." He just wanted to emphasize that it's "the punch line of this developmental story."

Even though there are many things in Kenrick's revised pyramid that people find objectionable—chief among them the implication that becoming a parent is the ultimate goal of human development—what's good about it is that it's a useful visual representation of the sequence of parenting, the notion that there are many things that need to be accomplished first before people feel ready to start a family.

The belief that you need to have all your ducks in a row before starting a family might be a distinctive characteristic of those more privileged, slower-to-mature emerging adults. When Martha McMahon, a sociologist at the University of Victoria, posed questions about the ideal sequence of transitions to motherhood to a group of 59 women, she found that the answers divided along class lines. "Whereas middle-class women indicated they felt they had to achieve maturity before having a child," she wrote, "working-class women's accounts suggest that many of them saw themselves as achieving maturity through having a child."

Drinking the Daddy Kool-Aid

Then once that family begins, all hell breaks loose.

In Daniel Gilbert's book *Stumbling on Happiness*, there's a line graph of the highs and lows of marital happiness over the life course of a marriage, based on data collected from four different studies. The pattern that emerges is what social scientists call a U-shaped curve. The lowest point in marital satisfaction coincides with the years when the kids are teenagers (though, in some studies, having preschoolers makes happiness drop almost as low). On the way to that trough is a steady decline in marital satisfaction. The happiest couples are at either end of the life cycle: young couples who have no children, and old couples who have an empty nest.

"None of this should surprise us," Gilbert wrote. "Although

parenting has many rewarding moments, the vast majority of its moments involve dull and selfless service to people who will take decades to become even begrudgingly grateful for what we are doing." The reason we expect otherwise is that the "belief-transmission network" of society insists that children are a source of incomparable joy— as it must, for the sake of its own perpetuation. The truth is, he wrote, we have kids "for reasons beyond our ken. We are nodes in a social network that arises and falls by a logic of its own, which is why we continue to toil, continue to mate, and continue to be surprised when we do not experience all the joy we so gullibly anticipated." Which is also why the cold, hard calculation of Jeff's and my pros-and-cons list didn't work; logic was no match for pure irrationality.

I saw the "belief-transmission network" in action a couple summers ago. We were on a family beach vacation, and at the dinner table one night were my parents, my dad's parents, my aunt and uncle, and my parents' closest friends: four couples and me on one big screened porch. I had just read Jonathan Franzen's Freedom, *and I mentioned that it made me think about the heartache of being a parent. It struck me, I said, that it's sort of a given that you will dote on and obsess about your children more than they ever dote on or obsess about you, and that if you do a perfect job raising them, then they will leave you, which is, in some ways, a cruel reward. My grandparents got agitated and insisted, quite emphatically, that I was wrong, that raising children was pure joy and had only ever brought them happiness. I tried to explain that I wasn't doubting the happy moments, but that surely there had also been times when they had been so intensely worried that it had hurt. Or maybe one of their kids had said something mean or snarky to them. No, they said. Pure joy all around.*

It was strange, this impenetrable unified front of positivity. (The other couples at the table, all parents of adult children, listened quietly to my grandparents' rant. I later found out that at least a few of them, including Mom, had thought I was right at least to raise the question, but they hadn't wanted to ratchet things up.) It reminded me of the hormone oxytocin that gets released after childbirth, which is said to make women essentially forget the pain of labor so they're

*willing to go through it again. Was this absolute denial of the hard-
ships of raising kids some biologically driven response, a baked-in
need to persuade the younger generations to go forth and multiply?*

The drawbacks of babies might be more obvious for Millennials
than they were for Baby Boomers, because having children later means
you're being forced to give up more. But we all gave up plenty, and most
of us continue to insist that we wouldn't have had it any other way. If
Gilbert is right, though, the recursive self-protection of the belief-
transmission network helps explain why parents express such shock at
the idea that kids are anything but worth every sleepless night and
every penny of that $226,920. Maybe we're just hoping for a reward of
our own after years of punishing work—grandchildren!—which leads
us to sugar-coat the truth and downplay the travails when we talk to
our children about children. Because it must be, mustn't it, that having
grandchildren is every bit as unmitigated a joy as everybody promises?

Round Five

NOW IS NEW:

- Modern medicine has made late-life childbearing possible.
- Which makes having kids in your twenties seem almost
  weird.
- There's a clear benefit to waiting to have kids.
- Which is good, because the "best" age to have a baby is sur-
  prisingly old.

SAME AS IT EVER WAS:

- Eggs don't lie, and women are most fertile in their twenties.
- Knowing this, many young women still feel pressure to start
  their families by at least their early thirties.
- Women continue to bear the brunt of child care responsibilities and career fallout.

- Twentysomethings still say they intend to have babies eventually.
- And fifty- and sixtysomethings still stress out about just when that will be.

Oddly, especially because the biological clock is the same no matter what era you live in, we're going to throw this one to the Now Is New camp. Even though fertility wanes as women creep past thirty, as it always has, there's been enough of a shift in the age at which Millennials expect to have children that thirty these days seems young. This is new, and may be the primary driver of the phenomenon that started our exploration of twentysomethings in the first place: the more distant horizon by which today's young people expect to be fully grown up.

Chapter 6

Brain and Body

I s it only in hindsight that the twenties glow as the height of physical perfection? You'll never again be as sexy, as clever, as beautiful. You're finally fully developed, past the adolescent acne, with limbs that have caught up with your torso and a metabolism that older, flabbier people can only envy. Everything's working at maximum capacity: heart, lungs, muscles, bones, reproductive organs, sexual equipment (though some studies suggest sex is already on the downward slide for men), cognitive functions, even lie-detection skills. It's harder to put one over on a twentysomething, and it works the other way, too—people in their twenties are better liars than they'll ever be again.

Many twentysomethings take their well-honed bodies for granted, the way they do their fertility, and find it inconceivable that things will ever change. Back in 1968, Paul Simon wrote a song called "Old Friends," about two elderly men observed on a park bench, that reflected a young man's narrow view. "Can you imagine us years from today," went the mournful lyrics. "How terribly strange to be seventy." When I first heard the song, I was fifteen years old, and to me, seventy meant decrepitude, tedium, pain, and the terror of staring into the great maw of your own mortality. Simon, in his late twenties, probably had similar ideas. But that was then. Time passes with disconcerting speed, and now some of my closest friends are in their seventies (as are Simon and his own old friend Garfunkel), and "to be seventy" doesn't seem so terribly strange anymore.

But while the *concept* of my own old age might have seemed bizarre, that didn't keep me from trying to picture it. It was all tied up with my eagerness to grow up and get on with my life. While we were in grad school, Jeff and I used to walk around Evanston and I would point out the old couples—so old! they must have been fifty at least!—and try to imagine what we would be like at their age. Would we, like some of them, still hold hands?

All that planning and imagining might have helped me take better care of myself—that and the first *Rocky* movie, in 1976, which inspired me to take up jogging, which I eventually downgraded to walking really fast. But a significant subset of young people aren't thinking that far ahead. One in ten, according to one national longitudinal study, doesn't even expect to live to be thirty-five. And social scientists have found that in the absence of a healthy respect for one's own future, age-related decline becomes almost a self-fulfilling prophecy. The less likely you are to expect to survive your twenties, the more likely it is that you'll treat your body badly: smoking, drinking, doing drugs, eating crap. Even young people who blithely expect to live to ninety sometimes have trouble with the Spartan, boring lifestyle it generally takes to get there.

Now Is New

This Is Your Brain on Google

With all the emails, tweets, chats, and status updates continually vying for brain space, young people these days are slave to what's been called "continuous partial attention." One study of college students found that 84 percent get instant messages, Facebook updates, texts, or other interruptions at least once in any given hour; 19 percent get them at least six times every hour. And for 12 percent, the interruptions occur so often that they've lost count.

Those incessant distractions don't bode well for the brain, wrote journalist Nicholas Carr in a controversial cover story in *The Atlantic* in 2008, "Is Google Making Us Stupid?" With our attention constantly splintered, he wrote, our brains might be subtly rewired, leading to a younger generation less and less capable of thinking deep thoughts.

"What the Net does is shift the emphasis of our intelligence, away from what might be called a meditative or contemplative intelligence and more toward what might be called a utilitarian intelligence," Carr wrote in an online symposium about his article hosted by the Pew Research Center's Internet and American Life Project. "The price of zipping among lots of bits of information is a loss of depth in our thinking."

Defenders of Google say it frees up people's brains for more important stuff than data entry and retrieval. "Holding in your head information that is easily discoverable on Google will no longer be a sign of intelligence, but a side-show act," wrote Alex Halavais of the Association of Internet Researchers in that same symposium in response to Carr's lament. Once your mind is clear of actual facts, goes his argument, you have room for sophisticated analysis and problem-solving. I'm reminded of my brother's uncanny ability to recite, since he was fourteen, the first thirty-six digits of pi. It was a cool trick, but it didn't make him any better at math than the guy with pi programmed into his TI-89.

Googling has, arguably, made Millennials less able than any previous group of twentysomethings to retain information. Recent research suggests that they use Google as a sort of auxiliary memory. In 2011 a team of psychologists led by Betsy Sparrow of Columbia gave 60 undergrads a bunch of trivia (on the order of "an ostrich's eye is bigger than its brain") and asked them to type all forty factoids into a computer. Half were told that the file containing these facts would be accessible later; half were told the file would be erased. On a subsequent test of memory, the ones who thought everything would be erased remembered much more. When they believed their document would be saved, Sparrow found, they didn't bother remembering it; they figured they could always find it (or, as it's called outside the lab, Google it) when they needed to.

And maybe it's not just pervasive Googling that interferes with memorization; it might be reliance on the computer keyboard itself. Some studies suggest that the best way to retain information is to write it out in longhand, which activates a tactile connection between the words and the brain that might be skipped by typing. Karin Harman James, a neuroscientist at Indiana University, recently asked a group of college students to transcribe a passage in one of three ways: by writing it out in cursive, by writing it out using print, or by typing it. One week later, she brought them back to the lab and asked them to recall as much of the passage as they could. Those who had written it out in cursive—the old-fashioned way, the way that's hardly even taught in schools anymore—remembered significantly more than either of the other two groups. This no doubt has implications for Millennials' ability to remember what they write, since even young people who use longhand, which is rare enough, tend to choose printing over script.

It's not the lack of memorization that bothered Carr, though. His concern, based on intuition rather than data, was the growing inability to focus on a piece of long-form writing in a way that allows the reader to resonate to the "intellectual vibrations" of an author's words. "In the quiet spaces opened up by the sustained, undistracted reading of a book, or by any other act of contemplation, for that matter, we make our own associations, draw our own inferences and analogies, foster our own ideas," he wrote. Those opportunities for mental improv are being drowned out, according to Carr, by noisy and distracting "content."

Carr's 2008 article appeared before Twitter really took off, before smartphones and constant texting and checking in and Googling became second nature, especially among twentysomethings. In just a few more years, distractions would be popping up not only on the laptop at your desk but on your mobile device everywhere—while you walked down the street, waited for a bus, rode the bus, went to the bathroom, stood still, all the quiet places where people used to let their minds wander for a bit and see where the musing led. (Even the shower, where I do some of my best thinking, is being invaded by waterproof iPods and smartphones.)

In 2009, *The Atlantic* published a rejoinder to Carr by Jamais Cascio, a fellow at the Institute for Ethics and Emerging Technologies. Not only are we not getting stupider, Cascio wrote; we're getting smarter, as the human brain evolves to take advantage of the hive mind of the web. Focus and attention might be sacrificed because of all the distractions and hyperlinks, he wrote, but they are being replaced by "fluid intelligence—the ability to find meaning in confusion and solve new problems, independent of acquired knowledge."

Only a handful of neuroscientists have looked directly at the brain in action to see if that's what's actually happening. Among them is a team from UCLA that used functional MRI scanning on a group of older adults to visualize electrical activity in their brains while they performed two cognitive tasks: reading a book and searching the Internet.

Led by psychiatrist and neuroscientist Gary Small, the scientists divided 24 subjects, aged fifty-five to seventy-six, into two groups: 12 who were experienced Googlers, and 12 who had never used Google before. In both groups, functional MRI scans showed that reading a book engaged regions in the temporal, parietal, and occipital lobes of the brain that were involved in language, reading, memory, and visual skills. So far, so good.

Next, the subjects were asked to do a Google search on a topic of interest to them, such as "What are the health benefits of chocolate?" While they were searching, their brains showed activation in the same regions that were involved in reading. But in some subjects, additional brain activity was recorded in the frontal pole, anterior temporal region, cingulate, and hippocampus—brain areas involved in decision-making, complex reasoning, memory, and vision. The subjects whose brains got more active while Googling were those from the web-savvy group, who were familiar with Google to begin with. The web novices didn't engage in searching in the same way, and Googling never managed to get their brains in gear.

"A simple, everyday task like searching the Web appears to enhance brain circuitry," Small said. People in the web-savvy group were using those circuits during the functional MRI scans because they already had them available to use, having strengthened them during previous episodes of Googling. Small and his colleagues were mostly interested in web searching as a way to stave off cognitive declines in old age—their paper was published in the *American Journal of Geriatric*

Psychiatry—but it's also possible to read these results as suggesting something about brain changes in the hyperlinked young. It was just a small pilot study, with only a dozen people in the Internet-literate group. But it might be a useful counterbalance to the conventional wisdom that Millennials have lost the ability to deal with anything more complex than screen-size bursts and 140-character thoughts. Google, it seems, might be doing something different to the brains of digital natives, creating a new set of neural connections and engaging young brains in an unprecedented way. With their brains thus wired, Millennials might be using the web as a vehicle for sophisticated thinking and higher-order cognition. And they might be even more mentally engaged while online than their elders are while reading a book.

The Quarterlife Crisis

We all know the clichés of the midlife crisis: red sports car, toupee, boob job, hot young fling. But the quarterlife crisis has not yet been burned into our collective cultural consciousness. (Nor would its signifiers be as glamorous: late-night pizza and nachos that you spend the next day regretting, maybe, or a string of unsatisfying hookups.) The term *quarterlife crisis* didn't even exist until Millennials got old enough to have one. Then it became an early-2000s meme, the subject of books, a web series, and Urban Dictionary's Word of the Day for May 17, 2005. The concept got some scholarly cred in 2010, when Oliver Robinson, a psychologist at Greenwich University, conducted in-depth interviews with 46 London-area young people and drew up a comprehensive map of the typical quarterlife crisis.

Much like the midlife variety, the quarterlife crisis often begins with the frantic realization that at least some of the big choices you've made so far have been wrong. It usually erupts after you think you have already moved past emerging adulthood and are engaged in the rest of your life, Robinson reported at the 2011 conference of the Society for the Study of Emerging Adulthood. "You are not thrashing around anymore; you have made some substantial commitment at home or at work that you feel is the basis of something long-term," he said. But then the home or work life you've built for yourself starts to feel "unsustainable."

Generally this is because, for one reason or another, the commitment you made was premature, like Jean Li's early devotion to chemistry research that we described in chapter 1. Maybe you made the choice of career or spouse for the sake of expediency, taking the road more traveled or the one you thought would get you out of a bind. Maybe you made the choice you thought would make your father or your girlfriend happy, not realizing how unhappy it would make you.

As Robinson described it, the typical quarterlife crisis has four stages.

- Stage 1: *the locked-in stage*, when you feel stuck in a straightjacket, living someone else's life.
- Stage 2: *traumatic separation*, which can be brutal, leaving you feeling lost and unmoored.
- Stage 3: *the chaotic period*, a kind of "emerging adulthood" all over again. It feels like backtracking, with many options once more up in the air.
- Stage 4: *transformative resolution*, when you experience a commitment to a new career or a new partner, and a clarified sense of self.

The psychologist Erik Erikson marked out a similar phenomenon in his scheme of adult development: the psychosocial moratorium, a period of socially sanctioned "free role experimentation" and "provocative playfulness" that can help the young person find "a niche which is firmly defined and yet seems to be uniquely made for him." The moratorium, according to Erikson, can take a variety of forms depending on the individual and on the culture: "a time for horse stealing and vision-quests, a time for *Wanderschaft* or work 'out West' or 'down under,' a time for 'lost youth' or academic life, a time for self-sacrifice or for pranks." (Funny to think that adult development might hinge on phoning someone and asking to speak to Amanda Huggenkiss.) Provocative playfulness would look different today: fewer pranks and horse stealing, more adventures along the lines of living in a village in Southeast Asia, trying one's hand at a tech start-up, canvassing for a congressman, surfing in Costa Rica, or sleeping till noon in your parents' basement and playing online poker all night.

The lovely thing about the psychosocial moratorium—and the

thing that makes it different from either emerging adulthood or the quarterlife crisis—is that the young person has society's explicit permission for this kind of undirected, "playful" exploration. As Erikson put it, it's in society's interest to grant this permission, since the moratorium is the best route for "young people who otherwise would be crushed by standardization and mechanization."

But the quarterlife crisis *does* resemble the psychosocial moratorium in that it involves twentysomethings stepping outside the flow of their lives, taking time out to assess who they are and where they're heading. It can be destabilizing to re-open options and start all over again, especially if that means undoing some prior commitments by getting divorced, moving to a new country, or going back to school. These major changes are accompanied by what Robinson termed "a real sense of trepidation," but I suspect he's employing classic British understatement here; in the case studies that formed the bulk of his presentation to the Society for the Study of Emerging Adulthood, there was a lot more panic and terror than there was mere "trepidation."

It might take years to get from the chaos of stage 3 to the resolution of stage 4, according to Robinson's map. The person might be as old as thirty-five by the time it's over. But the result of all that disruption and despair, he said, is "a greater sense of enjoyment and a new sense of self, and a more genuine expression of that self in daily life roles." Hopefully that new sense of self would give the thirty-five-year-old a respite (or maybe even a pass) on the midlife crisis that can start to loom at about age forty.

Darcy, a young woman who read about Robinson's work on a *Discover* magazine blog, had a quarterlife crisis that pretty much fit his pattern. "It hit me at 27," she wrote in an online comment, "after a bad breakup with a guy who I thought I was going to marry. I packed up, left my job and went to school 1,500 miles away. I struggled but had a bunch of fun rediscovering myself." Post-crisis, she thinks it was worth all the agony. "I am in debt from the student loans, but my eyes are now open. I am making better decisions, cutting out toxic frenemies, I enjoy my new career, I'm making more money and most importantly I wake up happy after being miserable at a dead end job/auto-zombie for the last 11 years." She said she feels "amazing."

Robinson has made a provisional analysis of the prevalence of the quarterlife crisis in a representative sample of 342 people over age thirty-five. He said that 55 percent recalled having had a "significant life crisis" in their twenties or early thirties—in other words, a quarterlife crisis. In a less scholarly survey conducted by Gumtree, the UK version of Craigslist, 86 percent of British twentysomethings said they felt under pressure to succeed in their relationships, finances, and jobs before they turned thirty. Forty percent worried about money; 32 percent felt under pressure to marry and have kids by age thirty; 20 percent thought they were in the wrong career.

If a quarterlife crisis is an inoculation against a crisis at midlife, that would be worth the upheaval. Because, as I know from experience, a midlife crisis is something to avoid. I had one myself, at about forty-five. Mine wasn't as bad as some, since it didn't end in any major rifts: no abandoning of my family, no divorce, no giving up on one career and starting something new. It was more of a deep undertoad of disappointment and dread, and it went on for a couple of doleful years. In my case, I doubt that a quarterlife crisis would have headed it off—but what might have is having had an emerging adulthood. Racing through my twenties, impatient for my real life to start, I had no time for provocative playfulness. I made my commitments early, and for whatever reason, whether devotion or lack of imagination, I stuck with them. Compounding this, and putting me on a sure track to midlife disappointment, was a string of early successes in my twenties, which led me to expect even more success in my forties. (My secret ambition, remember, was to be so famous I would be recognized *at the grocery store*.) My professional disappointments managed to seep into a sense of personal disappointment, too, as I looked around at other marriages, or at single fortysomethings, and found myself curious about alternative lives.

New Paul Simon lyrics swirled in my head during this time, two verses in particular. One line I sometimes found myself humming was from "Train in the Distance," a refrain for those stretches when I thought maybe I should just chuck it all and start anew—the kind of thought that is, according to Simon, "woven indelibly" into our human nature. At other times I knew deep down that chucking it all would be unbearable, and the lyrics that resonated were from another song, "Hearts and Bones." The entwining by midlife of yours and others' "hearts and bones" is why having a crisis at that stage of life can be so hard. The connections are more profound and more abiding than in your twenties, and there's so much more to lose.

Rx is the New LSD?

Every generation has its own defining drug, according to *New Yorker* writer Margaret Talbot. For Baby Boomers it was hallucinogens, which people used so they could blow their minds; the goal was to experience bursts of genius and a sense of transcendence, to get beyond one's own cramped, provincial ego and feel at one with the universe. For Millennials, the defining drugs are prescription medications, drugs taken not to "think different," but to think harder, faster, and longer. Talbot wrote that these drugs, which she called neuroenhancers, are tailor-made for today's twentysomethings, "perfectly suited for the anxiety of white-collar competition in a floundering economy."

When Millennials abuse an Rx drug such as Adderall, according to Talbot, it's not to experience any surges in genius; it's for absolutely prosaic reasons such as "squeezing out an extra few hours to finish those sales figures when you'd really rather collapse into bed; getting a B instead of a B-minus on the final exam in a lecture class where you spent half your time texting; cramming for the GREs at night, because the information-industry job you got after college turned out to be deadening." Her assessment might be an overgeneralization—most claims about entire generations are—but it's intriguing to think that the rise of various brain-boosting drugs is a response to the achievement-oriented, "grindingly efficient" world Millennials have inherited.

Baby Boomers had their fun with prescription or over-the-counter medications, too, such as speed and quaaludes, but at nowhere near the pace of Millennials. Between 1993 and 2005, according to the National Center on Addiction and Substance Abuse at Columbia University, the proportion of full-time college students who abused prescription drugs soared. Recreational use of Rx stimulants (Ritalin, Adderall) increased by 93 percent; Rx sedatives (Nembutal, Seconal) by 225 percent; Rx painkillers (Percocet, Vicodin, Oxycontin) by 343 percent; and Rx tranquilizers (Xanax, Valium) by a stunning 450 percent. Nearly a quarter of a million college students were abusing prescription painkillers in 2005, and nearly a quarter of a million were pulling all-nighters with the help of Ritalin and Adderall.

Not exactly in our defense, we also use prescription drugs for totally whimsical reasons, just like the hippies did. Ritalin and Adderall help you study harder and longer, but they facilitate the same sustained intensity for partying, too—sort of like cocaine lite. And then there are the drugs such as Ambien and Vicodin, which could fit into the whole work hard, play hard Millennial narrative if you wanted them to. But they're not only relaxation aids for people whose default state is tightly wound. They're also the modern-day equivalent of 'ludes, a way to relax for people who are already relaxed. And while we're talking about relaxing, that 450 percent increase in the use of Valium and Xanax hardly seems like the stuff of "grinding efficiency."

What determines which drugs people use and how often they use them? Often it's the folks you hang out with—especially the ones you're closest to. Married people start to resemble each other in their drug use, much the way dog owners gradually start to look like their dogs. Several studies have found similarities in husbands' and wives' exercise routines, alcohol intake, and cigarette smoking, and the same has been found for recreational drug use in married couples.

The similarities show up in couples who are just dating, too. Lauren Papp, a professor of human development at the University of Wisconsin, studied "the connections between romantic relationships and individuals' well-being" in 100 heterosexual young couples, mostly white and mostly in college or graduate school, 22 of whom were not only dating but also living together. None of the participants, who ranged in age from eighteen to thirty-six, had been married before or had children.

Papp found similarities in the misuse of prescription drugs within dating couples, especially for use in the previous year. She couldn't tell to what extent the partners were affecting each other's behavior, and to what extent they had originally chosen each other *because of* their similar attitudes toward drugs, something known in biology as assortative mating. Or it could have been as simple as having the Rx drugs lying around: If Fred is given Adderall for his ADHD, Ethel might more readily yield to the temptation to take it when she has a final paper due. And if Jill has a sleeping problem for which she was prescribed Ambien, Jack might pop some just to spend his waking hours feeling a little more chill.

Partners who engaged in more Rx drug abuse, Papp found, were also less satisfied with their relationships. This was true even after taking into account each partner's alcohol use, suggesting that the effects on relationship quality were related to abusing prescription drugs specifically, not abusing substances in general. But once again, it was hard to tell what was cause and what was effect. Rx drug abuse could have been a coping strategy to keep the relationship at a safe distance, or it could have been the *reason* for the distance.

Twentysomethings use more recreational drugs, proportionally, than any other age group. (This in itself is nothing new; Baby Boomers, too, used illicit drugs most heavily in their twenties, but their use fell off after that.) Recreational drug users also tend to be those most at risk for depression, and those least likely to plan for the future. They are probably a lot like the people we mentioned earlier, who gave a bleak response when asked how long they expected to live—and then revealed themselves, years later, as being much less likely to take care of themselves for the sake of a future they didn't expect to see.

Foodies to the Rescue

One important way to take care of yourself, and others, is by learning how to cook nutritious meals. Millennials seem to be more interested in this than young people from back in my day ever were. "I've noticed that many of my friends have a different relationship to food than our parents did," wrote Arline Welty, twenty-eight, of Chicago. "I think a lot of it is influenced by the organic/Michael Pollan–esque cultural influences. But I also think there is something more to it— something that is a signifier of adulthood, or a social cue that a twenty-something has achieved some level of independence."

Not long ago, a market research company surveyed 2,000 adults about their cooking habits, and found that more young adults described themselves as "casual cooking enthusiasts" than did the public at large—65 percent of young people compared with 53 percent overall.

The young people, who were aged eighteen to twenty-four, said cooking was a "pleasurable hobby," and reported cooking an average of 4.4 "elaborate" or "gourmet" meals every six months. They liked experimenting with new recipes, buying ingredients from other countries for specific dishes, and cooking with seasonal or local food. They were willing to spend more for high-quality ingredients, they said, and willing to buy new kitchen utensils or cookware for a specific recipe.

"Cooking gourmet meals makes them feel sophisticated and smart," said Fiona O'Donnell of Mintel, the company that conducted the survey. "Learning to cook and cooking for friends is viewed as a way to establish credibility among their peers."

Learning to feed yourself and your loved ones is part of feeling like a responsible, nurturing adult. Several of our questionnaire respondents mentioned learning to cook as one way they knew they'd finally grown up.

> *The first time I went to dinner at the home of married people who were my contemporaries was during my first year out of college, when I was living with R. in Cambridge. They were law school friends of his and they had invited over a handful of couples, most of whom were in some stage of pre- or early marriage. I can't remember what we ate, but I do remember the glassware (a different size for every drink you could think of) and the kitchen appliances: a bread maker, a rice maker, a Cuisinart, and a blender. If owning two devices for two different ways of smashing up food isn't adulthood, I don't know what is.*
>
> *The dinner party is an interesting measure of where you are on the spectrum of being grown up. Some of my twentysomething friends have already transitioned to matching plates and multicourse meals that begin with bruschetta with specialty olive oil and end with grappa and an after-dinner salad. (How European!) Others still expect guests to help with preparations, then dole out amorphous pasta dishes in mismatched bowls, which you eat sitting on the sofa if you're lucky or on the floor if you're not.*
>
> *As for eating alone, I tend to "assemble" meals rather than "cook" them. Like my thrown-together chickpea stew, which I recently posted about on the "Treats for the Disaffected 20-Something" series by* Vanity Fair *blogger Juli Weiner:*

Ingredients

1 can Goya chickpeas (also known as garbanzo beans)
1 jar tomato sauce

Open the can of chickpeas (also known as garbanzo beans). Don't worry, you don't need any opener because the can has one of those things at the top, like a can of tennis balls.

Pour some salt on the top layer of chick peas and eat as many as comfortably fit on a fork. (It's easier to get them to stay put in a spoon, but it's important to challenge yourself in the kitchen.) Some people may think it's gross to eat chickpeas right out of the can because of the gunk on the bottom, but that is why you're eating from the top of the can, obviously; plus the salt sort of mitigates the gunk. But fine, wash the rest of the chick peas in a colander.

Pour some tomato sauce in a pot (the bowl kind). It's best if there's something stewlike going on in the tomato sauce, like if it already has some vegetables in it. You can tell this by reading the type of tomato sauce it is, and also by peeking inside the jar. Does it look sort of like stew? Perfect.

Now pour the chickpeas in the pot. Maybe not all of them, since you'll want to nosh on some as an appetizer. (Keep that salt handy!) Once it's all warm, put some more salt on top, and even pepper—they're inside those decorative salt and pepper shakers you got when you got your first apartment. Stir. Eat. This time you can use a spoon, because it's stew now.

Same as It Ever Was

Mad Men Redux: Cigarettes and Booze

You'd think with all the damning evidence about the dangers of cigarette smoking, not to mention the social stigma borne by smokers who are banned from smoking in offices, hospitals, restaurants, bars, and even in parks, on streets, or in their own homes (at least if they live in certain co-op apartment buildings in New York)—you'd think with all that, young people would have long ago gotten the message that it's dangerous to smoke, difficult to quit, and a stupid idea even to start. And while it's true that rates of smoking have declined in recent years, the decline has been slower among twentysomethings than any other age group. In fact, in 2007 the highest prevalence of smoking was in young people: 22.2 percent of eighteen- to twenty-four-year-olds smoked cigarettes, according to the CDC, as did 22.8 percent of people aged twenty-five to forty-four, compared with 19.8 percent in the population as a whole. And the younger the smokers are, the less likely they are to give a shit about what they might be doing to themselves: in the fifteen years before that statistic came out, fewer and fewer eighteen- to twenty-four-year-old smokers were even *trying* to quit, a figure that fell from 59.3 percent in 1993 to just 52.1 percent in 2007.

They're not choosing to smoke out of ignorance. Young people today still may not know all the exact statistics—that smoking is the single most common cause of preventable death in the United States, and is associated with higher rates of cancer, heart disease, and osteoporosis— but it's hard to believe that a reasonably alert individual in the 2010s wouldn't catch the basic drift that smoking is very bad for your health. Some anti-smoking advocates think it might work better on young people to appeal to their vanity, emphasizing that smokers get more wrinkles and that their breath and clothing smell bad. Or that it interferes with fertility—new studies calculate that smoking ages a woman's ovaries by about ten years, and that it may lead to low sperm counts or abnormal sperm morphology in men. As Devora Lieberman, an Australian fertility specialist, told a reporter for *The Sydney Morning Herald*, "It's not OK to say I will smoke in my twenties and then give up in my thirties when I want to have a baby."

> *Those stats about fertility are troubling, but I don't think that's actually going to stop anyone from smoking. It sounds a little desperate, actually, to search around trying to find the one side effect that will scare people smokeless. It's not as if when Johnny doesn't respond to stats about heart failure, telling him some spleen stories will make him quit right then and there. The issue isn't lack of*

information (something the Manicures and Martini organizers from the last chapter failed to understand). The issue is young people feeling invincible, choosing to believe that the warnings simply don't apply to them. It's not unlike poor people supporting tax breaks for the rich. There's a disconnect there between the reality that should be inform- ing that decision (higher taxes on the rich will result in better social services for the poor) and the rosy imagined future ("But what if I'm a millionaire someday?") that drowns out the message.

Sam is right that a sense of invincibility is part of being young, and contributes to people making reckless choices such as smoking. But for a subset of young people, recklessness is a result not of a sense of invin- cibility but of its polar opposite: a sense that they will never grow old enough to see their bodies decay. If they project an early death, taking care of themselves seems beside the point—a statement at once self- evident and supported by data from the massive National Longitudinal Study of Adolescent Health (known as Add Health). Over the course of nearly twenty years, investigators have collected reams of data to help them see, among other things, how the health habits of two groups of twentysomethings compare: those who expected to live past thirty- five and those who did not.

Add Health began in 1994 with 20,745 subjects aged twelve to nineteen, who have been followed ever since, answering questions about health behavior (everything from exercise to drug use to sun exposure), family life, friendships, and goals. (Study participants were born between 1975 and 1982, which means they generally fall into the Generation X category, though the youngest of them, twelve years old in 1994, *could* be considered Millennials; it's all so squishy it's hard to say precisely.) Their parents answered questions, too, about their children's lives and about their own health habits, income, health insur- ance, and family dynamics. Every few years, subjects went through another round of interviews.

"What are the chances that you'll live to thirty-five?" participants were asked during the first interview, and they were given five choices: almost no chance; some chance, but probably not; fifty-fifty chance; good chance; almost certain chance. About 58.2 percent said it was "almost certain" they would live to age thirty-five, and 28.4 percent said there was a "good chance" they would. And there was indeed a good or almost-certain chance they'd live to thirty-five, and even long past that, since the average life expectancy for their age cohort was about 70.8 years for white men (65.6 for nonwhites) and 78.2 years for white women (74.0 for nonwhites).

But that left more than 13 percent of teens in the Add Health study who said there was only *a fifty-fifty chance or less* that they would live to see thirty-five. And that included 3 percent who said they had only "some chance" or "almost no chance" of living that long. Minority teenagers were most likely to fall into the I'll-die-young camp (19.0 percent of Hispanics and 25.7 percent of African Americans, versus 9.3 percent of whites), as were those whose parents had less than a high school education (23.9 percent, compared with 9.3 percent of those whose parents had college degrees). There was some truth in their self-assessment, since people with lower incomes, less education, and minority status tend to have shorter life spans. But dying before thirty-five? That's a long shot no matter what your race or class. Still, nearly one in eight of the teenagers in this sample thought there was a better than even chance of their dying that young. Am I alone in seeing despair hidden in that grim reply?

The forecast, Add Health researchers found, became a kind of risk factor, because these fatalistic young people engaged in behavior that put them on track for what public health experts call "premature death," which is any death that happens earlier than the norm. At the next round of interviews, when subjects were eighteen to twenty-six, those who had expected to die young were less likely to be taking care of themselves. Those who had expected to live past middle age were the ones who tended to exercise, refrain from junk food, and avoid cigarettes in young adulthood. This was also the case for those who had, as teenagers, expected to go to college; as young adults, they, too, lived healthier lives. If they saw their life chances as promising, they acted as though that life were worth protecting.

There's another part of *Mad Men* culture besides smoking that has echoes in today's twentysomethings: the use of alcohol. Drinking often starts in college, where it is getting progressively more dangerous. Between 1993 and 2005, according to the National Center on Addiction and Substance Abuse, binge drinking on campus (defined as five or more drinks at a sitting at least once in the previous two weeks) was up 16 percent, drinking on more than ten occasions in the previous month was up 25 percent, drinking to get drunk was up 21 percent, and getting drunk three or more times in the previous month was up 26 percent. This kind of big-league drinking leads to all the problems we already know about: car crashes, alcohol poisoning, sexual assault, and rape.

It keeps up in young adulthood. Three out of four drunk drivers in the United States are males aged twenty-one to thirty-five. Of this group, most of them are binge drinkers with very high blood alcohol levels. And these are just people who are picked up with levels above the legal limit for blood alcohol, which is .08 in the United States (about three drinks for a person weighing 140–160 pounds). Some anti–drunk driving advocates have urged that this standard be set lower, at .05 (about two drinks for that average person), the legal limit in most other countries. "If most people are buzzed with two drinks, that's roughly .05," said Barron Lerner, author of *One for the Road: Drunk Driving Since 1900*. "So just make the level there. Why we're cutting a break to people between .05 and .08, I just don't get. I don't see why even if a small number of people can hold their liquor at .08 we'd base public health laws on them."

J. L. Scott, twenty-eight, thought that she could hold her liquor, but soon watched her drinking spiral out of control. In a blog entry she called "Booze: My Final Farewell," she described why she was going straight. In her freshman year at a rural woman's college, J. L. started by drinking beer at frat parties, and she lost her virginity at one of those parties to a boy she hardly knew. She then transferred to a college in Manhattan, where she and her roommate drank their way through the city with cosmos and amaretto sours. "I loved the fact that five drinks could slide a Saturday night into a night of adventure, into so many firsts," she wrote: good firsts such as the first time making out in a cab or having sex outdoors; bad firsts such as the first blackout, the first time throwing up all over herself, the "first time having no clue whether or not I had sex (a flurry of text message exchanges the next day confirmed that I had)."

After college, J. L. stayed in Manhattan to work in publishing, and it only got worse. Endless open bars were the only perks of her low-paying job, and drinking made her feel as clever as her more sophisticated colleagues. When she was twenty-three, the guy she was sleeping with asked her which she preferred, drinking or sex. "I paused, silence hanging between us. The answer was so obvious. Sex was awkward, embarrassing. It was the opposite of drinking. 'I know,' he sighed and rolled away: A jealous lover. 'You love your booze.' "

Five years later, "it's not cute anymore," J. L. wrote. And having five blackouts in the space of just two months? That's "not okay." The blog post stops at the point she decides her drinking is a problem—something that Samantha and her friends, who tend to be as prodigious in their drinking as J. L. and her friends were, wonder about all the time.

> *Do my friends and I drink too much? How would we know? When does someone slip from being that fun guy who's always down to party to being that sad guy who's a sweaty, drunken mess? And how do we make sure we catch ourselves before we cross that line?*
>
> *It was almost immediately after graduation that this conversation started to pop up and repeat itself. Five and a half years later, we're still having the conversation. At a party recently, someone declined a drink, saying that he was "giving up alcohol." A friend with me laughed and said he'd never heard that before. "Really?" I said. "I feel like I hear that every weekend." "I just mean the wording," he clarified. "Normally people say 'I'm giving up drinking.' That I hear all the time."*
>
> *With all the swearing off and returning to and cursing and praising alcohol, I don't think we've gotten much closer to understanding the distinction between social drinking and problem drinking. And among all the reasons young people give for being unwilling to label ourselves "adults," I wonder if one big one is what that label would mean about our drinking. If we were adults, we would be considered alcoholics. But we're not alcoholics; we're just twenty-four or twenty-six or thirty-one or thirty-five, and this is what our lives are, this is what socializing is. The fact that we drink most nights just means that we're being social. But if we were adults, real adults, who drank like this, well, then we'd have a problem.*

One way to answer Sam and her friends' plaintive question is by taking a quiz such as AUDIT (Alcohol Use Disorders Identification Test). You add up your score and get an idea of how likely you are to be veering off into "problem drinker" territory. (By the way, what the quiz means by "one drink" is probably less than you'd think, given today's supersize wineglasses and cocktails. "One drink" means 12.0 ounces of beer, 5.0 ounces of wine, or 1.5 ounces of hard liquor.)

So here goes:

1.   How often do you have a drink containing alcohol?

> 0 = never
> 1 = monthly or less
> 2 = 2–4 times a month
> 3 = 2–3 times a week
> 4 = 4 or more times a week

2.   How many alcoholic drinks do you have on a typical day when you are drinking?

> 0 = 1 or 2
> 1 = 3 or 4
> 2 = 5 or 6
> 3 = 7–9
> 4 = 10 or more

Questions 3–8 are about your behavior in the past year. Answer them using this scoring system

> 0 = never
> 1 = less than monthly
> 2 = monthly
> 3 = weekly
> 4 = daily or almost daily

3.   How often do you have 6 or more drinks on one occasion?

4.   How often during the past year have you found that you drank more or for a longer time than you intended?

5.   How often during the past year have you failed to do what was normally expected of you because of your drinking?

6. How often during the past year have you had a drink in the morning to get yourself going after a heavy drinking session?

7. How often during the past year have you felt guilty or remorseful after drinking?

8. How often during the past year have you been unable to remember what happened the night before because of your drinking?

9. Have you or anyone else been injured as a result of your drinking?

    0 = no
    2 = yes, but not in the past year
    4 = yes, during the past year

10. Has a relative, friend, doctor, or health care worker been concerned about your drinking, or suggested that you cut down?

    0 = no
    2 = yes, but not in the past year
    4 = yes, during the past year

According to the World Health Organization, which developed the AUDIT measurement, a score of 8 to 15 indicates a "medium level of alcohol problems." More than 16 indicates a "high level." I scored a 6, which I guess is a "low level," due mostly to my fondness for red wine and bourbon, though usually not both in the same evening.

> *Samantha here. I scored a 12. "Medium level of alcohol problems" sounds about right.*

Slow-Growing Brains

Young people have a good excuse for not acting like full-fledged adults: their brains aren't finished growing. In 1991, Jay Giedd and his colleagues at the National Institute of Mental Health started mapping children's brains. They enrolled nearly 5,000 kids aged three to sixteen (average age ten) and brought them in for MRI scans every two years to track brain growth and development. The original plan was to stop the scans when the brain stopped growing, probably around age sixteen. "We figured that by sixteen their bodies were pretty big physically," Giedd said. But every time the children returned, their brains were found still to be changing. The scientists extended the end date of the study to age eighteen, then twenty, then twenty-two. The subjects' brains were still changing even then. Significantly, the most dramatic action was taking place in the prefrontal cortex and cerebellum, the regions involved in emotional control and higher-order cognitive function. Thanks in large part to this research, the scientific consensus now is that the brain keeps maturing at least to age twenty-five—and possibly even longer.

Growth and maturation are two different things when you're talking about the brain. Growth means the proliferation of new brain cells (neurons) and new branches between the cells (synapses). The cells and branches make up what's known as the gray matter of the brain: a hundred billion or so neurons and about a quadrillion synapses at its peak just before puberty.

But rampant growth without some organization is like a hoarder without a filing cabinet, and that's where maturation comes in. More cells or synapses is not the end point. There also needs to be a way to make sense of it, which happens via two processes: synaptic pruning and myelination.

Synaptic pruning involves molding the gray matter according to how the brain is used. Immediately after periods of rapid cell growth— first in childhood and again in adolescence and into the twenties— synaptic pruning starts cutting off pathways that are not used and yielding well-worn grooves along those most frequently fired. This is the mechanism for the so-called plasticity of the brain—its ability to change in response to the demands made of it.

Myelination involves the white matter, the bundles of axons (nerve cell projections along which the impulses travel) that link one brain region to another. The compound myelin is laid down along the axon for insulation, increasing by a hundred times the speed by which nerve impulses travel. An axon sheathed in myelin has a "signaling rate" that's thirty times faster, which means it requires less recovery time between firings. "This combination—the increase in speed and the decrease in recovery time—is roughly equivalent to a 3,000-fold increase in computer bandwidth," Giedd wrote in the journal *Cerebrum*.

So neural messages travel faster in the twentysomething brain than ever before—or ever again; most of the rest of adulthood is a story of gradual decline—and the connections become honed so that the things you've learned become easier to retrieve and act on. In this regard, the twentysomething brain just keeps getting better and better. But there's a hiccup in the pacing that causes some problems: a time lag in the early twenties between the maturation of the limbic system, where emotions originate, and of the prefrontal cortex, which manages those emotions. The limbic system explodes during puberty, but the prefrontal cortex keeps maturing for another ten years. This syncopation means that unrestrained emotions could occasionally wash over a young person who's not quite equipped yet to keep them in check. Feelings, in other words, might sometimes outstrip rationality.

"The prefrontal part is the part that allows you to control your impulses, come up with a long-range strategy, answer the question 'What am I going to do with my life?'" Giedd explained. "That weighing of the future keeps changing into the twenties and thirties." It's a neurological explanation for why it's so hard for twentysomethings to make the important decisions they need to: they just don't quite have the chops.

In one study Giedd conducted, the adolescent nucleus accumbens (part of the emotion-based limbic system) functioned like an adult's, while the adolescent orbitofrontal cortex (part of the rationality-based prefrontal cortex) was like a child's—a vivid neurological representation of the in-between nature of this age.

Why would a young person's brain have evolved to mature at such an uneven pace? What's adaptive about an adolescent brain that is so high on thrills and chills and so low on the cool restraint of "executive function"?

It might be good for the species as a whole, Giedd wrote in *Cerebrum*. Youth is a time of "increased novelty seeking, risk taking and a shift toward peer-based interactions." In the modern world, such behavior can be scary, but it's also a crucial part of growing up, he wrote, needed for "separating from the comfort and safety of our families to explore new environments and seek unrelated mates." It's adaptive, according to Giedd, for a brain to be so responsive to its environment, so nimble and capable of spontaneous reaction, so unfettered by the continual no-no-no impulses of the cautious, self-restrained cortex. We're no longer on the savannah, and the risk-taking involves different threats to life and limb than saber-tooth tigers; the modern correlates are drugs, alcohol, motorcycles, guns. But the benefits of a thrill-seeking brain are still basically the same. These days, they translate into a willingness to go for broke when it really matters, such as being willing to go through the chaotic phase of the quarterlife crisis: walking away from a career or a marriage that isn't working and starting over.

Youthful brains have always worked this way, of course. Modern sophisticated scanning machinery didn't *create* this odd pacing of brain maturation; it merely documented it. So why is it only now that slow brain maturation is being used as an explanation for why Millennials are taking longer than their predecessors to grow up? Didn't their grandparents have exactly the same brains, while managing to get jobs, get married, and start raising families long before they turned twenty-five? Why, then, is the youthful brain only now arising as an explanation for why people in their twenties are seeming a bit unfinished?

Maybe it helps to go back one more time to Abraham Maslow and his hierarchy of needs. Maslow theorized that people can pursue more elevated goals only once their basic needs of food, shelter, and sex have been met. What if the brain has its own hierarchy of needs? When people were forced to adopt adult responsibilities early, maybe they just did what they had to do, whether or not their brains were ready. That would mean it's only now, when young people are allowed to forestall adult obligations without fear of public censure, that the rate of social maturation can finally fall into better synch with the maturation of the brain.

While we're talking about the brain, let's return to the idea that the Internet is changing everything. What it isn't changing is this: there has always been an older generation that worries about what a new technology will do to the brains of the next generation, no matter what the new technology. My parents thought Baby Boomers' brains would turn to mush because we didn't have to memorize poems in school and could use calculators instead of doing arithmetic in our heads. They decried television as a "boob tube" that would, as Dutch psychoanalyst Joost Meerloo wrote in 1956, "catch the mind directly, leaving children no time for calm, dialectic conversation with their books." In the TV-saturated world in which Baby Boomers were raised, he wrote in *The Rape of the Mind,* "body and mind no longer exist. Life becomes only a part of a greater technical and chemical thought process."

My parents' parents had similar fears about radio, of course, and way, way further back, *their* ancestors were saying much the same thing about the printing press. But as technology makes one cognitive style outmoded, it can pave the way for a new and possibly better cognitive style—and the general historical trend has been toward more brain-power, not less. As Dan Tapscott put it in his 2009 book *Grown Up Digital,* Millennials are equipped with "the mental skills, such as scanning and quick mental switching, that they'll need to deal with today's overflow of information." Himself a Baby Boomer and the father of two twentysomethings, Tapscott wrote that young people "know when they have to focus, just as the most intelligent members of my generation did. They may think and process information in a different way than most boomers do, but that doesn't stop them from coming up with brilliant insights." His conclusion: young people's mental skills are different from their parents', but the kids are turning out to be impressive, sharp, quick-witted individuals who are destined to do just fine.

Letting Themselves Go

If you're like most young people, you might not want to hear that you should be living prudently to keep your brain and body from decline. It's way more fun to ignore the rules for now. Exercising, eating healthy, getting your teeth cleaned—you'll do all that later, when you're a true adult, when you have a better appointment calendar and decent dental coverage, and aren't so hungover.

> *I got my first cavity when I was twenty-four. It didn't require drill-ing, so the whole thing was pretty painless. Physically painless. But*

emotionally scarring. The dentist asked when I had last gotten my teeth cleaned. It had been about a year and a half—due partly to laziness, partly to switching jobs (and insurance coverage), partly to a naïve sense of invincibility. I think he caught on to the last bit. "You're not a kid anymore," he told me. "You can't just go two years without going to the dentist. You're twenty-four. The decay has begun." The decay. I was decaying from the inside.

It was more than just the word decay *that stuck with me; it was also the notion that the choices I make now can lead to permanent damage. These aren't my baby teeth; these bad boys will be with me, cavities and all, until the end. My cuts take longer to heal, and the scars don't fade. That cheap Chinatown massage I got four years ago, where she did something weird and my shoulder was popping and cracking for months—I never got that checked out, and my shoulder still pops. It might be like that forever.*

The "I'll get around to it someday" philosophy is not uncommon among twentysomethings. "I still, with great regularity, drink to get drunk," wrote Claire Gordon, twenty-three, in response to our questionnaire. "And drunk binge on pizza. I don't think adults do that." For Claire, living in Berlin as a graduate research fellow, "normal life tasks are a struggle. Chores like laundry, taxes, bills, grocery shopping I still accomplish with a wow-look-at-me novelty." So how is she going to fit in tasks such as a three-times-a-week jog, an annual Pap smear, and flossing her teeth every night? (She's also messy, Claire pointed out—"my room looks like it belongs to a 16-year-old with issues"—which might be another sign of her problems with routine maintenance.)

For a while, the lack of attention doesn't seem to matter much; your twentysomething body continues to do your bidding without complaint. Yale psychologist Daniel Levinson called the twenties a time of great "biological vigor" in his classic book *The Seasons of a Man's Life*. In Levinson's classification scheme, the twenties are summertime, and the days of summer are languorous and long. (Summer stretches into the thirties, too, wrote Levinson, but by 40 a man knows that "autumn is fast approaching.") "Biologists often use 30 as a reference point for studying age changes in adulthood," he wrote. And that was back in 1976, when thirty was practically midlife. Today forty, or maybe even fifty, is the new thirty. You have time.

At least you *think* you do. But let the basics of healthy living slip for too long and, like a car you haven't taken in for regular tune-ups, the well-oiled machine of your youthful body starts to sputter.

Preventive medicine takes money and organizational skills, neither of which a young person is likely to have in abundance. When people were asked in 2011 why they cut corners on routine health matters, nearly half of Millennials (45 percent, compared with 36 percent of Baby Boomers) said that they had neglected some aspect of medical care in the previous year because they couldn't afford it. Usually this meant not filling a prescription, not going to the doctor when they were sick, not seeing a specialist when they needed to, or not getting recommended follow-up care. And these stats are from *after* the first phase of the Affordable Care Act went into effect, letting young people stay on their parents' health insurance plan up to the age of twenty-six—an option that about six hundred thousand twentysomethings had chosen by the time of the survey. Cost also led 38 percent of Millennial survey respondents to delay or eliminate dental care, and led 15 percent to delay or eliminate routine health screening.

For whatever reason—whether it's inattention, lack of knowledge, the aggressive pursuit of cool, whatever—it's during the twenties that young people start sliding down the road to ruin. In 2000, when Add Health investigators did a new round of interviews, they found that study subjects, who were now young adults aged eighteen to twenty-six, had slipped on sixteen of the twenty standard indicators of healthy living. They had started smoking (25 percent of young men and 20 percent of young women smoked, versus 7 percent as teenagers), stopped exercising, stopped eating breakfast, started eating junk food and getting fat, stopped going to the dentist, and stopped getting annual check-ups. Compared with their behavior as adolescents, the twenty-something participants in the Add Health study engaged in more binge drinking, marijuana use, and hard drug use, and had higher rates of sexually transmitted diseases.

What happened? Mostly they were suddenly left on their own—and they were screwing up. The twenties were the first time a lot of these young people were making their own decisions about what to eat, when to go to bed, and whether to wake up early to work out. Previously, Mom or Dad had always done all the meal planning and enforcing of bedtime; Mom or Dad had carpooled them to soccer and basketball games, bringing along the orange slices for halftime. Being physically active was often what the kids did to please their parents or coaches (and, don't forget, college admissions committees). But for twentysomethings, making time for physical activity is hard, and making excuses is easy: too busy for spinning class, too old for team sports, too sleep-deprived to take up running, too poor to join a gym.

A 2011 study conducted by the American Stroke Association (ASA), which included young people all the way to their early forties, confirmed and expanded upon the Add Health findings, especially when it came to exercise. The ASA divided 1,235 participants into three age groups. In the youngest group (aged eighteen to twenty-four), only 48 percent said they exercised regularly, a number that dropped to 39 percent for the middle group (twenty-five to thirty-four) and 34 percent for the oldest (thirty-five to forty-four).

That's the bad news. But the good news is that as young adults moved through their twenties and thirties, they got more conscientious in other ways. They got better about eating their fruits and veggies (26 percent in the youngest group got their daily five, 33 percent in the middle, and 34 percent in the oldest), limiting their sugar-sweetened beverage consumption (from 40 percent in the youngest group to 50 percent in the middle and 58 percent in the oldest), and cutting down on alcohol (76 percent in the youngest group were deliberately drinking less, 77 percent in the middle, 84 percent in the oldest).

Still, there are already some troubling signs that the bad habits of the twenties will have some long-term consequences. Over the first decade of the 2000s, several chronic diseases, such as diabetes and high blood pressure, started to show up at progressively younger ages. And poor kidney function was a problem in 49 percent more twenty- and thirtysomethings at the end of the decade than at the beginning. In comparison, there was no increase in those ten years in problems with kidney function among people aged forty to fifty-nine.

In 2008–2010, when Add Health participants were aged twenty-four to thirty-two, they were interviewed one more time. They were still smoking—22 percent had smoked cigarettes every day in the previous month—and they were still sedentary, with 60 percent saying they had not exerted themselves in the last twenty-four hours. Three out of four had eaten fast food at least once in the previous month; 47 percent had engaged in binge drinking in the previous year.

And just as the researchers feared, the bad habits were showing up as health problems. Although only 11 percent said they had been told by a doctor or nurse that they had high blood pressure, the actual measurements done by Add Health investigators revealed a bigger problem: 44.4 percent had blood pressure readings the investigators called "prehypertensive," and 19.5 percent of the readings qualified as full-blown hypertension. If the numbers are showing up like this at ages twenty-four to thirty-two, this can't bode well for middle age.

Creaking Toward Adulthood

A face-to-face confrontation with your own declining prowess is sometimes what it takes to start looking after yourself. That's probably what happened to the ASA survey participants, who said they became progressively more concerned about their own cardiovascular health as they got older. My guess is that they hit the late-twenties wall, like Sam's co-worker Tony did.

> *I remember thinking Tony was being melodramatic when he talked about his deterioration. He used to be like Claire Gordon, able to stay out late drinking and drunk-bingeing on greasy food. But at twenty-six, he told me, it was starting to take a toll. He'd feel bloated the next day. He'd be horrified by his reflection. His body and face no longer covered for him. His nights on the town were now apparent the next morning.*
>
> *I was twenty-three at the time, and scoffed at the notion that his body would react so much differently to things than mine. And on the days he claimed to feel haggard, Tony looked the same to me as on any other day. But I have thought of his warning often in the last year or so, as my own late-twenties decline has become apparent. My body*

now reels from drinking, my face expands and contracts visibly from one day to the next, and my eyes droop and darken from just one rest- less night. If I mentioned this change to the twenty-three-year-old colleague in the cubicle next to mine, would she think me as delu- sional as I once thought Tony?

Sometimes it's your body that forces you to reassess your attitude toward it, the accretion of small aches, pains, and bags under the eyes that lead you to get more serious about things. Sometimes it happens when you start having babies, and decide you have to get your act together. Sometimes you just start to realize that growing up means learning to delay gratification. "I take responsibility for my health and well-being," Elise of Boston, twenty-six, wrote when we asked in our questionnaire whether she felt like an adult. She lives a thousand miles from her parents and pays all her own bills, and she contributes regu- larly to a retirement account and an emergency fund—so, she reasoned, all that's pretty grown-up, right? Plus, she takes charge of "visiting the doctor and dentist regularly, exercising, flossing, cooking healthy food, wearing a bike helmet, and generally doing for myself what parents do for children. What else is really required?"

What else indeed. In a way, Elise's actions are the very definition of adulthood: they represent prudence, self-control, and an orientation toward the future, the same traits that lead people to do grown-up things such as save for a house or think about the person they're dating as a potential life partner instead of someone just for now. Yet many of the constraints that work against saving or marrying—lack of funds, lack of time, a certain live-for-today recklessness—can also work against adopt- ing healthy habits. Good habits are so sober, so boring, so damned responsible. Isn't it more fun to drink that second manhattan or skip the condom than to think about calories, your liver, or STDs? Isn't it cooler, both in terms of style and comfort, to ride your bike without a helmet than to fret over the remote chance of traumatic brain injury?

But whatever prompts the wake-up call, the question is whether it comes too late. That's the real concern: that blithely mistreating your body in your twenties, when it doesn't seem to really hurt you, might undermine your future health in ways that can't be undone.

Round Six

NOW IS NEW:

- Google and smartphones are messing with everyone's brain.
- After "emerging adulthood" may come the "quarterlife crisis."
- Every generation gets the drug of abuse it deserves, and this one gets Ritalin.
- It's hip to eat healthy.

SAME AS IT EVER WAS:

- People still smoke too much and drink too much.
- Maybe it's because their brains don't fully mature until at least twenty-five.
- When young people are responsible for their own health, good habits go to hell.
- And their bodies show the effects.

While we agree that the Internet has had a significant impact on the way Millennials focus, think, and remember, it strikes us as not all that different from how technologies of the past changed the cognitive styles of previous generations. The biggest influences on twentysomethings' physiology—drug and alcohol abuse, poor health habits, and the slow, unsteady maturation of the brain—are as important today as ever. This round, we think, goes to the camp of Same as It Ever Was.

Chapter 7

Friendship in Real Life

Ask a group of old people what it was about their lives that made them happiest overall, and they'll probably mention some close, warm relationships with family and friends. If you're satisfied with your social life, according to psychologists, you tend to be satisfied with life in general. And much of that relationship-building work is done in the twenties. According to Bernice Neugarten of the University of Chicago, who earned the world's first doctorate in human development, people choose most of their adult relationships, both friends and lovers, between the ages of twenty-two and twenty-eight.

The friends we make in our twenties are not only BFFs; they're also our first truly *chosen* friends, people we discover as a result of our own adult decisions—where to go to college, where to live, where to work— as opposed to our parents' decisions and their accompanying school districts. Choosing how to reconfigure and commit to these friendships is an essential psychological task of the twenties. Finding intimacy— the basis and by-product of good friendships—is one of the five major life tasks of young adults aged eighteen to thirty, according to Robert Arnstein, a Yale psychiatrist who was, like Neugarten, a pioneer in the study of development through the life span.

There's a more utilitarian reason for seeking out friends in your twenties, too. In a decade of quick career changes and romantic reshuffling, expansive friend networks improve your chances of making the connections that could precipitate life changes. It's an unsentimental view, to be sure, but spending time with friends (who have friends, and whose friends have friends) can be a handy way to find a future boss or a future mate.

Now Is New

Friend as a Verb

Oldsters like me love to bemoan the sacrifice of true friendship on the altar of Facebook. How many more times can opinion writers make some snide comment on the order of "How can anyone have four thousand 'friends'?" Even Zadie Smith, who's not so old (born in 1975), wrote a 5,700-word essay in *The New York Review of Books* lamenting the loss of "person as mystery" that Facebook represents. "When a human being becomes a set of data on a website like Facebook, he or she is reduced," she wrote. "Everything shrinks. Individual character. Friendships. Language. Sensibility. In a way it's a transcendent experience: we lose our bodies, our messy feelings, our desires, our fears." While Facebook defenders say the site is a way to keep in contact with distant friends, Smith says we all know better. "If we really wanted to write to these faraway people, or see them, we would. What we actually want is to do the bare minimum."

The problem for Smith and for her elders, the Baby Boomers, is that we don't really *get* it, this social media kerfuffle. But for those who are fluent in Facebook, something significant is going on. Rather than supplanting friendship, Facebook seems to be supplementing, enriching, and redefining it.

"No matter if it is a wall post, a comment, or a photo," wrote Craig Watkins and Erin Lee in *Got Facebook? Investigating What's Social About Social Media*, "young people's engagement with Facebook is driven, primarily, by a desire to stay connected to and involved in the lives of friends who live close by, far away, or have just entered into their lives."

The stats in *Got Facebook?* are staggering—five hundred million Facebook users worldwide spending seven hundred billion minutes and sharing thirty billion pieces of content every single month. And those figures are from mid-2010, probably outdated the moment the report was published that November, and doubly outdated when I read it fifteen months later and typed the numbers here. Still, it's an indication, even if the precise numbers are off, of how the world has accepted Facebook, and other social media, as an irrefutable fact of life.

People often use Facebook to facilitate real-world encounters, Watkins and Lee found. This is no surprise, of course. What *is* a surprise is the length to which some people will go for those encounters. ArLynn Presser, fifty, made it her New Year's resolution for 2011 to meet all 325 of her Facebook friends in person—a challenge she set for herself as a way to cure her agoraphobia. "I can and frequently do spend days not interacting with my friends in a 'real' way," wrote Presser, a former lawyer, romance novelist, and divorced mother of two from Winnetka, Illinois, who kept a blog and video account of her progress. "I probably use Facebook to keep in touch with my friends in a way that may be good or might just give me a false sense of intimacy." She worked through her fear of flying and of anything new, and by the end of the year she had traveled to 51 cities in 12 countries on her friend-finding mission. "I'm not going to get to all 325 friends," she wrote three days before New Year's 2012. "Some are spambots and don't even really exist." But she managed to meet 292 people, about 90 percent of her "friends," over the course of one frenetic year.

About one-third of the 900 people in the *Got Facebook?* study used the site to organize what Facebook calls "events": happy hours, movie outings, picnics, parties. "Even as social media is accused of making young people anti-social," Watkins and Lee wrote, "they often use the site to arrange face-to-face social interactions with friends." Similarly, the vast majority of the respondents (nearly 80 percent) post photos on Facebook, and three out of four of those who post photos include pictures of social gatherings with friends. Slightly less popular are photos involving family (which about half of the respondents also posted). The rest are photos that have nothing to do with a social life: photos of hobbies, animals, scenery, concerts, news items. One strange factoid: of the 459 respondents who had jobs, about 6 percent actually said yes when asked if they posted photos on Face-book of "work-related meetings." Hard to imagine what these might be photos *of*, but now I understand why the news feed has a "hide" func-tion.

With all those photos, Facebook creates one more thing for appearance-conscious young people to fret about. "I see other 20some-things feeling pressured to constantly keep up a public image, espe-cially a cyber-public image," wrote Ariana Allensworth of Brooklyn on *the twenty-somethings*, a group blog edited by Rachel Mathews, the paralegal from New York. "Folks are always keeping the world in the loop one way or another about what they're up to, where they're at, what projects they're working on. It can be a bit much at times."

I don't apologize for how much time I spend checking Facebook and Twitter or chatting online. It feels more productive than other forms of unwinding, such as watching TV—I'm not just relaxing, I'm also maintaining relationships! Multitasking! And, as they found in the Got Facebook? study, what happens with e-friends can seep out into the real world in a positive way. There are a number of people I've never met but feel close to because we often reply to one another on Twitter, and a few people for whom that feeling of closeness has transferred into real-world hangouts. And my friends and I have actual conversations about our most noteworthy Facebook observations: an atrocious dye job, an unexpected marriage, a garishly self-promotional stream of status updates.

What I do mind is the way social networks make me think about, to an off-putting degree, the image I'm projecting. I hate that some-times I say something clever and actually think, I should tweet that. Or that when my friend sends an email of a flattering photo he took of me, I get annoyed that he didn't post it to Facebook, where others could see it. (I'm not yet so vain that I would post it myself.) In much the way that My So-Called Life hijacked my brain, making me silently narrate all my thoughts in Claire Danes's voice, social networks have inserted themselves as an unwelcome filter through which I view the world and myself.

I'm not about to die for love of my reflection anytime soon, but social networking does seem to amplify my narcissistic tendencies. It doesn't help that the more you talk about yourself on sites such as these, the more successful you are (if success is defined in terms of "likes" and "followers," which I'm sure Mom and her Boomer friends would argue it isn't). Given all this, it's probably no surprise that Facebook attracts narcissists. A number of studies have found that people with narcissistic personalities—and, contrarily, people with low self-esteem—are more active on Facebook, and more likely to engage in the kind of self-promotional activity I feel so weird about (posting extra-flattering photos—you know, the duck-lipped, deep-cleavage, shot-from-above kind—or crowing about their accomplishments or those of their brilliant babies). That doesn't mean Facebook makes you more self-absorbed; it just means self-absorbed people spend more time on Facebook. But it does explain why sometimes it feels like your feed is less a virtual living room than it is a hall of mirrors.

Fear of Missing Out

Social media has also created a new way to be a lousy friend. The proliferation of e-connections and e-commitments has turned digital-age Millennials into "flakes," according to a 2010 article in *The New York Observer*. Reporter Leon Neyfakh called them "reliably unreliable," falling short according to a whole new set of e-rules. You're expected to respond instantaneously to emails, Neyfakh wrote, since everyone knows you have a smartphone. You're expected to respond just as immediately to texts and G-chats, and to keep tabs on all the Tumblrs of your closest friends. "As obligations proliferate and ordinarily meticulous people find themselves unable to maintain the social vigilance they expect of themselves," he wrote, "small emotional injuries are inflicted with unprecedented frequency."

Neyfakh described several twentysomethings who knew they were drifting into flaky-friend territory but seemed unable to find a detour. Eugenia Ballve, twenty-five, who worked in an art gallery, was too popular for her own good: "I'll get an email from someone who is asking me to hang out that night, then the next thing I know I have a text message from someone else who's like, 'Oh, what're you doing tonight?' And then I'll get a Facebook invite or something like that. It's just really hard to keep up." Mike McGregor, twenty-six, who worked at the tech company Kickstarter, added, "We're so hyperconnected that you're expected to respond instantly, and if you don't, people think you're blowing them off. A lot of times, it's just that you have hundreds of messages to sift through, and not enough time in the day to deal with them."

> It might not be so hard to "keep up," as Eugenia put it, if people didn't try to maintain eighteen half-plans at once, juggling them all until the last minute so they can pick the best one. Is it possible that the failure to commit to a single social activity for the evening is twenty-somethings' way of dealing with what's happening in the rest of our lives? We have to pick a career and a lifestyle and eventually a mate—but damned if we're going to close any doors on what to do on a Friday night!
>
> In Mom's day, even if you knew in theory that people were some-times doing fun things without you, you didn't have to see photo-graphic evidence of it, unless your friends invited you over for a slide show of their trip to Europe. Now you see that stuff daily: look, there are eight of your friends in some Facebook photo together at . . . is that a barbeque? Who had a barbeque? Why wasn't I at that bar-beque? By keeping tabs on a wide group of people's every check-in, you feel you're less likely to miss out on something awesome—or even just mildly better than whatever you're currently doing. But you're also more likely to spend much of your night preoccupied with smoke signals arriving via cell phone and wondering which are worth follow-ing, rather than just settling in and focusing on the choice you've already made.

Fear of missing out on something better going on somewhere else—a rowdier party, a more interesting conversation, a funnier movie, a better hookup—is no doubt part of being young. For me it goes back as far as elementary school, when we'd go on field trips and the more appealing crowd was always the one in the back of the bus if I was in the front—or in the front of the bus if I was in the back. Why were they all singing and laughing and carrying on, and we were all so quiet?

But when fear of missing out becomes pervasive enough to get its own acronym—FOMO, Urban Dictionary's Word of the Day for April 14, 2011—it can make for some serious intrusions into ordinary life. And it brings out the grumpy old lady in me when I see high-tech FOMO being used to rationalize behavior that strikes me, in my general disdain for all those distracting screens, as just plain rude.

Not long after *The New York Observer* reported about constantly wired twentysomethings turning into flaky friends, *The New York Times* declared that this nefarious FOMO mentality is turning Millennials into smartphone-addled cybersluts, constantly texting and emailing, always on the prowl for the next better thing. It's so bad that one twentysomething admitted to zoning out entirely while he was with people, because he was spending so much time attending to people he wasn't with.

"You're passing in and out of consciousness, listening for the key words, the meat of the conversation, but letting the ancillary parts drift off," this young man, Spencer Lazar, told *Times* reporter John Leland. "You can miss important details or offend someone by not being present." Yes, it does seem like a good bet that you might offend people by slipping in and out of consciousness as they talk. The irony is that Spencer—who was practically addicted to the constant quest for his "information edge"—was at the time starting an online service to help friends connect with other friends in person. If they all act like him once they're in one another's presence, why even bother?

I know not to read too much into trend stories, even when they appear in the venerable *New York Times*. But this one really troubled me—especially because I asked Sam if it sounded like the way she and her friends behaved, and she said, yeah, it pretty much did.

Just last night I was with some friends at the Museum of Modern Art, where there was a nighttime event with music and free beer and wine. As we were standing around in a small group talking, my friend Annie pulled out her BlackBerry and began reading something. "I'm reading an email that doesn't matter," she said, sort of instantly baffled. "I don't know why I'm reading this email." I didn't, either. But I've been there.

In describing the Spencer syndrome, which apparently has also infected Annie, Leland pointed to a study that found that 30 percent of young adults sometimes use their smartphones to avoid interacting with the people they're with. Seventy percent use them when they're bored. And we parents just aren't getting it. As twenty-nine-year-old Jordan Cooper told Leland, when he's with his mother and spends all his time texting and tweeting and checking Facebook, she tells him— no doubt hurt in the way we dinosaur fiftysomethings get hurt when our beloved children treat us this way—that he's being anti-social. But Jordan puts her in her place. "I'm being social," he tells his mother, "just not social with you."

The constant-texting phenomenon can be particularly frustrating with suitors—or, to use a less euphemistic term for it, booty calls. Take this infuriating exchange from a couple weeks ago. At 5:14 p.m., Michael, who lives in D.C. but is visiting New York, texts and asks if we "dare" talk about making plans. (The last few times he's been in town, our plans never went beyond planning to make plans.) I text back, "We could try. It doesn't tend to go well," then give a full rendition of my own agenda for the night: to go to Paragon Sports after work to buy running gear, and then no plans. I even go so far as to mention that I have no plans after work the following evening, either. Silence until 8:13 p.m., when he texts, "How many times has it not gone well?" (Nothing about, say, when or if we should actually meet up.) Silence. Then this, at 10:33 p.m.: "Plans now?" Was he asking about my plans? I had already told him my plans. The texting devolved into what we were each doing: I was at home reading; he was in Williamsburg, drunk. One hour and twenty-seven texts later (literally; I counted), he was still stalling, and still acting as though we might eventually meet up. I played along, despite being in my pajamas by this point and under the covers. "It just keeps getting later!" I texted. "You around tomorrow?" His answer: "Yep. Let's try that." Fed up, I texted that if he wanted to hang out the next day, he should contact me with a general place and time by 1:00 that afternoon. "No planning to plan," I ordered. He agreed. And that's the last I ever heard from him.

Digital connections might make it easier to be a bad friend, or a bad booty call, but they also make it easier to be a good one. "I am terrrrrible at keeping in touch with friends by email and phone," twenty-seven-year-old Veronica Lee told us. If too much time passes between emails, she wrote in response to our questionnaire, "it gets harder because I have to update them on everything that's been going on in my life for however long we've been out of touch. Facebook (I don't use Twitter or MySpace or anything else) lets me easily keep up with or get back into relationships that may have otherwise lapsed."

Friends Are the New Family

When you're young, you never know which connections will lead where, so you make an effort to accumulate lots of them. You go out to bars and join volleyball leagues to meet new people, you stay in touch with old friends and old co-workers, you set a low bar for Facebook friends—all because you never know what might happen next.

The connections have worked amazingly well for Samantha, who has never lost track of a friend. Her current job came from a tip she got from her college friend Jonah's girlfriend's former boss—someone Sam kept up with even after one of those crisscrossing paths had already diverged. She dated a guy she met through Elizabeth, her best friend in fourth grade and someone she still sees regularly for dinner; she dated someone else she met through Elizabeth's former co-worker. And whenever she has a question about the internal workings of Facebook, she can call one of several old friends who actually *work* there, the geeky guys she knew from their math/science magnet program in high school with whom she's stayed in touch (via Facebook, of course) for all these years.

*Sometimes I wish I kept more space between friend groups. I
tried to when I started taking improv classes, which seemed like a
chance to do something entirely new, with people who didn't know me
or my other friends or what I did for a living. And I planned to keep it
that way. I would be aloof in class, and wouldn't tell my friends what
I was doing every Thursday night. To make the alter-identity complete,
when the roll call presented another Samantha in the class, I said I
could go by "Scooter," or "Scootes" for short.*

*My cover was quickly blown. Before we had even gotten through
the introductory name game, the boy beside me said, "I know you."
His name was David and he had gone to college with my friend Ben's
girlfriend Sarah; he also knew Ben from when they both lived in D.C.,
and by the way he also went to high school with my college friend
Matt. Oh, and he knew Elizabeth from journalism school. And also the
guy who had preceded me in my job at* The New Yorker.

So much for boundaries.

*This sort of small-world encounter is mostly amusing, and I won-
der if it comes from the way all of us keep tabs on our friends so
aggressively these days. But it can be a bit claustrophobic, sometimes
feeling like everyone once hooked up with everyone else, and you
can't even take a secret improv class and pose as "Scootes" without
facing someone who knows your real byline, résumé, and romantic
history.*

For many twentysomethings, especially those who are single,
friends can be a kind of chosen family, which is often even better than
the biological kind. Young people who move away from their home
towns, where childhood friends and family members might once have
offered social support to get through lonely times, are especially
beholden to their friends. And the longer they remain single and childless, with no need to focus on a new nuclear family, the more expansive
and essential their circle can become. "It's interesting to me that you
asked about marriage and children as points of consideration in your
20s, but not friendships," Sara, the twenty-five-year-old photographer
from Brooklyn, wrote in response to our questionnaire. "This makes
sense in a way," she wrote, "as my friends and I are realizing that

[marriage and children] can really take over now and shape our decisions moving forward. But both due to the ease of long-distance communication and the potentially transient nature of our lives, I have found friendships to be an increasingly important factor and something that I plan to work hard on throughout my life."

Sara's friends are pretty far-flung; in the preceding twenty-four hours, she told us, she had been in touch with friends in New York, the Bay Area, North Carolina, and Palestine, and she felt close and connected to all of them. But other Millennials aspire to being part of a posse of proximate twentysomethings all hanging out in the same place, like the ones we loved on *Seinfeld* and *Friends* in the 1990s, *Sex and the City* in the aughts, and *Girls* in the 2010s.

In 2001, three years after Jerry and Elaine and Kramer and George retired together to syndication heaven, a young journalist named Ethan Watters called this kind of open-all-hours friendship an "urban tribe." He was part of such a tribe, which he described as an essential survival strategy for modern, middle-class, sort-of-hipster youth.

"We met weekly for dinner at a neighborhood restaurant," Watters wrote in *The New York Times Magazine*. "We traveled together, moved one another's furniture, painted one another's apartments, cheered one another on at sporting events and open-mike nights. One day I discovered that the transition period I thought I was living wasn't a transition period at all." He had made a permanent, meaningful connection to his circle of friends; he relied on them, made plans around their collective needs, gave them priority over almost anything else going on in his life, including girlfriends. His was "a tight group, with unspoken roles and hierarchies, whose members think of each other as 'us' and the rest of the world as 'them.'"

Urban tribes seem in part an outgrowth of the longer path toward marriage these days, with more twentysomethings in need of the kind of immediate company (and an automatic support system) that spouses used to provide. Such tribes are common among singles no matter what their sexual orientation, but twenty-eight-year-old Arline Welty told us she had always assumed it was a phenomenon specific to the gay community she's part of. "I really didn't know this happened outside of queer culture," wrote Arline, who lives in Chicago, "because it definitely happens among queer friends." She and her "chosen family," she wrote, "have family dinners on Sunday nights and get together for cocktails and homemade meals—and we rely on each other. But nobody is closer to me than my partner, so I think of her as my real urban tribe member. And everybody else kind of encircles us." The night before Arline wrote to us, she had gone out with one of the women in her "chosen family" and found herself thinking about how precious real-world contact is. "The exchange was so different than it would be if we were emailing—just intense and fluid and funny, and like we're both pushing toward each other with these ideas and questions—much more intense and intimate." That's one of the nicest things about urban tribes: the chance they offer for face-to-face interaction with people you care about, looking up into one another's eyes instead of down at a glowing, unresponsive screen.

Same as It Ever Was

Isolated or Intimate?

One thing is eternal about friendship in the twenties: making new friends is hard. Especially if you're shy, especially if you're married, especially if you're in a new city with no easy way to meet people. All those things conspired to give me, in October 1974, when I turned twenty-one, the most pitiful birthday of my life.

I was living in Evanston at the time and had virtually no friends. My office was not the kind of place where you found them, and I wasn't sure where else to look. The crazy ophthalmologist who published the journal I worked for had his solo medical practice up front, and in back was the editorial office, with a gorgeous view of Michigan Avenue and a staff of three: me, a pleasant middle-aged guy named Don, and Joann, who was about my age. When I asked Joann if she'd mind limiting her chain smoking to just one cigarette an hour, she was polite about it. For me, that was enough for her to count as a work friend.

As for other places to find friends, Jeff was no help. He was busy all the time with his doctoral program, and no one in his department seemed to be friend material, either too dorky or too dull. There was one couple in our building who seemed interesting—she was a weaver, he a harmonica player—but we hadn't really tried to socialize with them, mostly because in our new grown-up lives we couldn't figure out how. Invite them over for dinner, when we barely knew out how to cook for ourselves? Go to a restaurant together, which we couldn't really afford? Ask them to join us for a picnic at the lake? That seemed so . . . I don't know, childish. It's as if there was a language to adult friend-making that we hadn't learned yet.

A party seemed like the perfect solution—other than that one pesky detail of my not having any friends. I invited Joann, whom I barely knew. I invited Marji, the only friend I'd made in graduate school the previous year. I invited my college roommate Chris, who was living in Chicago that year and taking theater classes at Northwestern, and asked her to bring some actor friends I'd once met who seemed cool. Joann arrived early, Marji bailed, and Jeff and I sat around waiting for Chris and the rest of the party for two hours, making awkward small talk with Joann, with whom I turned out to have almost nothing in common. Chris and three of her actor friends finally appeared at nearly eleven, laughing and offering a bottle of cheap red wine in apology, but what I took away from that mortifying night was a bitter lesson about friend-making in adulthood.

Difficult as it can be, though, making friends is a crucial part of psychological health at this stage of life. Erik Erikson famously described each developmental stage in terms of the particular "crisis" that characterizes it—that is, in terms of the conflict between two opposing impulses that need to be resolved before you move on. The stage he called young adulthood (when the psychosocial moratorium we discussed in the previous chapter will happen if it happens at all) focuses on the crisis of intimacy versus isolation, when the individual commits to, among other things, meaningful, emotionally close social bonds. Many of those bonds will last a lifetime. Even Marji and Chris, who didn't quite come through for me on that miserable twenty-first birthday, are today the kind of friends with whom I can be comfortable within five minutes of re-connecting, despite the fact that we live hundreds of miles apart.

All that comes later; it's in the twenties when things can be so hard. Twentysomethings are more transient than at any other age, and more in need of friendships and tribes wherever they happen to land. But the rules aren't so clear about how to be the "new kid" when you're not actually a kid anymore.

"It's a poignant thing to be a full-grown human and realize you're deficient in something that seems so effortless for children," Ryan Blitstein wrote in an essay in *Salon* in 2009 about also being new to Chicago, in his twenties, and friendless. Ryan and his girlfriend had taken on friend-finding as a mission, "a platonic version of dating. . . . I search for wedding rings on the fingers of women I like—not because I'm hoping they're single, but because I'm hoping they're not, and that maybe their husbands will be willing to double date." They even trolled Craigslist and MeetUp for couples to befriend. "My girlfriend wants to volunteer at a green festival to meet new people. I'm more into the hiking clubs. Then we see a post by a woman wanting to trade nerdy theories about *Lost*. That's us! We recently started watching the show. We love trading nerdy theories."

The *Salon* essay ended ambiguously, with Ryan, then twenty-eight, about to have a drink with Andy, a guy he'd met through friends. "The relationship may lead to nothing. It may lead to something great. But I know that Andy and his crew have given me a small sense of belonging— something I hadn't craved so badly since I was a teenager." I wrote to Ryan recently to see how things had turned out. Very well, apparently. He married his girlfriend and they started making friends, together and separately, without forcing anything. "I was too impatient," he told me. "Most of the friends we have now are, of course, people we met without proactively *looking*." Ryan and his wife have "a thriving network of friends," and while he hangs out with them less often than he did when he was in his early twenties—about once or twice a week, he estimates, rather than every night as he did when he was fresh out of college—he values it more.

As for Andy—he has become one of Ryan's closest friends, the kind of friend you watch TV with, turn to in a career crisis, help through the death of a loved one, and, even though you haven't known each other long, invite to your wedding.

The Friendship Narrative

Our idea of the meaning of friendship is etched early in life, gleaned from both pop culture—the way Bert bosses Ernie around, the way Frog is always there for Toad—and from one's own life, such as when your friend Nick is only nice to you when no one "cool" wants to play. (Sam says she's forgiven Nick, but a mother never forgets.) Childhood experiences create a "relationship schema," the story you tell yourself about what kind of friend you are and what kind you expect your friends to be.

Psychologists have studied relationship schemas for insight into what people value about friendship. As the need for friendship evolves with age, the schemas evolve, too. To study how this happens during the transition between adolescence and young adulthood, a group of Harvard psychologists collected narratives from 40 young people. They interviewed them first in the early 1990s, when the subjects were aged fourteen to sixteen, and again in the early 2000s, when they were twenty-five. A lot had changed in those ten years. At twenty-five, the subjects tended to be more socially assured than in their teens, more tuned in to the complex nature of their identities, more concerned about peer relationships, and more at peace with themselves in terms of their peers.

The Harvard investigators kept track of every "relationship episode" in their subjects' narratives (stories prompted by questions such as "What is the biggest decision you and your closest friend have ever made together?"), coding the predominant theme in each episode in terms of the wish it expressed, how the narrator felt about it, and how the friend responded to it. As teenagers, 48 percent of the subjects told friendship narratives that touched on themes of opposition to or rejection by others. That is, nearly half the episodes described by teens involved one party wanting to be either close or distant, and the friend wanting the opposite. When the subjects were twenty-five, themes of opposition and rejection appeared in their stories only 27 percent of the time, indicating a better fit between how close they were to their friends and how close they wanted to be. Along with that fit came the ability to lean on rather than rub up against other people, as indicated in the words the subjects used to describe their friends. For teenagers, according to the researchers' coding, the second-most popular word for peers was *bad*. For twenty-five-year-olds, the second-most popular word was *understanding*.

Settling into healthy friendships rather than struggling through strained ones starts in the twenties and continues throughout life. Psychologist Laura Carstensen of Stanford calls it the theory of socioemotional selectivity. People need different things from their friends at different stages of development, the theory states, and as they age they eliminate the relationships that don't work for them. In their twenties, she wrote, people use friendships for gathering cultural information and for arriving at a better sense of who they are and how they fit into the world (which requires lots of friends, including lots of new ones). In their eighties, they need social contacts primarily for emotional comfort (which requires only a few very dear, very familiar friends).

> *I have my fair share of friendships-for-the-purpose-of-gathering-cultural-information. But even in your twenties there's something to be said for those few very dear, very familiar friends. When I moved to New York, my college roommate Katie and I found a cramped two-bedroom in Brooklyn. It amused me that she kept calling it "our first grown-up apartment," because it seemed a lot like the places where we'd lived together as undergrads. (She insisted the Clorox wipes in the bathroom made all the difference.) In some ways it was less "grown-up" than my arrangement the previous year, living in Cambridge with my boyfriend R. But Katie and I were proud of the place. We painted and decorated, and bought a sectional couch on Craigslist, each piece light enough that we could transport it entirely on our own in Katie's Honda CRV. Katie called it the No-Boyfriend Couch. We were single grown-up ladies, doin' it on our own.*
>
> *And that, we soon discovered, was often misinterpreted. In college, our relationship was easy to understand: we were apartment-mates, best friends, co-editors of a magazine we'd created together that took up much of our free time. After college, in the world of introductions to work friends or kickball teammates, we fumbled for*

labels. "Best friend" sounded so cheesy to me, like something one should swear to by finger blood and doodle on her Lisa Frank trapper keeper. I tried to signal my level of friendship with Katie by mentioning that we lived together. But it didn't take long for us to realize that didn't quite work; people kept mistaking us for a lesbian couple. Not that there's anything wrong with that. But each awkward correction underscored the feeling that the type of close friendship we had might not make as much sense in this new, grown-up world.

As Sam and Katie learned, external ideas about friendship change as you grow up. Internal expectations change, too, according to the theory of socioemotional selectivity. Carstensen arrived at the theory with an experiment involving card-sorting. She gave a group of subjects, aged eighteen to eighty-eight, a stack of eighteen cards, each with a general descriptor—brother, new neighbor, old friend. "How would you feel about getting to know each of these people better?" Carstensen asked her subjects. "Sort the cards into as many piles as you need in order to categorize them according to the feelings they spark in you."

Unprompted by anything more specific than these instructions, Carstensen's older subjects primarily sorted the cards along a like/dislike dimension. Younger subjects used more dimensions for sorting, which included like/dislike but also the potential for emotionally meaningful contact, the potential for future contact, and the potential for information-gathering. Whereas old people did their sorting primarily in terms of emotions, young people gave all three dimensions equal weight. It was, in other words, as important to twentysomethings for a friend to be someone they could learn stuff from as it was for a friend to be someone to confide in.

Socioemotional selectivity is "a developmental phenomenon that has considerable adaptive value," Carstensen wrote, a way of differentiating among types of friends and culling only the ones you really need. Adolescence and young adulthood represent "the peak emphasis on the goal of information-seeking and, consistent with the theory, is a time when people are establishing their independence from long-time family and friends and seeking out new social contacts."

So twentysomethings might have lots of friends who bug them, but they hold on to them nevertheless, because at this stage of life they can derive some benefit even from the irritating ones. Having wide social circles, despite a few duds, helps young people figure out cultural roles and expectations, meet new social prospects (both professional and romantic), and cultivate second-tier friends to hang with if their first-tier friends aren't around. But how many duds are too many duds? Is hanging out with someone who irritates you really better than staying home alone with a good book? Is this big-tent approach another instance of twentysomethings trying to keep all their options open indefinitely? And when do they finally close some doors on so-called friends who just aren't worth the effort?

Two Roads Diverge

Friendship bonds may buckle when relationship statuses change. This happens when one friend is married and stressing out about whether to start a family while the other is preoccupied with analyzing last night's hookup. Or when one wants to continue the hard-partying, close-down-the-bar friendship they had in college, while the other, with a boyfriend or girlfriend waiting at home, is ready to pack it in at eleven.

Tim Smith, twenty-six, calls it a friendship disconnect. Tim was a second-year law student at Penn State, living in his mother's basement, watching friends sail away on the road not taken. "I have friends getting married and buying homes," he wrote on *the twenty-somethings* blog. "I have friends moving around the world to 'find' themselves, I have friends having children, others that are working and being single. Things just have a different feel when you are still in school and a person you were friends with in college is married, with a home, and talking about having kids."

On the one hand, Tim wrote, he's happy for his friends, and glad to see how far they've come since college. On the other hand, their achievements make it look as if he's far behind, and lead to an emotional gulf that saddens him. What he loved about his group was the sense of "accomplishing our goals together," he wrote, "but now we are all on our own paths, with different goals, and different timetables for those goals." Even if his friends don't like to admit it, Tim said, this difference in their life choices "dramatically changes the dynamic of the relationship."

Having your dear friends take off in new directions that don't include you is a common theme in literature. Movies, too, such as the hit *Bridesmaids* from 2011. After Annie (Kristen Wiig) agrees to be the maid of honor for her childhood best friend, Lily (Maya Rudolph), she must organize events for a wedding party that consists of Lily's new friends from her new stage of life—a rich, snobby, very annoying new stage dominated by rich, snobby, very annoying people. Annie feels that this new Lily, who plays tennis at fancy clubs, orders designer dresses from Paris, and bleaches her asshole, doesn't resemble the friend she grew up with. But that's precisely the point. With her new friends, Lily is able to try out new selves—athletic, entitled, bleached—without feeling chained in by who she used to be, or who other friends took her to be.

The Hollywood ending to *Bridesmaids* is a variation on what often happens to twentysomethings: Lily realizes that she needs both the old friend—to dance with to corny '80s rock, just like when they were kids—and the new one—to pay for corny '80s rockers to come sing in the backyard. People who bridge your two worlds, childish and adult, become especially important when you're feeling awfully in-between yourself.

The *When Harry Met Sally* of Platonic Friendships

With the increased emphasis on coupling off, and with social engagements more often taking the form of one-on-ones rather than big group events, the twenties can be a strange time to have friends of the opposite sex. There might be a moment, after yet another after-work drink with that "just a friend" guy to dish about yet another dating disaster, when a young woman (or her mother) wonders if maybe he's been the right one all along. Hollywood certainly would have you think he is: Harry and Sally, Monica and Chandler, even Mulder and Scully (after nine seasons of sexual tension) ended up in bed together. Wouldn't that be the perfect ending to the story, your own true love sitting right there under your nose?

But maybe he's *not* the right one. Maybe he's just a fantastic friend.

More than half of young adults say they have close friends of the opposite sex, one study reports, and such relationships can be wonderful—often less competitive and more affirming than same-sex friendships. A "you look great" from a guy friend, if you're a straight woman, has a different impact than the same compliment coming from another woman. Cross-sex friendships can be particularly valuable in the twenties, when people are starting to figure out how the other sex thinks. And it's not necessarily a bad thing for there to be a frisson of flirtation in such friendships, a way to heighten the bantering pleasure without taking any real risks.

It can be much harder to maintain these cross-sex relationships, or to cultivate new ones, after you've paired up or married. "The older you are, and the more married you are, the more difficult it is to become friends with someone of the opposite sex," Ryan Blitstein, my Chicago correspondent, told me. "I mean, can you go on 'friend dates' with them? It's just weird to say to your wife, 'I'm going to go hang out with Lucy.'"

I'm not as reticent as Ryan about my cross-sex friendships; "I'm going to go hang out with David" has never been an especially weird thing for me to say to Jeff. Maybe it's because Jeff is a rare and trusting man; maybe it's because I ignore signals he might be sending out that this bothers him, since my male friendships are so important to me that I don't want to actually *know* if he'd rather I stayed home. Conversation with a male friend is for me a safari into unknown territory, a way to become intimate with a variety of men without the sexual shenanigans that were taken off the table when I married so young. Sometimes I think I might have felt more strangled in my super-early marriage if I hadn't had these close male friends, chatty guys who give me insights into alternate lives—and who are in many ways better listeners than a lot of my female friends are.

The trick in cross-sex friendships, whether you're married or unmarried, is to keep things platonic. "The unique challenges faced by cross-gender friends include the need to discuss, and yet downplay, sexuality in the relationship (for heterosexual friends)," wrote psychologist Aurora Sherman of Brandeis. (While I agree with her that the sexuality needs to be downplayed, especially if you're married, I totally disagree with the notion that this is something that merits discussion; that way madness lies.) The judgment of others can also make it harder to keep cross-sex friends, Sherman and her colleagues wrote, since there are "outside pressures on the relationship to move either into a romantic relationship or to give up the friendship entirely in favor of more 'legitimate' relationships with spouses or partners." It's hard for some people to understand that cross-sex friendships still "count" even if they don't turn into something more.

Jonah and I have remained strictly friends ever since we met in our freshman year of college. Drunk or sober or transitioning in between, we always have fun together. Asexual fun. It's not that I don't think he's a good-looking dude—just not one that I could ever imagine kissing, let alone, you know, the other stuff. We confide in each other about job frustrations, wrinkle fears, relationship tics, social insecurities. I find it easier to open up to him than to my women friends, in part because he seems less eager to engage fully. Standing on a street corner one night, I blurted out to him "I think I'm depressed." "I think I am, too!" he exclaimed. We laughed and hugged and kind of cried, and it was exactly what I needed. If I had mentioned my sadness to Katie or Elizabeth, they would have wanted to parse my feelings. But with Jonah it was enough just to hold each other for a while and then go home.

It was on a family trip to his uncle's West Palm Beach mansion that Jonah and I decided on a new form of introduction: "This is Sam. My platonic wife." It didn't exactly explain our situation, but it was enough to signal to Jonah's relatives that, yes, I was a girl accompanying him on their vacation—but, no, it's not what you think.

The label fit so well because the "wife" bit communicated a certain sense of my always being there: I was around for the last girlfriend, and I'd be around for the next. "Platonic girlfriend" would sound coy, confusing. "Wife" signaled something permanent and intimate, but also easy to take for granted. I was expected to be there for him when he needed me, and to fill in when he was between relationships and had no one to take the extra spot on his uncle's private jet. But I was also meant to stand back demurely when his attention was diverted to another woman, as happened a few months later—a woman who'd actually put out.

But what if you wake up one day, take a look at your dear platonic friend, and are . . . um, turned on? This sexual attraction, if mutual, could be the basis for a solid romantic relationship, one made sturdier by the friendship foundation. Or it could turn into "friends with benefits," a sort of casual and sporadic sexual side note. People say no-strings-attached arrangements can work—and I'm talking here about arrangements where both parties are single; when one or both are married or in a committed relationship, this sliding from friends into lovers is an entirely different thing. If it were really that easy, though, why would there be so many articles in men's magazines that list the "rules" for friends with benefits, or FWBs, such as the advice to "take your eggs out of the basket" after three months? And why are the plots of so many Hollywood films, including the 2011 rom-com *Friends with Benefits* (and the barely distinguishable 2011 rom-com *No Strings Attached*) specifically about how hard it is to keep sex from ruining everything?

Friends with benefits have always existed, of course, but without the social acceptance and without the clever name. James Bradac of the University of California, Santa Barbara, tried back in the 1980s to coin *flovers* to describe people who were "simultaneously friends and lovers." But *flovers* never caught on—maybe because it was hard to pronounce ("fluvvers," Bradac helpfully wrote in his article introducing the term), maybe because even when it was pronounced correctly it sounded kind of dumb.

Just as "emerging adulthood" had more staying power than "youth," "friends with benefits" is a whole lot catchier than "flovers."

Mother Nature Has a Say

For all that Millennials are staying superconnected with every person they've ever known—and, to an extent, with every person that every person they've ever known has ever known—there's a limit to how far a true social network can extend. This is another way that friendships for Millennials, even if they feel different, are a lot like friendships have always been. Back in the 1990s, anthropologist Robin Dunbar of Oxford University calculated the maximum number of friends it's possible for any one person to have. That upper limit, which has come to be known as Dunbar's number, is based on his observation that in primates, the size of the social group is directly proportional to the size of the neocortex of the brain—the bigger the neocortex, the more individuals any primate can keep track of. In humans, Dunbar's number is 150—well, 147.8, plus or minus.

"Partly it's a cognitive challenge just to keep track of more people than that," Dunbar has explained. "And it's a time-budgeting problem: we just don't have the time in everyday life to invest in each of those people to the extent where you can have a real relationship."

Dunbar's number was calculated pre-Internet, but it applies to social networks, too. A study conducted in 2009 for *The Economist* found that people with 500 Facebook friends had actual interaction—such as leaving comments on people's walls or "liking" their links or photos—with an average of just 17 friends for men, 26 for women. (I've just checked; I have 260 Facebook friends, but I generally "like" or comment on the walls of only Sam; her sister, Jess; and my good friend Judy.) And one-on-one communication, such as individual messages or Facebook chats, was even more limited: men had two-way contact with an average of just 10 of those 500 friends, women with just 16.

What to make of this? Maybe Dunbar was right. Keeping tabs on people is hard, and even the most promiscuous friender has the time and mental energy for only a handful of actual relationships. Facebook itself has figured this out and has developed an algorithm that restricts the updates you'll see on your friend feed to those from the people whose updates and links you most commonly interact with. Other social media start-ups are also trying to capitalize on the desire for a less dauntingly large friend group, companies such as Path, Highlight, GroupMe, Frenzy, Rally Up, Shizzlr, Huddl, Kik, Disco, Beluga, and Bubbla. These apps (some of which might already have bitten the dust by the time you read this) offer ways to limit groups to a more manageable size, a reflection of how friendships work in real life: an inner circle for true intimacy, an outer circle for all the benefits of a community at large. And when Google+ launched in 2011, many early adopters were excited about the chance to start sorting their e-friends from scratch.

Hansel and Gretel Grow Up

A new kind of friendship that dawns in the twenties is friendship with siblings. When kids are little, brothers and sisters are the people you torture, play with, get annoyed by, get embarrassed by, and put up with because they're always around. But if you're lucky, you enter your twenties and realize that your sibling is someone you actually *like*, and *want* to spend time with. Then you become more like friends than siblings—better than friends, even, because of all that shared history.

"Families are bound by ties of obligation that are generally much stronger than those tying together friends," Jack Woods, a thirty-one-year-old graduate student from Brooklyn, wrote in response to our questionnaire. Estrangement from one's brother, he wrote, is "taken to be remarkable and sad in a way that estrangement from one's friend is not." If you live far away from siblings and depend on friends to be your urban tribe, it can feel a little tenuous, he wrote. "Your family has a moral obligation to be there for you in a way that your friends don't." Jack has lots of friends, but sometimes he wonders what would happen if they all suddenly stopped liking him, or if he suddenly stopped liking them. "In the case of family, that wouldn't destroy the felt bond of obligation. In the case of friends, I think it might."

The quality Jack is alluding to is something Ingrid Connidis calls "a taken-for-grantedness." Connidis, a sociologist at the University of Western Ontario, has interviewed 60 sibling pairs, ranging in age from twenty-five to eighty-nine, to see how the relationship changes over the life span. Feelings of loyalty and love tend to remain dormant, she wrote, "to be rekindled or 'mobilized' only when needed." And it doesn't matter how often the siblings see each other in person or communicate by phone; even if they barely talk to their brothers or sisters, they still know they can rely on them in a way they can rely on no one else. Connidis called it "intimacy at a distance."

A few years ago I called my sister on a Sunday, just to chat. This was not something we did as a rule, and she answered with a tentative "What's up?," trying not to sound alarmed. "Nothing," I said. "I just decided that we should talk on the phone every Sunday." "Oh." Jess went along with it, and I kept it up for a few weeks. I hate talking on the phone, and so does she, but I felt we should do something. She was my sister, and I mostly found out what was happening in her life via our parents, our grandparents, or Jess's Facebook wall.

The Sunday chats didn't last long. But since then, there have been two phone calls I remember. One was on a Tuesday evening in March 2011, after I had just spent a few hours at New York Hospital with our grandmother, who had been brought to the ER with a bad fever that turned out to be pneumonia. I knew Jess was getting all the same email updates I was, so I didn't have any new information to impart. Nor did I expect that she, down in Maryland, had any new information for me. But I just wanted to tell her, as close to in person as I could, how scary it was to see Grammy looking so weak and to have a flash of what should be fairly obvious about an eighty-seven-year-old woman but that somehow, with Grammy, never is: that eventually she's going to die. It was the sort of conversation that could happen only with someone who knew Grammy as well as I did, and in the same way: as a grandmother. Basically, only with a sibling.

This taken-for-grantedness was tapped into by the National Survey of Families and Households, which asked 7,730 adults whom they would call for help in the middle of the night. Almost 30 percent said they would call a sibling first.

The other phone call was in the early morning on September 14, 2008. I know the date because the previous evening was Jess's wedding, at which I drank too much, and after which I went out to some dive bar in Baltimore with the best man and my younger cousin Ben and did shots of something, and moved on to another bar, which wouldn't let Ben in because he didn't have his ID, and then somehow I lost Ben, and maybe lost the best man, too, and didn't have either of their phone numbers, and didn't know where I was, and so I called

*my sister. On her wedding night. And she answered, and she helped
me, and she never made me feel like the drunk and fairly thoughtless
idiot I was. I'm pretty sure neither of us has mentioned it since.*

No, neither Sam nor Jess has ever mentioned it, at least not to me.
But while I might not be pleased with the picture of Sam staggering
around blind drunk in a strange city at 3:00 a.m., I'm glad to hear that
her big sister was there to rescue her. And that Jess kept Sam's secret.

A good relationship with a sibling can be even more important in
young adulthood than earlier in life. During childhood and adolescence, having close ties to siblings can do little to ease troubles with
parents or friends. If you're a sixth-grader aching to be in the cool
clique, being close to your equally uncool brother doesn't compensate;
if you're a teenager who hates his parents, your older sister's sympathy,
sent through emails from college, won't be enough. For teens and
tweens, it's kind of pathetic to have to turn to a sibling for friendship
because no one else wants to play.

But in the twenties, siblings are every bit as socially acceptable as
friends, and there's nothing pathetic about going to dinner, or on vacation, or even rooming with them. (On *Friends*, Ross and Monica are
brother and sister, and they hang with the same gang without anyone
thinking it's weird.) For young adults, "Sibling support compensates for
low levels of support from other relationships," wrote Avidan Milevsky,
a psychologist at Kutztown University in Pennsylvania, who conducted
a study of sibling relationships in 305 people aged nineteen to thirty-
three. Siblings were excellent friend substitutes; young people in his
study who had no friends reported a lot less loneliness and depression,
and higher levels of life satisfaction and self-esteem, when they were
close to their brothers or sisters. Close sibling relationships compen-
sated for bad parent relationships, too, but less so. Because siblings
make up for the lack of friends better than they make up for the lack of
family, Milevsky concluded that in the twenties, brothers and sisters
are more like friends than like relatives.

Better than friends, actually, in that they require less upkeep—that
taken-for-grantedness again. Not long ago, Robin Dunbar and his colleague at Oxford, Sam Roberts, tried to assess the "cost" of two types

of relationships, kith (close friends) versus kin (close relatives). The cost of a relationship is evolutionary biologists' term for the personal resources, such as time or expense, required to sustain it. Those that have the highest cost are the ones we recognize as high-maintenance relationships—the mother who insists on a phone call every evening, the drama queen roommate who needs constant hand-holding but never asks how *your* life is going.

Roberts and Dunbar looked at the social interactions of 25 young people at three points in time: when they were about to graduate from secondary school; nine months later (when 6 of them were working and the rest were at university); and nine months after that, or a year and a half after the study began. They were asked to list all members of their family circle and all members of their social networks, from close friends to casual acquaintances. For each person listed, friend or family, the subjects were asked how long it had been since they had last had direct contact, and were asked to check off the activities they had engaged in together over the previous six months. Possibilities included physical activity (football, keeping fit, mountain biking), leisure activity (shopping, going to the cinema, going to see a gig), social activity (going to the pub, going round to their flat, meeting at a social event), work activity (going to lectures, studying together, working together), and going on holiday (away for more than one night). Then the investigators got a sense of the subjects' inner and outer networks by asking two questions tied to emotional closeness: "Would you seek support, advice, or help from this person in times of severe emotional or financial distress?" and "Would you find this person's death personally devastating?"

As it turns out, for young adults, friends are higher-cost than relatives. Without frequent joint activities, the emotional tie to friends, even supposedly close friends, wanes. But that's not the case with the emotional tie to relatives. "The emotional closeness of friendships over time, as compared to that of kin relations, is more sensitive to changes in frequency of contact," Roberts and Dunbar wrote, and is also "more sensitive to changes in the number of different activities performed together." Friends, they concluded, require more maintenance than relatives. You might not see or talk to your brother for months, but you know he loves you and that you can pick up where you left off when you both have more time.

Some siblings, though, are very high-maintenance—for example, those who are unable to live alone, due to mental illness, addiction, chronic illness, developmental disability, traumatic brain injury, or some other serious problem. Laura Passin, a thirty-one-year-old grad student in Evanston, Illinois, has a brother whose cognitive impairments make him unable to hold down a job or live on his own. He lives in a group home in North Carolina now, but after their mother died, Laura realized there was a good chance she would become his legal guardian while still in her thirties. "I've never particularly wanted kids of my own," she told us (nor does her boyfriend, whom she's been with for eight years), but her responsibility for her brother has eclipsed whatever maternal urge she might have had. "I do not want to take on more caregiving responsibilities."

Others in Laura's position make similar adjustments. A recent study of siblings of people with developmental disabilities found that having a needy sibling profoundly affects a young person's decision-making—or, more accurately, a young *woman's*. Robert Hodapp of Vanderbilt University and his colleagues studied nearly 1,200 sibling pairs and found that the sisters, but not the brothers, of disabled siblings got married and had children significantly later than the norm. Thirty-six percent of the women with disabled siblings were single at age thirty-four—twice that of the general population of white women. (Most people in the study were white.) They were also twice as likely as the general population to be childless at thirty-four—68 percent of women had no children at thirty-four, compared with 28 percent of women overall.

"One explanation may relate to a cautious stance toward major life decisions," the researchers wrote. "Anticipating . . . future caretaking responsibilities, female siblings may need to be more careful when entering into marriage or having children. Unlike their non-disabled brothers, who will usually not be responsible for the care of the brother-sister with disabilities, these women have more to think about than just themselves." So the taken-for-grantedness in sibling affection can sometimes turn into a huge obligation, which colors a twentysomething's decisions for a lifetime.

Round Seven

NOW IS NEW:

- With Facebook, you can have a gazillion friends.
- And smartphones provide new ways to obsess over FOMO.
- Friends can be thicker than blood.

SAME AS IT EVER WAS:

- Friends don't come easy.
- Luckily, it gets better, and friendships change over time.
- Harry was wrong; men and women can be friends.
- Our brains limit the size of our social networks.
- Brothers and sisters are the closest thing in the world.

In our view, the Same as It Ever Was camp wins this one. Even though there's compelling evidence that friendship behavior has changed in the age of social media, the fact remains that most human interactions are still occurring in real life, and people are still restricted by time, space, personal preferences, and the limits of the neocortex—restrictions that mean they can have only a limited number of true friends. And although technology makes it easier to keep tabs on a massive crew of acquaintances, the reason for maintaining that large network, and winnowing it down in later years, is tied to a desire for identity exploration that is part of being young, not just for Millennials but across the eras.

Chapter 8

Parents as Co-Adults

In a book about twentysomethings' momentous, life-altering decisions, what's this chapter doing here? What decision-making is involved where parents are concerned? We're born into the families we're born into, something that none of us asked for (and, truth be told, some of us might have requested a few alterations if we *had* asked); we're linked to them inextricably. Even people who deliberately sever ties with parents or siblings forever bear a crusty scar where the connection used to be.

But that's just the point: the severing, while painful, is still a choice. And staying together and interacting as adults is a choice, too.

Now Is New

Opting In

Once a twentysomething grows up and moves away, subsequent interaction with family members is pretty much voluntary. The connection might be loaded with guilt, obligation, or resentment, or it might be something of deep, abiding sustenance. Either way, this is a relationship that, like that dog your mother never let you get, is now yours if you want it—but it requires care and feeding if it's to survive.

"As adults, [twentysomethings] have the power to distance themselves from their parents, and they use that power when they need to," wrote Jane Isay in 2007 in *Walking on Eggshells: Navigating the Delicate Relationship Between Adult Children and Parents.* "They can no longer be forced to accede to parental authority, and they have the right, and in some sense the responsibility, to make their own decisions, even if they make mistakes in the process." The trick for parents is to sit back and let their adult children make those mistakes, trusting them to be mature enough to face the consequences. Now is the time to adopt the parenting mantra Jeff intones, which used to drive me crazy when the girls were little but is fitting now that they've grown: That which doesn't kill you makes you stronger. For twentysomethings, almost every hard knock will teach them something, and parents have to learn to back off.

When the connection is voluntary, there's nothing quite as profound, or quite as much fun, as the parent-child bond reconfigured as a bond between adults. The kids are a direct line to energy and excitement for the parents, and the parents are an endless source of amusement for the kids. "Honey, I just want to let you know that if you have any, you know, QUESTIONS, you can ask me anything," one mother wrote to her about-to-be-married daughter, who posted the email to *Postcards from Yo Momma,* a website where twentysomethings gently tease their mothers for being so, well, mommish. "Your father isn't the best lover in the world, so I also know a lot about toys. Let's get dinner tonight. Love, Mom."

The very existence of *Postcards from Yo Momma* is pure twenty-first-century. The site feeds on the slightly mangled texts, chats, and emails that mommas send, to the merriment of their daughters and sons. In the interest of full disclosure, I should point out that Sam once submitted one of our G-chat exchanges to *Postcards;* at least she was kind enough to send it in anonymously.

I may have sent it anonymously, but I think it's too amusing not to include here. The backstory is that Mom and I were on a family cell phone plan that included my grandmother. We were shuffling around the accounts for boring reasons having to do with a new job that paid for my phone plan. Also important to know: my grandmother, Mom's mother, was very much alive.

> **Momm:** I just canceled the -1043 phone, and the guy asked me in such a chipper voice why I was doing that ("what's going on?") that I told him it was because my mother died. Do you think God will strike her dead? or strike me dead?
> **Me:** whoa
> **Me:** why'd you say that??
> **Momm:** I don't know. He was being so damned chipper
> **Me:** wow
> **Me:** weird, momm
> **Momm:** yeah, maybe

And that's the second reason *Postcards from Yo Momma* is quintessentially twenty-first century: it couldn't exist if parents and their adult children weren't so close, constantly in touch with each other and on the same wavelength. It was different in my day. Yes, we Baby Boomers tended to stay in regular contact with our parents, but for those of us who moved far from home, regular contact meant snail mail or long-distance telephone calls—and we were very careful not to overshare. Long distance was expensive in the 1970s, so catch-up phone calls were generally limited to once a week, both parties clock-watching the whole time. (If you waited till the weekend to "reach out and touch someone," a cross-country call in 1970 cost 70 cents plus tax for the first three minutes—$3.89 in 2010 dollars, and that's just the discount weekend rate.) I had a few friends in my twenties who phoned their mothers almost every day, but to me that was just bizarre. What could you possibly be telling her? And why would you want her to *know?*

Technology has changed all that. Cell phone minutes don't differentiate long distance from local, text messages are speedy, G-chat is instantaneous, and if Mom misses seeing her son's sweet smile, she can always Skype him.

The same technology that makes it possible for Millennials to keep their parents intimately involved in their lives can make it difficult for them to pull away. It also makes it possible for parents to know too much about our kids' lives—and hard, even when we try, to know how to give our kids the e-privacy they deserve. The etiquette is confusing with social networking, especially when parents and children are in the same circles. I've always known it was wrong to read my daughters' journals, for instance, but is it okay to read blog posts they send out to the world at large? Can you comment on your kids' Facebook walls? Do you acknowledge that you know more about that new guy your daughter's dating than she told you, because you Googled him? Do you ask why your son's relationship status has suddenly shifted back to "single"? And what about Twitter? May a mother retweet? It's always been tricky to re-negotiate the parent-child relationship at the twenties crossroads; Facebook and its ilk make it even trickier.

Constant Comment

Then there's the cell phone, which allows Mom to take up residence in her adult children's pockets so naturally that neither of them bats a proverbial eye. The Pew Research Center reports that seven in ten Americans talk to at least one family member with whom they're not living *every day*. Four in ten speak daily to a parent, either in person or by telephone—up from just three in ten fifteen years ago. Those high-tech apron strings are getting awfully hard to unknot.

This isn't necessarily how young people pictured their independence. In 2005, investigators at Middlebury College in Vermont polled the incoming freshmen to see how often they expected to be in touch with their parents in the coming year. The typical answer: once a week. "I'm trying to have a realization with my parents that they're not always going to be the support system, the control system," one young man told the investigators, led by psychologist Barbara K. Hofer. "I'm trying to create my own support system."

But at the end of first semester, when the students were interviewed again, it turned out they'd been communicating with their parents not once a week but *ten times* that, an average of 10.4 times a week. "Students [had] envisioned college as a parent-free zone and an important step in growing up, an altogether exhilarating prospect," wrote Hofer and journalist Abigail Sullivan Moore in *The iConnected Parent*. Were they disappointed to discover that college wasn't parent-free after all? No, the authors found. In fact, students wished they could communicate with their parents more often, not less. "It's hard to get everything in a simple telephone conversation," one student told them. "If there was a way to meet for coffee every day and chat, then things would be perfect." The researchers were dumbfounded by such an attitude. Baby Boomers, they wrote, "are not likely to recall wishing they could have met mom and dad at their version of Starbucks every day to process their college experience." You've got *that* right.

Calling their parents daily was a deliberate choice for these Middlebury students—or, perhaps more accurately, the deliberate response to a plethora of choices. After a lifetime of being overscheduled, Hofer and Moore wrote, the freedom of campus life was a bit much for them. Classes occupied no more than a few hours a day, and the rest of the day was a succession of decisions about how, when, and whether to study, eat, exercise, or party. It could all get a bit overwhelming—remember the trap of decision fatigue from chapter 1?—so why not just call home? Parents were always willing to drop everything and chat, Hofer and Moore observed, and a quick phone call could "easily fill the void" caused by not quite knowing what to do next.

Like our children, we Baby Boomer parents are just feeling our way through these new grown-up relationships, aiming for the right balance between close and not-too-close. A lot of us think we're managing that balance pretty well. In 2005, the Pew Research Center asked 3,014 adults nationwide, aged eighteen and up, how they felt about the quality of their family life. Seventy-two percent said they were "very satisfied"—more than the proportion who were "very satisfied" with their housing situation (63 percent), standard of living (42 percent), or household income (32 percent). Family was a source not only of pleasure, but also of support. When people were asked to whom they'd turn (besides a husband or wife) if they had a serious problem, 45 percent named a family member, twice the proportion that named a neighbor or a friend.

I contact my parents—by email, phone, G-chat, text—pretty damn often. Take this email that I recently sent to my mother:

From: Samantha Henig
To: Momm
Subject: motherly advice

so, three maternal questions:

1- bloating. i'm not sure i'm entirely sure what it is. is it always accompanied by gas/ discomfort? or sometimes does your belly just swell up for like three days for no reason? because that seems to have happened to me, so it's either bloating or that i gained a lot of weight very rapidly.

2- soap scum. what does one do about it? i feel like suddenly i'm having to thoroughly clean my bathtub every couple weeks because it has already gotten disgusting. is there a spray i should be using that'll keep that from happening? or is it just a matter of frequent cleaning?

3- towels. i bought two about a year ago so that i could rotate them and launder them more often than i used to. and i've been doing that. but they still smell sort of moldy! why?? (actually, i might know the answer to that: i don't think my bathroom has any circulation, so nothing really dries in there.)

> love,
> your daughter

Is that the sort of email an adult sends? Um, maybe? I do sometimes worry that I lean on my parents too heavily for guidance, but it's just so tempting when they are, as the Middlebury researchers found, so quick to drop whatever they're doing to help me, and so unflinchingly on my side.

Many of our exchanges have reached more equal footing. I don't meet them daily at Starbucks, but I do spend more time with my parents than a lot of my friends do with theirs—and often in contexts not unlike how I hang out with peers: meeting for a drink or dinner or, yes, sometimes coffee. It helps, of course, that we live in the same city. But it's more than that; I enjoy their company. I love going to football games with my father, and sometimes I sleep over just so he and I can run together in Central Park the next morning. Mom and I are in a book club together, have volunteered to be mentors together, and, for God's sake, are writing this book together. So although they do still advise me on soap scum and occasionally do my laundry, my parents have also become partners in sport, work, and play in a way that wouldn't have made sense earlier in life.

In a way, we need to stay close to our kids—not so we can help them out, but so they can help us. The speed of technological advancement is downright dizzying, and it takes a digital native to keep up. So parents rely on our kids to keep us abreast of all the changes, patiently explaining the difference between Wi-Fi and 3G, or what exactly Instagram is for. (We used to do it for our own parents, who never seemed to be able to figure out how to program the VCR, but the speed of change is exponential now, and affects every corner of our lives.) Thank goodness for the twentysomethings, magpies in the Internet cloud who bring home trinkets of news and trends to their sclerotic, befuddled parents.

My parents are hip enough to watch The Daily Show *(though my father can't stay awake for the whole thing). They usually get why Jon Stewart is hilarious. But they were confused by a report by Ed Helms a few years ago that played off a congressman's comment about the "level of taint" in Washington. "When Tom Delay or Bob Ney walks into the gym, you can't help but whisper, 'Jesus God would you look at the size of that guy's taint,'" said Helms—and my parents didn't get it.*

Mom emailed me the next day to ask why that segment was so funny, and I felt a combination of amusement and dread. It probably wasn't so different from how she felt in 1990 when I came home from kindergarten and asked her about "that sex thing" that Ian had mentioned at school. Back then, Mom had turned to a book to help her through the awkward birds-and-bees talk. I got off even easier, pointing her to urbandictionary.com—which she's old enough to read all by herself.

Okay, so now I know the modern definition of *taint*, as well as *tossed salad* (don't ask)—not especially edifying, but at least I won't inadvertently embarrass my daughters by using either one the old-fashioned way. This is how it's supposed to work, according to sociologist Lauren Rinelli McClain of Savannah State, with the young patiently educating the old and telling us that no one calls marijuana "grass" anymore. Young people are exposed to cutting-edge "attitudes, values, and behaviors" and then bring them home, she wrote, "thus socializing their parents and encouraging change in parental values and attitudes" in politics, religiosity, and gender roles.

In attitudes toward cohabitation, too. Rinelli did a study involving 275 parent-child pairs, in which the adult child was aged eighteen to thirty-three and the parent was single (most were divorced, 16 percent were widowed, and 10 percent had never married). Some of the parents had romantic partners, and those who did were seven times more likely to be living with them if their adult children were cohabitating, too. This is partial support for the theory of "reciprocal socialization," McClain wrote: "There appears to be a possibility that some parents are learning cohabitation behavior from their children." That's not all we learn from our kids. Who else is going to teach us about social media, clothing, music, and words for parts of the anatomy we didn't even know existed?

Parents as Safety Net

Despite the headlines about twentysomethings lazing about in their childhood bedrooms, there's some good that comes from young people rooming with Mom and Dad. The refuge of home can be a lifeline, sometimes meaning the difference between barely getting by and falling over the edge into poverty. In 2009 the U.S. Census Bureau tried to quantify the benefit of living at home for young people at the bottom of the income heap. At a time when the poverty level for twenty-five- to thirty-four-year-olds was 8.5 percent, demographers calculated that if twenty- and thirtysomethings had not been living with their parents, the poverty rate in this age range would have been a stunning 42.8 percent.

Parents are a safety net for twentysomethings even when they're not all living under the same roof. In 2008 psychologist Karen Finger-man of Purdue asked parents of young adults who were living on their own whether they had provided significant "social support" to their sons or daughters in the previous month. She defined social support as practical assistance, money, advice, logistical help, emotional support, companionship, or lending an attentive ear. The proportion of parents who gave their grown children various kinds of social support on a monthly basis was much greater than comparable studies had found twenty years earlier. In 2008, she found, 70 percent of parents had given their grown children practical assistance and 90 percent had offered advice—compared with 31 percent who had given practical assistance and 46 percent who had offered advice in 1988.

Fingerman, now at the University of Texas at Austin, saw this as a good thing. "Families become stronger in a world that's more compli-cated," she said. Parents tend to give help to the kids who need it most—those at the younger end of this age range, those who are unmar-ried, or those who have faced setbacks such as divorce, trauma, or men-tal illness. To Fingerman, there's a certain logic to it. "Parents have invested two decades of their lives in these kids," she said. "After all that investment, parents are still investing." It upsets them to watch their children suffer, she said, so the "social support" parents offer their needier children is partly to relieve their own distress.

There's a serious downside to this arrangement, though: the entrenchment of the gulf between the haves and the have-nots. Young people who can count on their parents' aid if things get tough have the freedom to take some risks in their twenties: trying out low-wage, low-security jobs, or taking time off for grad school or internships. No parental cushion—whether in the form of a regular allowance, monthly help with the rent, or emergency-only backup—means no chance to dabble.

I was especially aware of being on the lucky side of this unfair divide the summer after my freshman year of college. My parents were newly living in Manhattan, so spending the summer "at home" meant I couldn't be around all my high school friends in Maryland. At the time, not yet settled into a new group and nostalgic for the old one, that seemed just about the worst thing ever. But whatever, I'd deal.

Decked out in my mother's ill-fitting but work-appropriate clothes, I started an unpaid internship at a now-defunct trade publication covering the youth fashion industry. (My sole bylined article that summer: "Spring Trends for Infants and Toddlers.") I was younger than the other interns, and one of only a handful of people whose parents lived in town. But we were all equally unpaid. I couldn't figure it out—how did these people afford housing in New York City when they spent their days working for free?

With each passing summer, the value of accruing those internship credentials increased, and each time it was clear that, except for a few great fellowship programs, the internships were all going to people with relatives who could put them up or bankroll their summer, or both. My parents might not have been writing me checks, but their free place to stay and dinners on demand were what allowed me that early start to my career. Totally lucky—what if my dad taught at Kenyon instead of Columbia? what journalism internships could I get there?—and totally unfair.

The nonmonetary investments Fingerman looked at, such as advice or logistical help, similarly divide the classes. Think of the young person facing her first job interview or annual review, and the payoff that comes from having a knowledgeable parent who can coach her on how to negotiate a raise. It's yet one more instance of the rich getting richer, benefiting from their parents' largesse in ways that go beyond remaining on the family cell phone plan.

Same as It Ever Was

First, About That Basement

My parents both lived at home until they married in 1950. My father had a sick mother with chronic breathing problems, and he had been helping support his family from the age of fifteen, when his father died. Except for his time in the army during World War II, Dad lived with his mother and two brothers in Coney Island, where they'd moved because the "sea air" was supposed to be good for her lungs, until the day of his wedding, when he was not quite thirty-one. My mother, too, lived at home in Brooklyn until she married. She'd graduated from high school at sixteen and gone straight to work as a secretary. Every week, Mom would come home with a paycheck, and Grandma would take five dollars of it, which she said was for the family upkeep. Whenever my mother got a raise—which was often; she was a great secretary—Grandma would take out a bigger chunk: ten dollars, fifteen. My mother thought it was all terribly unfair, since her two younger sisters weren't helping out at all. But it turned out Grandma wasn't spending that household contribution; she was saving it. On the day of my mother's wedding, when Mom was twenty-six years old, my grandmother did what she'd always intended: she gave it all back, $4,000 stuffed inside an envelope (the equivalent of nearly ten times that in today's dollars), enough to get my parents started on their married life.

My parents were typical of their generation in living at home until they married. For the first half of the twentieth century, young men and women lived at home far into their twenties, working, contributing to the household upkeep, caring for younger siblings, waiting to marry. It was common, too, for at least one of the children (usually a daughter) to remain single and, almost by default, to stay with the parents and take on caregiving responsibilities as they aged. In a way, Millennials still living in their parents' basements at twenty-four or twenty-five are not that different from their great-grandparents. Today they're called "slackers." In 1940 they were called "farm help."

In the prosperity of the post-war years, because jobs were plentiful and mortgage rates were low, people were able to move out of their parents' houses and into their own, spouse and baby in tow, at historically young ages. By 1960, white men were leaving home at a median age of 20.5 (and black men even younger: 19.7), compared with age 24.5 twenty years earlier.

Since that post–World War II blip, the median age of home-leaving has crept upward. But the rise has been slow. The median age at which white men left home in 1980 was still almost a year and a half *younger* than it had been a century before (20.9, compared with 22.3 for white men in 1880). And now, the median age of home-leaving remains less dramatically different from previous standards than the headlines would have you think.

Whenever I read about home-leaving and boomerangs, I recall Robert Frost's wistful lines in my head about the haven of the family: "Home is the place where, when you have to go there, / They have to take you in." What's resonant about these lines is that they include both points of view—that of the returning, and of the returned-to—and neither one is happy with the arrangement. Hence the repetition of the words "have to." (These lines, by the way, are not actually about returning to the family nest at all; they're from the poem "The Death of the Hired Man," in which the "you" is not a ne'er-do-well twentysomething son, but an aged, broken handyman dragging himself "home" to a resentful employer.)

The return to the nest—or the delay in flying away in the first place—is not all that new for Millennials; neither is the complaint that failure to launch is the parents' fault. That's the attack on the "helicopter parent," the current derisive term for heavily invested parents who hover over their children, swooping down to take over and solve problems at a moment's notice. Helicopter parents have been the subject of a raft of trend stories, with teachers and coaches complaining about their intrusion at every stage of Millennials' lives, from preschool through college. Now, apparently, the trend stories tell us that helicopter parents have landed in the workplace, coming in to HR to drop off a kid's résumé, accompanying Junior to his job interview, or buttonholing the boss to negotiate a higher salary.

But our own parents came in for much the same criticism back in the 1950s and '60s, when they were accused of spoiling us and making us feel like the center of the universe, creating, as one critic called us, "a generation of coddled infants who developed into demanding little tyrants." The person who bore the brunt of the blame for our spoiled egomania was Benjamin Spock, whose *Baby and Child Care* sold twenty-one million copies between 1946 and 1968 and instructed a lot of our parents about how to raise us. As a 1968 essay in *The New York Times* summarized the general lament, the haters said that Dr. Spock's permissive ways—on-demand feeding, no spanking—is what caused Baby Boomers to grow up to be "unkempt, irresponsible, destructive, anarchical, drug-oriented, hedonistic non-members of society—dropouts from the accepted codes of moral, social, political, academic and economic behavior. And besides, they don't want to fight in Vietnam."

The characterization of my generation as hedonistic druggies was no more accurate then than the criticism of Samantha's generation as entitled, navel-gazing narcissists is now. And blasting Baby Boomers for ruining our kids is no fairer than criticizing our parents for ruining us.

New Ground Rules and a Little Role Reversal

According to the American Dream, kids are supposed to grow up, move out, and then, equipped with a better education and a broader worldview, eventually outstrip their parents. Some of this Dream script, as we've already mentioned, has been thwarted by the recession, and there might not be as much outstripping as there used to be. But the recession has had an impact on the parents as well as the kids—and every now and then, the result has been a more familiar story, with the younger, stronger, less-cash-strapped twentysomethings rushing in to try to help their parents, just as in the past.

Camille DeMere was twenty-two when her parents asked her for a loan of $4,000 to repair a storm-damaged roof on their house. "I'm a young, single person with no responsibilities," Camille told a reporter from *Business Insider* in 2011. "I don't even have a cat." Camille's parents had had a tough year (her father was a freelance writer and her mother was a physical therapist), and she was glad she had saved enough to be able to help them out. "They've put down a lot of money for me, so it was the least I could do," she said.

When financial ruin flips the roles and forces kids to become their parents' patrons, the kids grow up fast. Winston, twenty-five, had to re-adjust his plans for a career on Wall Street, he told us, to help get his widowed mother out of the financial hole she'd fallen into to the tune of $80,000 in debt. He moved back to his Chicago home in the summer of 2009 to become the man of the house—a role he didn't want, and one that forced him to put a lot of his other plans on hold. He found work in Chicago as a contracts manager for a large IT company and persuaded his mother to file for bankruptcy. A year and a half later he found a better job in Indianapolis, as an IT guy for a large data warehouse company, and he moved to his own apartment with his college girlfriend, his mother moving into another apartment nearby. But instead of spending the summer of 2010 nesting, Winston and his now-wife spent it crazily fixing up his mother's house to get it in shape to sell, which meant throwing out three Dumpsters full of crap. His mother was a hoarder, with whole rooms "piled floor to ceiling with old newspapers, magazines, lotto tickets, dollar store trinkets, empty plastic bottles, unsolicited mail, 'as seen on TV' junk, unused exercise equipment." Winston and his wife put the house on the market and held their breaths, knowing it was a bad time for real estate. Finally, in late 2011, the house was sold: one less financial burden for the young couple to shoulder and a years-long experience that had made them grow up double-time.

When twentysomethings are forced to become their parents' caregivers—either financially, emotionally, or medically—their own internal timetables suffer, which can be maddening. "We've all been placed at the mercy of her disease," wrote Robin Romm in *The Mercy Papers*, a memoir about her fury at moving back home at age twenty-eight to help her mother die of cancer after a nine-year illness. "[I]t's trapped us in this house, warping even our arguments. . . . I wish I were somebody else—one of my fresh-cheeked friends in graduate school who for the last nine years took time for granted. Someone who didn't have to think about each day, whose cup of coffee on the deck in the morning didn't feel so fucking temporal."

Some who responded to our questionnaire saw signs that they, too, might have to put their plans on hold in the not-too-distant future to help out their parents. "My parents were very hard hit by the recession and by my father taking early retirement," wrote Renee Autumn Ray, thirty-three, the urban planner in Tupelo, "so their disposable income is much more limited, although they still have significant savings and have not made many sacrifices (like moving into a smaller house . . . they can't sell theirs anyway)."

With an inheritance from her grandmother, Renee has managed to pay off $47,000 in student loans, put 3 percent down on a $65,000 house in Tupelo, and have enough left over to put away $300 a month into a retirement account, in addition to the mandatory 8 percent the city takes out of her paycheck for her pension plan. Her parents still usually pay when they go out to dinner, she told us, but "it is a point of pride that I sometimes treat them to meals when we eat out." In a way, she might be practicing for the day when everything changes and she'll need to help support her parents, instead of the other way around.

Parent-Child Disconnect

Many of the fifty- or sixtysomethings who responded to our questionnaire observed that their grown children felt much closer to them than they'd felt to their parents when they were young. It became such a familiar litany that I'd almost think they were protesting too much—if not for the fact that I say much the same thing about my own daughters.

"I don't know exactly why but my relationship with my children is like night and day to my relationship with my parents," Marji, a sixty-year-old from suburban Washington (and my only friend from grad school), told us. "My parents and I fought about everything—when I came in at night, where I went, who I dated, what I wore, whether I was too fat, whatever." But she said that her two sons, ages thirty-two and twenty-eight, have a totally different attitude. "They want to do things with us. They are happy to go on vacation with us, spend long weeks at the beach together, go out to dinner, etc. They are definitely part of our social life. I would not have wanted that with my parents."

Annie, sixty-three, feels the same way. "There is quite a bit of difference between how our children relate to my husband and myself from how I related to my parents," wrote Annie, the mother of two twentysomethings. "First of all, our kids really treasure their family time, feel quite close to us, seek out our company. Secondly, there's a real sense of being adult friends. We share thoughts about our work—everyone in the family is engaged in some form of creative, artistic endeavor. Unlike my parents, I know a great deal about what my children are up to."

But some parents worry that this feeling is partly wishful thinking. "I like to think my kids are more direct with me, more able to show me when they are angry, and more able to tell me outright when they need me for something," Susan from Massachusetts, a fifty-one-year-old mother of three twentysomething sons, wrote in response to our questionnaire. "But maybe I am fooling myself."

Maybe we're all fooling ourselves, at least a little. A lot of the young respondents to our questionnaire had nice things to say about Mom and Dad, but gushing was rare. And there are signs that our kids aren't quite as flat-out honest with us as we'd like to think. It's like that *Saturday Night Live* sketch "Damn It, My Mom Is on Facebook"— a fake commercial for an app that translates ordinary Facebook status updates into phrases that would make any mother proud. "There isn't enough beer in the world for me to deal with Glenn Beck's holy roller b.s." magically gets posted on Mom's wall as "Boy, do I need new dungarees."

The mother in that sketch, played by guest host Jane Lynch in a Hallmark-sweet pink sweater, is sure that her Facebook activity gives her insight into her son's twentysomething life. She's delighted to be in his network, cheerily typing back on his wall, "I've got a $5 coupon from Kohl's. I'll send it to you." Cut away to the kids back in the dorm room, snickering about how cleverly they put one over on Mom. The video has nearly 300,000 "likes" on Hulu. But to the parent of a twentysomething, there's an edge to the humor.

> My mother is all up in my shit. If I put an inside joke in my G-chat status, she asks me to explain it. She's Facebook friends with my friends, and, at least when she first joined in 2007 and was on Facebook all the time, she kept better tabs on them than I did. (When my old friend Jesse changed his status to "in a relationship," Mom is the one who told me.) If I mention that I'm going on a date, she wants to know what he does and where his parents live—even when I insist that it's just a first date and not likely to go anywhere. And it's even worse with exes: she met up with R. for coffee after we broke up,

which I learned about from him. (Granted, he had been the one to suggest it, since he always liked her. But still.)

For the most part, I can handle it. I'd rather she understood what actually was going on with me than guess. In the past few years, though, I've learned to hold some stuff back. If I tell her about friends hurting my feelings or otherwise behaving badly, she holds on to that, often long after I've forgiven them. Sometimes there's great comfort in her mother-lion tendencies. But I've learned not to give her too much ammunition, lest she fire it off, inappropriately, years later.

And it's easier to impose some distance and keep those secrets now. Mom and Dad don't know who sleeps over, or what time I wake up. I may tell them I had a bad day at work, but I don't explain that I rolled in to the office an hour late because I'd been out until 4:00 a.m. on a Tuesday for no good reason. I can spend hours talking to them—which might make them think we're having a major bond session—but still keep undisclosed entire sets of friends or chunks of my life. But it's not like they're telling me everything, either, right?

Sam is probably right that our relationship isn't as no-holds-barred as I like to think it is. (And no, I'm not going to ask who she was out with until 4:00 a.m. on a Tuesday.) It pains me to admit this, since being close to my daughters is one of my deepest, most unalloyed pleasures. But, alas, scientific studies show again and again that twentysomethings consistently rate the parent–adult child bond as more distant and more contentious than their parents do. We really might be kidding ourselves.

Noted sociologist Vern Bengtson of the University of Southern California and his colleague J. A. Kuypers tried to explain this disconnect with their "developmental stake" hypothesis. Middle-aged parents and their young adult children are at different developmental stages, they wrote in 1971, and come to the parent-child relationship with different needs. The primary task for twentysomethings is to establish autonomy from their parents; they have a "stake" in making sure the relationship is none too cozy. For fiftysomethings, the task is what Erik Erikson called generativity: finding a way to pass on their knowledge, values, and nurturance to the next generation. So their "stake" is for the relationship to be loving and close. As a result, Bengtson and Kuypers wrote, parents "tend to overstate affectual and consensual solidarity with their offspring." And the offspring, with their need to pull away, tend to understate it.

Interestingly, the same disparity in how parents and adult children view their relationship has been found even when parents and children are older—long after the parents have passed the generativity stage, long after the kids most vociferously need to assert their independence. Elderly parents tend to think their relationship with their middle-aged children is smoother than the children do. Adult grandchildren, who have little stake in pulling away from their grandparents, tend to describe that relationship as less rose-colored than do Gram and Gramps. So psychologists now call it the "intergenerational stake phenomenon," since factors other than one's own developmental stage might also be at work in creating the imbalance.

No matter how they describe their relationship, parents and their adult children still can annoy the hell out of each other. Kira Birditt of the University of Michigan, working with colleagues from Purdue and Penn State, interviewed 158 families in Philadelphia—each one consisting of a mother, a father, and a child over twenty-two who lived within fifty miles of the parents. They asked parents and kids what it was that bugged them about each other, and grouped the irritants into two categories: relationship tensions and individual tensions.

Kids' complaints focused on relationship tensions: parents wanting more contact, offering unsolicited advice, intruding on their kids' lives. This might have been because parents were more invested in the relationship, Birditt and her colleagues wrote, so they did things to try to make the relationship closer—things that turned out to be annoying to their children. Parents, for their part, talked most about individual tensions, mentioning the myriad ways young people managed to fall short: job or education, finances, housekeeping, lifestyle, and health. Or, as the kids might have heard it: you're poor, you're messy, you eat crap, you drink too much, and when are you going to settle down and start a family already?

Mothers were found to be more annoying to (and more annoyed by) their daughters than their sons, and more annoying than fathers were to children of either sex. "Children feel their mothers make more demands for closeness," the investigators wrote, "and they are generally more intrusive than fathers."

Demanding and intrusive? *Moi?* All right, all right, I admit it: Jeff is the quiet, kind, accepting parent, and I'm the one who wants so much to be part of our daughters' lives that I can't even let them finish a story without interrupting.

Birditt and her colleagues hypothesized that problems would be more intense when the grown children were young (aged twenty-two to thirty-three) than when they were older (thirty-four to forty-nine). They thought tensions would ease as the young adults grew up and their parents were less stressed out about them, and therefore less intrusive and less likely to offer superfluous advice. But it turned out to be the opposite: the irritation and annoyance only grew as the kids got older. Maybe it's because the relationship actually becomes less important to children as they move into middle age and are diverted by the demands of their own families, the researchers wrote. As relationships are valued less, minor irritants have a way of taking center stage. Or it might be that as children move through their twenties and thirties, they accumulate spouses and babies and jobs, a whole panoply of new topics about which parents can be irritating.

A Few Deadly Sins: Pride and Envy

The old saw that you're only as happy as your unhappiest child—even if the child is an adult—has some scientific underpinning. There's research that shows that middle-aged parents' sense of well-being is intimately connected to how their grown children are doing, rising and falling along with the children's well-being. Back in the 1990s, researchers at the University of Michigan asked 215 fiftysomething parents how their twentysomething children were faring. Were the children well-educated? Well-employed? Financially independent? How about their overall adjustment: Were they happy? Self-confident? Discouraged? Anxious? Well-liked? And they asked whether the parents thought their kids had made the most of their abilities.

The researchers, led by psychologist Carol Ryff, also asked the parents how their children's accomplishments compared with those of other kids their age. And there was one more question, which turned out to be the juiciest: they asked the parents how their kids compared with what *they* had been like back in the day, when they themselves were young.

Most of the findings were pretty much what anyone who's been stuck in an elevator with that "proud parent of an honor roll student" would expect: the more well-adjusted and accomplished the child, the happier the parents. Parents who were pleased with how their kids had turned out had higher levels of self-acceptance, a feeling of environmental mastery, and a sense of purpose in their lives. But there was one finding that was not only surprising but a bit disconcerting. The parents who thought their kids were better adjusted than they themselves had been in their twenties weren't all that pleased. In fact, thinking their kids were faring better than they had made them downright grumpy.

Isn't this counterintuitive? "Why would parents not feel better about themselves," the researchers mused, "if their children were doing better than they had done, as the American Dream suggests?"

The answer, it seems, is that parents aren't quite as self-effacing and pure of heart as the Dream would have it. Yes, we want our children to have better lives than we did—at least, that's the official party line. But life is complicated. People are complex. And parents—yes, even parents—can hold two competing emotions at the same time.

"Children who are accomplished and well-adjusted may occasion pride, and even vicarious enjoyment, among parents," Ryff and her colleagues wrote. "Yet, these same wonderful children may evoke envy and the sense of missed opportunities in parents' own lives." When you get right down to it, parents' attitude toward their children's success is a lot like their attitude toward anyone's success: it sort of makes them feel worse about themselves.

The anthropologist Lionel Tiger once described parenthood as "a set of radically unselfish and often incomprehensibly inconvenient activities." And as we discussed in chapter 5, there's a rumor going around that the dirty little secret of parenthood—the secret that other parents won't tell you, because misery loves company—is that those first eighteen years of parenting are the most difficult, most exhausting, least fulfilling years of anyone's life. That's a debate for another time. But Tiger is right about this: parenthood *does* require a certain amount of selflessness and inconvenience. And after all those years of devoted attention, it can be difficult to shift gears—especially when we wake up, look at our adult children, and see a stark reminder of our own mortality.

Look at Loudon Wainwright III. He's one of my favorite folk singers, and he has made a career of admitting to feelings of envy and regret about almost everything he's ever done, including his relationship with his father, a writer and editor for *Life* magazine, and with his son, Rufus, who is now a bigger pop star than Loudon. He's been quite blunt in interviews, too, about his less-than-noble reaction to Rufus's success. "[I'm] both proud and jealous," he admitted to *The New York Times* the year after *Rolling Stone* named Rufus the best new artist of 1998. "I guess in a way I wish I was 25 starting all over." In one song addressed to Rufus, Loudon evokes the eternal struggle between fiftysomething fathers and their sons by remembering his own adolescent fights with his father, "his life half over, mine about to begin."

The whole trouble, as Loudon notes so pithily, is that the children are young and the parents are middle-aged. There's excitement and pride and unconditional support after every one of a beloved child's accomplishments, but there's a bittersweet feeling, too. "You're starting up," Loudon sings ruefully in his song to Rufus, "and I'm winding down."

On my worst days, that's how I feel: like a member of the generation passing into oblivion (in my profession, in my health, in my looks) as my young, beautiful, accomplished daughters, with more of their lives still stretching ahead of them than coiling up behind, gently nudge me along and out of the way, please. I'm not proud of these feelings.

When Mom's envy about my youth slips out, it's often in the form of backhanded compliments: "My clothes always look better on you than on me," or "I don't think I'm hip enough for that bar you go to." But as our careers have circled in on each other, from the same field to the same city to the same magazine, things have become progressively more fraught.

Mom has written regularly for The New York Times Magazine *since she was my age, dozens of articles in the past thirty years. But when a new editor was hired recently, he killed the first article she wrote for him, a long feature that was meant to be a cover story. He didn't ask for revisions; he simply said it wasn't going to work. Mom read this as a brush-off: if he'd wanted to keep her on as a contributing writer, she reasoned, he would have told her how he wanted the article changed, and she would have changed it. But she concluded that he was trying to sever ties because she was old, and past it, and he wanted to find the next fresh young thing.*

And when the next fresh young thing turned out to be me, that was pretty awkward.

Just a few weeks after the new editor dissed my mother, he started courting me for a job. It was as the web editor of the magazine, not a writer of cover stories. But for both of us, the similarities outweighed those fine distinctions. "It's just a bit too literal for me," Mom told me apologetically over sangria the weekend after I accepted the job. She had encouraged me to go after it, and had advised me on drafts of memos and follow-up emails along the way. But the tension was obvious to both of us. We had spent years in this dynamic of me as the up-and-comer and her as the former up-and-comer (with the added complication of her also being the coach and cheerleader of her own next-generation replacement). And now, at the very moment she was worrying that she had crossed over into has-been terrain, the very man who had pushed her there was embracing me. As she said, too literal.

The act of a parent helping a child grow up has been compared by psychologist Brad Sachs, maybe a bit melodramatically, to "digging one's own grave." Parents of twentysomethings, Sachs wrote in *Emptying the Nest*, "are laying the groundwork for the growth of those who are eventually going to replace us. Our children's departure from the family nest nudges us inexorably towards our *own* departure from this mortal coil, and forces us to conclude that we are moving farther and farther away from the start of our lives, and closer and closer to its conclusion."

A better way of thinking about this, of course, is to think not about conclusions, but about new beginnings. It's all that cycle-of-life stuff, the eternal perpetuation of the species, adult children moving on to start their own households, their own families, their own next generation. This is the real wonder, and profound pleasure, of parenting adult children: being able not only to watch them spin off on their own, but to be a part of it, walking alongside them as co-adults into their new, grown-up adventure.

Round Eight

NOW IS NEW:

- Kids want to stay in touch with their parents.
- Texting and email make constant contact easy, and that's okay.
- Having parents as a safety net can make all the difference.
- The help goes both ways, and parents have a lot to learn from their grown children.

SAME AS IT EVER WAS:

- There have always been twentysomethings who still lived with Mom and Dad.
- Twentysomethings and their parents need to set new ground rules for a new relationship.
- Kids are closer to their parents than kids used to be, but maybe not as close as their parents think.
- And making way for the next generation is hard.

It would have been cool to give this one to the Now Is New camp, since that would have meant that twentysomethings and their parents had achieved an unprecedented level of closeness, interdependence, and trust. Sadly, things are less uniquely close-knit today than Boomers think, and the strains between parent and adult child, including different expectations of the relationship and the bittersweet feelings that come from watching a child grow up, are with us still, giving the parenting round to Same as It Ever Was.

Chapter 9

What's Different, and
Why It Matters

After all is said and done, the definition of adulthood is a personal matter. You might look around and see people your age engaged in activities that sure *seem* grown-up—getting themselves to work every morning, cooking dinner, figuring out how to keep enough toilet paper in the house—but from the inside, those folks might feel they're just pretending, same as you. Even twenty- or thirtysomethings who have taken on the full complement of adulthood signifiers, such as a spouse and a child, might be feeling deeply uncertain about whether they're doing any of it the right way.

So how do you know when you really *are* an adult? The definition these days, even from the experts, seems to focus on subjective measurements rather than the five traditional milestones of adulthood. So Sam and I began our questionnaire with this opening line: "How will you know when you're an adult?" We got a range of responses from Millennials, most of them reflections of still feeling awfully in-between.

- Am I an adult? Yes-ish, I guess. (male, 31)
- I can no longer find a significant difference between myself and other people that I consider to be adults. So, I guess it's time to call it what it is. (female, 32)

- It's less "I'm an adult!" than "Yeah, I guess I must be an adult." . . . [It was] just a slow process of asking myself the question "Am I an adult?" from time to time and each time moving further away from "Nah! Couldn't be. Not yet" and closer to "Yup, guess so." (male, 28)

- Just because I'm not very good at being a grown-up doesn't mean I'm not one, I guess. (male, 29)

- I am not sure. I definitely have some adult responsibilities. Also, I have a beard. (male, 25)

- I have this idea that buying a new couch will make me feel like an adult. I still have an old hand-me-down. But as soon as I do that I'll probably come up with a different benchmark. (female, 29)

- I'm an adult who thinks I should be better at every aspect of being an adult. (female, 28)

- There are bars of adulthood measurement that I simply do not reach. For example, I fail to keep my closet organized for a full week. (female, 28)

- I still like to party, I like to daydream about what my life will be like when I'm "grown-up," I like to ride my bike . . . I don't know why I equate bike riding with being young, but for some reason I do. (female, 24)

- I see nothing wrong with staying in on a Saturday night. This makes me feel like an adult. (male, 28)

- The first time I got reamed out by a boss in my first job after graduation. Definitely felt the crushing weight of adulthood then. (male, 27)

- The condom broke and I took Plan B a few hours later, and while the statistics were in my favor, I think adulthood is about realizing that, if enough time has passed (25 years, for example), at some point you will come out on the wrong side of the statistics. (female, 26)

- Do I feel the way adults appeared to me when I was a kid? Not at all. But in retrospect, they obviously didn't feel that way at the time either. (female, 26)

- Indecision may be a sign of not being an adult. Maybe not though. (male, 26)

In the 1980s, Cheryl Merser asked the same question while she was working on her book about young Baby Boomers, *"Grown-Ups": A Generation in Search of Adulthood.* She got a variety of responses from her fellow twenty- and thirtysomethings when she asked them to define adulthood. The answers Baby Boomers gave Merser were a lot like the answers Millennials gave us.

- An adult is somebody who, when eating alone, doesn't do it standing up and uses a plate.
- You're a grown-up when you're accountable to yourself.
- If you don't keep your socks under the bed.
- I never buy wine or Scotch because I only drink gin and tonic. But when my friends come over, they never want gin. I guess I'd be a grown-up if I bought what my friends like, not just what I like.
- Why are you asking *me?*

This echo of young Baby Boomers in the lives and thoughts of young Millennials has struck Sam and me again and again as we've researched this book and tried to tease out to what extent youth-hood today is different from the past and to what extent it is, as the Talking Heads refrain goes, same as it ever was. Some differences are clear. The timing on the road to adulthood is slower (slower, even, than for Cheryl Merser's "generation in search of adulthood"), driven in large part by a series of changes affecting women. Reproductive technology allows young women to put off childbearing decisions for longer, which in turn allows them to put off marriage decisions, which in turn lets them devote more time to their jobs, and to explore the wider range of career options now available to them. In addition, because of a more widespread acceptance of premarital sex and cohabitation (even in comparison to the Swinging Sixties), neither women nor men have to go without regular sex just because they're getting married later.

The Internet and always-on connectivity have made the twenties different for Millennials, too. There's more social activity to keep up with than ever before; you're expected to be available to your employer round-the-clock and to respond to emails all night and on weekends; friends and family are in constant touch; and young people rely more on Google and Outlook calendars and less on good old-fashioned introspection, memorization, and rumination.

Millennials are also grappling, for the first time ever, with the inversion of the American Dream, the realization that they probably won't be as well off as their parents were. Their houses will be smaller, if they can afford them at all; their jobs will be harder to get, more demanding, less secure; they might not have the fancy cars and fancy vacations their parents could afford. Some of the downsizing is actually in keeping with what Millennials say they want; many polls report that they hope for more urban lifestyles, smaller homes, and fewer cars than their parents did. But it's a harsh realization nonetheless, and the need to face it is something that's new to this generation.

Sam and I also found that a lot of things about this period of life are evergreens, including many that seem at first glance to be unique to Millennials. The fact of having to choose mates and friends and careers in the twenties, the fact that doing so is really hard, the fact that closing doors goes against our nature—all these truths have applied to young people for generations. Also true is that even though parents of twentysomethings think we get along with our kids way better than our parents did, we're kind of wrong. Our parents thought they were getting along with us pretty well, too, even if that's not what *we* thought.

Considering what neurotic worriers we both are, Mom and I have ended up with some pretty laid-back conclusions—the opposite of all those screaming headlines about "kids today." If it seems that young people are taking longer to grow up . . . well, we are, in some respects, but maybe we're right to. There's less of a need to rush marriage, either for the sake of financial stability or for beating the biological clock. There's a greater number of accessible options to explore, both for careers and for partners, so it's not a bad idea to sample a few paths before committing. And taking the time to do so now could help prevent major crises of confidence later in life.

This trial-and-error period can't last forever, though. If you keep clicking, indefinitely, to restore shrinking doors, you'll rapidly fall behind those people with the sense to let a few of those doors disappear— to commit to the room they're in, and reap the rewards.

We know that many members of the Baby Boom generation went down a path in their twenties that looks a lot like the path of Millennials, sputtering and veering and taking surprising and circuitous turns. Many of those who meandered and explored, such as my friend Mitch, ended up doing really well, possibly even better than folks such as Jeff and me, who followed a pathway to adulthood that was straight, narrow, and fast. Getting there first might be overrated. And the tortuous paths of post-adolescence might be exactly what people need to become grown-up.

After filtering through all the evidence, we've concluded that some things about being twentysomething are unique to Millennials, and some things are not. Here are the areas where we ended up ruling that Now Is New:

- **Decision-making.** Many of the decisions faced at the twenties crossroads are familiar, and the unwillingness to close doors seems almost instinctive. But there are far more choices now, and the fact that young people are generally permitted a longer time to make their decisions only makes the endless weighing of options more agonizing.

- **Schooling.** Higher education costs more than ever before, leads to more crushing debt than ever before, and has to go on for longer than ever before just so a person can keep up.

- **Babies.** The biological clock still ticks, and even though young women expect to have babies far into their forties, it's much more difficult then. Still, the general expectation among better-educated Millennials has been to wait at least until the thirties to start having children, which is older than ever before.

And in these areas, we came down on the side of Same as It Ever Was:

- **Careers.** Even though Millennials are facing the prospect of long-term underemployment and downward mobility, previous generations, including Baby Boomers, have faced the same prospect before and gotten through it.

- **Marriage.** Love is timeless, and though the pacing of marriage is different for Millennials, many of the choices they fret about regarding marriage—when, with whom, and whether—are the same as those their parents and grandparents faced.

- **Health.** Lifestyle decisions that most directly affect the health of Millennials—drug abuse, alcohol abuse, cigarette smoking, bad diet, lack of exercise—are made no more wisely now than they used to be. And the twentysomething brain is still a work in progress, not quite finished with its maturation.

- **Friends.** Facebook hasn't changed things as much as it first appears; Millennials still need friends more in their twenties than they ever will, still use friends for different purposes at different ages, and still can have only a limited number of real friends in real life—or, for that matter, even on Facebook.

- **Parents.** Parents may think they get along with their kids much better than their parents did when they were young, but it turns out that's an old story—midlife parents always see the parent–grown child relationship as rosier than the grown child does, and fiftysomethings can never completely "get" twentysomethings.

In other words, certain things about today's world make being twentysomething different from how it's ever been: the staggering number of options available, the crush of student debt, the long lead time before deciding about babies. But on other measures—career options, marriage, health, friendships, and relations to parents—we think that Millennials are more like preceding generations than they are different. The Same as It Ever Was side wins by a nose.

Why does it matter that the slow route to adulthood is generally not that different from the route earlier generations took? Maybe it will ease people's minds—both for the twentysomethings themselves, who might worry that they're doing it wrong, and for their parents, who are worrying even more, and even more vocally. It's easy to forget what it was like to be young, and understandable to want to keep your kids from making the mistakes you made. But being young is confusing, and mistakes are inevitable. Not only mistakes, of course; triumphs and lessons learned are a pretty good bet, too. And one thing is almost certain: these floundering twentysomethings will become adults eventually, just like their parents did.

When we started on this project, it was because we thought there was a book's worth of stuff that Mom's article had left out. Now, one book later, we fear there is a volume still to go. (And, no, we're not just setting ourselves up for the sequel here; I'd rather enjoy what's left of my twenties than keep dissecting it.) For all that we've uncovered, we still have a lot of questions. So we'll borrow from the format of all those academic papers we've been reading, and allow ourselves the luxury of pointing out opportunities for further research. If social scientists look at this generation again in twenty years or so, to see how smoothly we've made the transition from quarterlife to midlife, will they find that the people who tried more paths when they were young are behind financially? Or ahead psychologically, less likely to be suffering from midlife regret about the road not taken? Will the cohabitation effect diminish as living together becomes more commonplace even for casual relationships, and therefore less likely to trigger a slide into marriage? If our generation struggles into middle age to attain the financial comforts that we took for granted growing up, will we raise our children with strict demands for clear signs of success (straight As, Ivy League, medical school), in the model of immigrant parents like my great-grandparents, and end up being even less accepting of the next generation's grab at emerging adulthood than our parents were of ours?

We don't know what kind of fiftysomethings today's twentysomethings will be. We fiftysomethings probably aren't quite the way we'd have pictured ourselves back in the day, when we were telling one another not to trust anyone over thirty. That's the great thing about human nature. For all that the psychologists and economists and sociologists try to explain it, there are still some elements that remain inexplicable, with twists and variations that are impossible to predict.

So there's no telling what exactly awaits Millennials. Exciting, isn't it? Right now the future is wide open, as today's twentysomethings grapple with the choices that twentysomethings have always made— albeit with some distinct hurdles and distinct advantages. Surprises await as they deal with the options they've been given, and as they figure out and shape the unfolding of their own story.

Appendix

Our Questionnaire

We're a mother-daughter writing team working on a book together about 20-somethings. Robin, the mother half of the team, wrote a cover story for *The New York Times Magazine* last year on 20-somethings, which is what got us started on this topic. The book will look at the culture, science, and economics of being young, both today and in previous generations. Its working title is "Twenty-Somethings: Millennials on the Cusp of Adulthood."

We're hoping to incorporate a broad range of voices from 20-somethings, and former 20-somethings—and that's where you come in. Could you please take a few minutes to answer some questions that will help in our book research, and to **forward this email on** to others (ideally in their 20s or early 30s) who you think have interesting stories to share?

First, we're asking everyone to answer these specific questions. IF YOU'RE SHORT ON TIME, YOU CAN STOP AFTER THIS!

- Do you think of yourself as an adult?

- If you do, what was the single thing that **made you realize** you were, and how old were you then?

- If you don't, **how will you know** when you're an adult?

Then, we're hoping you can fill us in a little on your life now or, if you're a fair bit beyond your twenties, your life back then.

- **Please start with your age and where you live.**

- Then feel free to tell us as much or as little as you like about **what it's been like (or was like) to be in your twenties**.

- And please let us know if you'd like your replies to be **anonymous**.

Here are some aspects of your life we're interested in, to get you started.

- **Are you working?** How many jobs have you had since college? What were they? What is your current job? Do you expect this job to be something you stay at for a while? How is it related to what you studied in school, and to what you intend to do as a career?

- By what age do you think you should be ready to **commit to a career**? Why?

- Have you gone to or considered **graduate school**? What are the pros and cons?

- How many **student loans** do you have? If you have loans, how much is your monthly payment? How much does your debt affect your other life decisions?

- How much have you thought about, or started, saving for retirement? How **financially independent** are you from your parents? In what ways do they help you out financially (who pays when you go out for dinner, for instance)?

- How close are you to your **parents**? How does your relationship compare to when you were younger? How big a role do your parents play in your daily life?

- Do you have a **healthy lifestyle**? How would you describe your health habits in terms of exercise, diet, medical check-ups, **smoking, drinking**, drug use? Have you gotten more or less attentive to a healthy lifestyle compared to when you were in your teens?

- Are you **married**? in a relationship? How many **sexual partners** have you had? How many more do you **expect to have**? When did you (or when do you expect to) **commit** to a long-term serious relationship?

- Have you ever **moved back home** to live with your parents after college? Why? For how long?

- Do you live alone? with roommates? with a romantic partner? Do you own or rent your home? How many times have you **changed residence** in the past two years?

- Do you **have kids**? At what age did you (or expect to) have them? Do you think there are more benefits to having kids **early, or waiting** to have them until your late 30s or 40s? What do you think should go into the decision to have children?

Those're just some prompts—you can answer as many of them, in as much detail, as you like. The more the better, of course—we're trying to get a fair view of what life is like for 20-somethings today, especially the choices people make about **either committing to a particular path or continuing to explore their options**. And please remember to tell us if you'd like your replies to be anonymous.

Also, if it's OK with you for us to **follow up** with further emails or maybe a **phone interview**, please include your best contact information.

Thanks for your help!

Robin Marantz Henig (58) and Samantha Henig (27)

Acknowledgments

We took a risk, Samantha and I, embarking on this mother-daughter project. As she already mentioned, our professional lives have been orbiting around each other for years now, and recently I've started to feel that Sam's career has managed to eclipse mine long before I was ready for it to be eclipsed. (I think that's how a lot of fiftysomething print journalists feel these days about twentysomething web journalists, but it was all made much more complicated for me by our biological and emotional bond.) And then we entered into a book collaboration, with all the weird ups and downs of co-author power plays looming scarily on the horizon.

We avoided the worst of it, I think. For my part, I had tons of fun, and came out of it still crazy in love with my daughter, and with more respect—if more was even possible—for her intelligence, cheerfulness, commitment, equanimity, grace under pressure, and consummate editorial skill. I know she gave up a lot to stick with this project, especially mid-book, when she took her new job at *The New York Times Magazine*, a demanding position that kept her at the office late almost every night. There were a lot of after-work indulgences and weekend trips that Sam had to put off until the book was done.

My husband, Jeff, had to give up a lot, too, but he's used to that. I'm never an especially nice person while I'm working on a book, but I keep doing it anyway, and Jeff never complains. When Sam and I had our occasional weekend "writers' retreats," either in Manhattan or at my sister-in-law Julia's beautiful house upstate, Jeff sometimes came along, fetching dinner when we needed it, joining us for bourbon when we were too frazzled to write another word. And Jeff is a full-service errand boy; he read several sections of the draft and offered the insightful editorial direction and objectivity I've come to rely on.

We were lucky to have a couple of other wonderful readers on this book, who helped improve it immensely. First and foremost was my older daughter, Jess Zimmerman, a brilliant writer and editor; everything she touched got better. Even though Jess insisted at the outset that she didn't want to collaborate with Sam and me, we're both so grateful that she was willing to get past her initial reticence and join forces with us as a book doctor par excellence.

Thanks to our other readers, too, who read part of the book and offered helpful advice: Sarah Ball, Katherine Bouton, Julia Gray, Paul Marantz, Peter Schubert, Bob Schwab, Matt Shaer, and Mitch Weiss. And a special thanks to Dan Menaker, who read a nearly complete draft and showed us how to reframe the whole shebang. Dan's help made all the difference.

As with everything else in this book, Mom has already done the heavy lifting in the acknowledgments section, and leaves me with only one person left to thank: the woman who made this book happen, and invited me to ride her coattails.

Mom basically bred her own co-author, teaching me from childhood how to write and edit, and training me (less intentionally) how to handle her sensitivities when she's deep in a writing project. At my mother's knee, I have learned to recognize and hone long-form writing, the way some kids learn to brine a chicken or knit a scarf. And now, by her side, I've learned how to write a book—or at least to poke at a book being formed and shaped by an expert hand. Many of my friends in this industry have parents who don't quite get what they do. I'm lucky to have a mother who gets it even more than I do.

I'm also hugely grateful to my friends Brian, Chad, Dan, Jonah, Julian, Katie, Rishi, and Tony for letting me tell their stories so I didn't just have to prattle on about myself. Thanks, too, to all my friends who served as focus groups during the writing process, especially Nancy Cook, Elizabeth Green, and Annie Karni, who always seemed genuinely interested, and Andrew Marantz, who was the first to quote me back to me. Thanks, also, to Jake Bronsther, for assuring me that even if people made fun of me for writing a book about twentysomethings with my mother—and even if Jake himself was leading the mockery brigade—I should still feel good about it.

We're also grateful to everyone who responded to our questionnaire for their generosity and frankness. Some of the stories they shared were quite personal; all were touching, insightful, and helpful. Even those whose responses we didn't quote directly informed our understanding of this exciting, shape-shifting stage of life.

Our agent, David Black, was, as ever, a stalwart advocate and a true mensch. Thanks also to the people at Hudson Street Press: Caroline Sutton, for taking the book from the glimmer-in-our-eye stage all the way to publication; and Brittney Ross, for offering it the fresh perspective of a smart Millennial.

I'm grateful to my editors at *The New York Times Magazine*, who first assigned me a cover story on twentysomethings back in early 2010—and who then made me revise it, and re-revise it, and then revise the re-revision. It was torture of course, the way these endless rewrites always are, especially since most of it was taking place while I was supposedly on a long family vacation at the beach. In retrospect, though, I know how indebted I am to their insistence that I get it right; it's why the piece was so widely read and why it touched so many people. So my thanks to Vera Titunik, Alex Star, and Gerry Marzorati, even for the torture.

Notes

Introduction

Alpha Boomers . . . and [their] $2 trillion in buying power: "Don't Trust Anyone Over 50," Maureen Callahan, *New York Post*, Jan. 23, 2011.

in their twenties, Gen Xers made up . . . 15 percent of the population: In 1992, people aged twenty to twenty-nine totaled 39,239,000, and the total population was 255,082,000; www2.census.gov/prod2/statcomp/documents/1994-02.pdf.

Millennials . . . born between 1980 and 1990 . . . make up about a quarter: "Occupy Movement Must Get Support from Millennial Generation to Survive," Morley Winograd and Michael D. Hais, *Christian Science Monitor*, Nov. 29, 2011, www.alaskadispatch.com/article/occupy-movement-must-get-support-millennial-generation-survive.

"the obvious trappings of growing up . . . are neither obvious nor automatic": Cheryl Merser, *"Grown-Ups": A Generation in Search of Adulthood*, New York: Signet, 1990, p. 59.

11 percent of twenty-five- to thirty-four-year-old men were still living with their parents: "Facing a Financial Pinch, Moving in with Mom and Dad," Sam Roberts, *The New York Times*, March 22, 2010, www.nytimes.com/2010/03/22/nyregion/22singles.html?_r=1&scp=1&sq=facing%20a%20financial%20pinch&st=cse; also "Recession Threatens Generation of Young Adults, Inspires 'Occupy' Protests," Bob Sullivan, *Red Tape*, Nov. 2, 2011, redtape.msnbc.msn.com/_news/2011/11/02/8586286-recession-threatens-generation-of-young-adults-inspires-occupy-protests.

the rate for adults under twenty-four living with their parents has been generally stable: "On the Road to Adulthood: Leaving the Parental Home," Krista K. Payne, published by National Center for Family and Marriage Research, Bowling Green State University, 2011, FP-11-02, ncfmr.bgsu.edu/ pdf/family_profiles/ file98800.pdf.

Time magazine's cover line "They Just Won't Grow Up": The cover, dated Jan. 24, 2005, featured a picture of a twentysomething in a sandbox, and was probably the first use of the term *Twixters*, which never quite took off. The cover line: "Meet the Twixters, young adults who live off their parents, bounce from job to job and hop from mate to mate. They're not lazy . . . THEY JUST WON'T GROW UP, by Lev Grossman," www.time.com/time/covers/0,16641,1101050124,00.html.

Young people aged twenty to twenty-four are making less today: "The Young and the Jobless," Bob Herbert, *The New York Times*, May 12, 2005, query.nytimes.com/gst/abstract.html?res=fb0915fc3b540c718dddac -0894dd404482.

an estimated 17 percent lower than if [they] had graduated into a better economy: "The Long-Term Labor Market Consequences of Graduating from College in a Bad Economy," Lisa B. Kahn, *Labour Economics* 17, no. 2 (April 2010): 303–16.

Twentysomethings comprise more minorities than any other age group: "On Life's Way: The Contemporary Context of Young Adulthood," keynote address by Richard Settersten, presented at "Emerging Adulthood in a Family Context," Penn State University, Sept. 29, 2010.

The proportion of blacks and Asians is also higher among Millennials: "The Generation Gap and the 2012 Election: Angry Silents,Disengaged Millennials," Section 1, "How Generations Have Changed," Pew Research Center for People and the Press, Nov. 3, 2011, www.people-press.org/ 2011/11/03/section-1-how-generations-have-changed/.

42 percent of people aged eighteen to twenty-nine are living in poverty or near-poverty: We're defining "near poverty" as 200 percent of the federal poverty level; see www.census.gov/hhes/www/poverty/data /incpovhlth/2010/table6.pdf.

In Great Britain . . . young people choose their educational track earlier: According to Project Britain, "British Life and Culture," by Mandy Barrow, kids in grade ten (age fifteen to sixteen) take the General Certificate of Secondary Education, after which they either leave school, go to technical college, or stay in high school for two more years and then take A levels to see if they go to university; see www.woodlands-junior .kent.sch.uk/customs/questions/education.html.

70 percent of single Italian men: Charles B. Hennon and Stephan M. Wilson (eds.), *Families in a Global Context*, NewYork: Routledge, 2008, p. 149.

In Israel, roughly two-thirds of eighteen-year-olds: David Pollock of the Institute for Near East Studies, an expert on Israel, gave the two-thirds estimate, pointing out that most Arab Israelis, Orthodox women, and Haredi Jews do not serve in the military.

Senegal, where the average age of first childbirth is nineteen: "Family Planning: The Progress of Nations, Many Are Mothers at 18," UNICEF report from 1995, www.unicef.org/pon95/fami0009.html.

Chapter 1: The Twenties Crossroads

undergraduates are getting paid money to open and close doors: Jiwoong Shin and Dan Ariely, "Keeping Doors Open: The Effect of Unavailability on Incentives to Keep Options Viable," *Management Science* 50, no. 5 (May 2004): 575–86.

Millennials pass through all the Big Five . . . about five years later: A Canadian study reported that a typical thirty-year-old in 2001 had completed the same number of milestones as a twenty-five-year-old in the early 1970s. Among thirty-year-olds in 2000, fewer than half of the women and one-third of the men had done so. James Coté and John M. Brynner, "Changes in the Transition to Adulthood in the UK and Canada: The Role of Structure and Agency in Emerging Adulthood," *Journal of Youth Studies* 11, no. 3 (2008): 251–68.

having options like this improves . . . overall life satisfaction: Sheena S. Iyengar and Mark R. Lepper, "When Choice Is Demotivating: Can One Desire Too Much of a Good Thing?" *Journal of Personality and Social Psychology* 79, no. 6 (2000): 995–1006.

Barry Schwartz . . . calls it "the paradox of choice": Schwartz writes about this subject in *The Paradox of Choice*, New York: Ecco, 2003 (the quote is from the preface), and he gives a great TED talk on this topic at www.ted.com/talks/lang/eng/barry_schwartz_on_the_paradox_of_choice.html.

in . . . a gourmet market in California: Iyengar and Lepper, "When Choice is Demotivating," pp. 995–1006.

a phenomenon known as "decision fatigue": John Tierney, "Do You Suffer from Decision Fatigue?" *The New York Times Magazine*, Aug. 17, 2011, www.nytimes.com/2011/08/21/magazine/do-you-suffer-from-decision-fatigue.html?_r=1&scp=2&sq=tierney%20willpower&st=cse.

Daniel Kahneman writes about the shortcuts we take: Daniel Kahneman, *Thinking Fast and Slow*, New York: Farrar, Straus and Giroux, 2011.

a Google search for "jam": The exact numbers vary from day to day; we got 789 million hits for "jam" on March 15, 2012.

the Internet is a fundamental resource for the human race: "Cisco Connected World Technology Report for 2010," www.cisco.com/en/US/netsol/ns1120/index.html#~2010.

they "refuse to consider themselves adult": Kenneth Keniston, "Youth: A New Stage of Life," *American Scholar* (Autumn 1970): 635–38.

youth **wasn't a very convincing term**: Jeffrey Jensen Arnett, "Emerging Adulthood: A Theory of Development from the Late Teens Through the Twenties," *American Psychologist* 55 (2000): p. 470.

"The parallels . . . are too clear to ignore": James B. Stewart, "An Uprising with Plenty of Potential," *The New York Times*, Nov. 18, 2011, www.nytimes.com/2011/11/19/business/occupy-wall-street-has-plenty-of-potential.html.

"At 40, I'll be ready for marriage and family": Sylvia Ann Hewlett, "Executive Women and the Myth of Having it All," *Harvard Business Review*, April 2002, pp. 66–73.

a pattern that has held true in studies around the world: Shamsul Haque and Penelope A. Hasking, "Life Scripts for Emotionally Charged Autobiographical Memories: A Cultural Explanation of the Reminiscence Bump," *Memory* 18, no. 7 (2010). Other examples of the reminiscence bump can be found in Yayoi Kawasaki, Steve M. J. Janssen, and Tomoyoshi Inoue, "Temporal Distribution of Autobiographical Memory: Uncovering the Reminiscence Bump in Japanese Young and Middle-Aged Adults," *Japanese Psychological Research* 53, no. 1 (March 2011): 86–96, onlinelibrary.wiley.com/doi/10.1111/j.1468-5884.2010.00451.x/full#fn1.

the children had the most to say about their young adulthoods: Annette Bohn and Dorthe Berntsen, "The Reminiscence Bump Reconsidered: Children's Prospective Life Stories Show a Bump in Young Adulthood," *Psychological Science* 22 (2011): 197, originally published online December 30, 2010, at pss.sagepub.com/content/22/2/197.

"Know your own bone": Henry David Thoreau, *Letters to a Spiritual Seeker*, New York: W. W. Norton, 2004, p. 38.

"What a man *can* be, he *must* be": Abraham H. Maslow, "A Theory of Human Motivation," *Psychological Review* 50 (1943): 370–96.

"Being well-suited to one's job didn't always predict a longer life": Howard S. Friedman and Leslie R. Martin, *The Longevity Project: Surprising Discoveries for Health and Long Life from the Landmark Eight-Decade Study*, New York: Hudson Street Press, 2011, p. 144.

"sometimes they are wrong": Author interview with Daniel Gilbert, available at www.randomhouse.com/kvpa/gilbert/author.html.

Regretted something they *had not* done that they wished they had: Thomas Gilovich and Victoria Husted Medvec, "The Experience of Regret: What, When, and Why," *Psychological Review* 102, no. 2 (1995): 379–95.

Chapter 2: Schooling

two out of three expected to have a worse life than their parents did: Jessica Godofsky, Cliff Zukin, Carl Van Horn, "Unfulfilled Expectations:

Recent College Graduates Struggle in a Troubled Economy," May 2011, John J. Heldrich Center for Workforce Development, Edward J. Bloustein School of Planning and Public Policy, heldrich.rutgers.edu.

drive down wages for an entire generation: Richard Freeman, *The Overeducated American,* New York: Academic Press, 1976.

a student . . . would have to work 40 hours a week: Robert Hiltonsmith, "Generation Y Bother," *The American Prospect,* Nov. 14, 2011, at ht.ly /7vzSC.

"We just woke up one morning and it had happened": Pat Callan spoke in an interview that appeared on the Project on Student Debt website, projectonstudentdebt.org/voices_home.php.

In the space of just ten years: Various stats about student loans come from the following: "Quick Facts About Student Debt," Project on Student Debt, Jan. 2010, Debt_Facts_and_Sources.pdf; Tamar Lewin, "Burden of College Loans on Graduates Grows," *The New York Times,* April 11, 2011, www.nytimes.com/2011/04/12/education/12college.htm?_r=2; Matthew Reed, "Student Debt and the Class of 2007," The Project on Student Debt., projectonstudentdebt.org/files/pub/classof2007.pdf.

even if you declare bankruptcy: Michelle Singletary, "Students Trapped in Private Loans, with No Bankruptcy Protection," *Washington Post,* April 29, 2010, www.washingtonpost.com/wp-dyn/content/article/2010/04 /28/AR2010042804396.html; also Christina Mulkin, Dick Durbin Press Office, "Durbin, Cohen and Others Introduce Legislation to Restore Fairness in Student Lending," projectonstudentdebt.org/files /pub//Durbin_2011_Bankruptcy.pdf.

the only recourse seems to be default: "Sharp Uptick in Federal Student loan Default Rate," Project on Student Debt, Sept. 12, 2011, projectonstudentdebt.org/pub_view.php?idx=780.

Among 900 twentysomethings polled by the Gallup organization: Jeff Jones and Frank Newport, "USA Today/National Endowment for Financial Education Young Adults' Finances Poll," Oct. 26–Nov. 14, 2006, Gallup Poll #06-10-045, www.nefe.org/Portals/0/NEFE_Files /USATodaySurvey.pdf.

"When I have a boyfriend": Cait Flanders, "Why I Can't Afford to Start Dating," on the blog *Give Me Back My Five Bucks,* Dec. 2, 2011, www .givemebackmyfivebucks.com/2011/12/02/guest-post-why-i-can% E2%80%99t-afford-to-start-dating/.

urging young people to consider other, cheaper ways: Daniel B. Smith, "The University Has No Clothes," *New York,* May 1, 2011, nymag.com /print/?/news/features/college-education-2011-5/.

Thiel said when he announced the fellowship program: "Peter Thiel Launches Innovative Thiel Fellowship to Foster Next Generation of Tech Visionaries," Thiel Foundation press release, Sept. 29, 2010.

no more than your expected annual salary your first year: Zack O'Malley Greenburg, "How Millennials Can Survive This Economy," *Forbes*, Nov. 30, 2011, today.msnbc.msn.com/id/45465033/ns/today-money /t/how-millennials-can-survive-economy/#.TtpBsOrgLog.

people who go straight to grad school: Cecilia Capuzzi Simon, "R.O.I.," *The New York Times*, Education Life supplement, July 22, 2011, www .nytimes.com/2011/07/24/education/edlife/edl-24roi-t.html?page wanted=all.

all peak between ages twenty-five and thirty-four, before the slow decline: Bruce J. Avolio and David A. Waldman, "Variations in Cognitive, Perceptual, and Psychomotor Abilities Across the Working Life Span: Examining the Effects of Race, Sex, Experience, Education, and Occupational Type," *Psychology and Aging* 9, no. 3 (1994): 430–42.

having a college degree slows the aging of the brain: Patricia Cohen, "The Sharper Mind," *The New York Times*, Education Life supplement, Jan. 22, 2012, pp. 20–21, www.nytimes.com/2012/01/22/education/edlife /a-sharper-mind-middle-age-and-beyond.html?_r=1&scp=5&sq=patri cia%20cohen&st=cse.

the important premium . . . attached to a master's: Louis Menand, "Live and Learn: Why We Have College," *The New Yorker*, June 6, 2011, www.newyorker.com/arts/critics/atlarge/2011/06/06/110606crat _atlarge_menand?currentPage=all.

The earnings bump for a graduate degree: Anthony Carnevale, Jeff Strohl, Michelle Melton, "What's It Worth? The Economic Value of College Majors," Georgetown University Center on Education and the Workforce, 2011, cew.georgetown.edu/whatsitworth; also Bruce Watson, "Grad School Math: Which Degrees Are Worth the Debt," *Daily Finance*, Dec. 29, 2011, www.dailyfinance.com/2011/12/29/grad -school-math-which-degrees-are-worth-the-debt/.

grad school . . . an additional $31,700 in debt: Adelle Waldman, "In Debt from Day One," *Christian Science Monitor*, March 9, 2004, www .csmonitor.com/2004/0309/p11s01-legn.html.

"The One-Year, Self-Directed, Alternative Grad School Experience": Chris Guillebeau, "Skip Graduate School, Save $32,000, Do This Instead," *Powells Books* blog, Sept. 28, 2010, www.powells.com/blog/guests /day-2-skip-graduate-school-save-32000-do-this-instead-by-chris -guillebeau/.

that Rutgers poll of 571 recent college graduates: Godofsky, Zukin, and Van Horn, "Unfulfilled Expectations."

A different survey, funded by the Lilly Foundation: Arthur Levine and J. S. Cureton, "When Hope and Fear Collide: A Portrait of Today's College Student," San Francisco: Jossey-Bass, 1998; also A. W. Astin, L. Oseguera, L. J. Sax, and W. S. Korn, "The American Freshman:

Thirty-Five-Year Trends," Los Angeles: Higher Education Research Institute, UCLA, 2002.

Alison Monahan, takes issue with this old trope: Alison Monahan, "Law School Myth #3," Sept. 7, 2011, *The Girl's Guide to Law School* blog, Sept. 7, 2011, thegirlsguidetolawschool.com/09/law-school-myth-3-law -school-gives-you-three-more-years-to-decide-what-to-do-with-your -life/.

$129,000 (the average cost of a law degree): David Segal, "Is Law School a Losing Game?" *The New York Times,* Jan. 8, 2011, www.nytimes.com/ 2011/01/09/business/09law.html?scp=6&sq=law%20school& st=cse.

the average law school loan was $80,000 to $100,000: Law School Admission Council website, Financing Law School, Repayment: An Overview, www.lsac.org/jd/finance/financial-aid-repayment.asp.

about fifteen thousand legal and staff jobs . . . disappeared: Kevin Kiley, "Objecting to More Lawyers," *Inside Higher Ed,* June 21, 2011, www .insidehighered.com/news/2011/06/21/law_schools_shrink _enrollments_in_face_of_poor_job_market_fewer_applications, also the study from Northwestern University, www.law.northwestern. edu/career/markettrends/#Attorney%20Hiring.

The average debt of new physicians . . . was $158,000: Pauline W. Chen, "The Hidden Costs of Medical Student Debt," *The New York Times* Well blog, July 28, 2011, well.blogs.nytimes.com/2011/07/28/the-hidden -costs-of-medical-student-debt/.

med school is so expensive . . . only the rich can afford to go: S. Ryan Greysen, Candice Chen, Fitzhugh Mullan, "A History of Medical Student Debt: Observations and Implications for the Future of Medical Education," *Academic Medicine* 86, no. 7 (July 2011): 840–45, journals.lww .com/academicmedicine/Abstract/2011/07000/A_History_of_ Medical_Student_Debt_Observations.16.aspx.

physicians. . . earned 70 percent more than lawyers: Freeman, *The Overeducated American,* p. 117.

their student loans are staggering: George Mannes, "Young Doctors in Debt," *Money,* Nov. 16, 2007, money.cnn.com/2007/11/16/pf/young _doctors.moneymag/.

the National Health Service Corps: Information about the current scholarship program is available at nhsc.hrsa.gov/scholarships/index .html and at www.hhs.gov/recovery/programs/nhsc/nhscfactsheet .html.

One study followed 1,410 Michigan kids from birth onward: D. Wayne Osgood, Gretchen Ruth, Jacquelynne S. Eccles, Janis E. Jacobs, and Bonnie L. Barber, "Six Paths to Adulthood," in *On the Frontier of Adulthood: Theory, Research, and Public Policy,* Richard A. Settersten Jr.,

Frank F. Furstenberg Jr., and Rubén G. Rumbaut, eds., Chicago: University of Chicago Press, 2005, p. 335. According to Osgood and his co-authors, seven out of ten in the "fast starter" group were, at age twenty-four, already working at jobs they expected to be at for the long haul. And their annual income was significantly higher than that of other twenty-four-year-olds: $674 a week (in 1996 dollars) compared with an overall average of $471 a week.

"college education has been an important influence": Jeffrey Jensen Arnett, *Emerging Adulthood: The Winding Road from the Late Teens Through the Twenties*, New York: Oxford University Press, 2004, p. 121.

The articles usually featured someone like Sally Cameron: The original article Kevin Carey followed up on was Karlyn Barker, "The Underemployed: Working for Survival Instead of Careers," *Washington Post*, Dec. 9, 1982.

Carey wondered what had happened to Sally: Kevin Carey, "Bad Job Market: Why the Media Is Always Wrong About the Value of a College Degree," *The New Republic*, June 9, 2011, www.tnr.com/article/economy/89675/bad-job-market-media-wrong-college-degree.

the 1967 *Time* Man of the Year: *Time* editors named as the Man of the Year the generation "Twenty-five and Under" in the issue of Jan. 6, 1967, vol. 89, no. 1.

Today it's almost 70 percent: College attendance rates are from the Bureau of Labor Statistics, www.bls.gov/news.release/hsgec.nr0.htm.

"There is stuff that every adult ought to know": Louis Menand, "Live and Learn: Why We Have College," *The New Yorker*, June 6, 2011, www.newyorker.com/arts/critics/atlarge/2011/06/06/110606crat_atlarge_menand?currentPage=all.

"the signal accomplishments of humankind": Rebecca Mead, "Learning By Degrees," *The New Yorker*, June 7, 2010, www.newyorker.com/talk/comment/2010/06/07/100607taco_talk_mead?printable=true#ixzz1bASNpAai.

in a follow-up study, 36 percent still showed no . . . improvement: David Glenn, "New Book Lays Failure to Learn on Colleges' Doorstep," *Chronicle of Higher Education*, Jan. 18, 2011, chronicle.com/article/New-Book-Lays-Failure-to-Learn/125983/.

time spent studying was a little over twelve hours a week: Kimberly Dvorak, "A Nation of Dummies?" *San Diego Examiner*, Jan. 18, 2011, www.examiner.com/county-political-buzz-in-san-diego/new-study-says-students-should-skip-first-2-years-of-college.

the most popular undergraduate major in America: Menand, "Live and Learn."

the outcome everybody is looking for: This is from an excerpt published in *The Chronicle of Higher Education*, Jan. 18, 2011, from the book *Academically Adrift: Limited Learning on College Campuses* (Chicago:

University of Chicago Press, 2011), by Richard Arum and Josipa Roksa, chronicle.com/article/Are-Undergraduates-Actually/125979/.

undergraduate course called Fundamentals of Reality: James S. Kunin, "The Rebels of '70: Confessions of a Middle-Class Drifter," *The New York Times Magazine*, Oct. 28, 1973.

The financial benefit of college has actually doubled: David Leonhardt, "Q&A" The Real Cost of College," *The New York Times* Economix blog, Nov. 19, 2009, economix.blogs.nytimes.com/2009/11/19/q-a-the -real-cost-of-college/.

a typical college graduate is said to earn about $800,000 more: Derek Thompson, "What's the Best Investment: Stocks, Bonds, Homes . . . or College?" *The Atlantic*, June 27, 2011, www.theatlantic.com/business/archive/2011 /06/whats-the-best-investment-stocks-bonds-homes-or-college/241056/.

a return on investment . . . of 15.2 percent: Michael Greenstone and Adam Looney, "Where Is the Best Place to Invest $102,000—In Stocks, Bonds, or College?" Washington, DC: Brookings Institution Press, The Hamilton Project, June 25, 2011, www.brookings.edu/papers/2011/0625 _education_greenstone_looney.aspx.

Generation Limbo includes Amy Klein: Jennifer 8. Lee, "Generation Limbo: Waiting It Out," *The New York Times*, Sept. 1, 2011, p. E1, www.nytimes.com/2011/09/01/fashion/recent-college-graduates-wait -for-their-real-careers-to-begin.html?_r=1&scp=1&sq=generation% 20limbo&st=cse.

G. Stanley Hall . . . a prominent American psychologist: G. Stanley Hall, *Adolescence: Its Psychology, and Its Relation to Physiology, Anthropology, Sociology, Sex, Crimes, Religion and Education*, Englewood Cliffs, NJ: Prentice Hall, 1904.

the child labor protection movement: A comprehensive history of the movement, which began in the 1880s, can be found at the Child Labor Education Project, a website managed by the University of Iowa Labor Center and Center for Human Rights, www.continuetolearn.uiowa .edu/laborctr/child_labor/about/us_history.html.

He described a "curve of despondency": Jeffrey Jensen Arnett, "G. Stanley Hall's *Adolescence*: Brilliance and Nonsense," *History of Psychology* 9, no. 3 (2006): 186–97.

Hall . . . went through emerging adulthood: Jill Lepore, "Twilight: Growing Old and Even Older," *The New Yorker*, March 14, 2011, www.new yorker.com/reporting/2011/03/14/110314fa_fact_lepore.

Chapter 3: Career Choices

people change jobs in their twenties more than . . . in any other decade: Robert H. Topel and Michael P. Ward, "Job Mobility and the Careers of Young Men," *Quarterly Journal of Economics* 107 (May 1992): 439–79.

A poll of 872 people commissioned by . . Demos and Young Invincibles: "The State of Young America: Economic Barriers to the American Dream," Nov. 2, 2011, Demos and Young Invincibles, complete report available at www.demos.org/sites/default/files/publications/State-of -Young-America-TheDatabook.pdf.

an "animus that threatens to poison . . . a generation": Landon Thomas Jr., "For London Youth, Down and Out Is Way of Life," *The New York Times*, Feb. 16, 2012, www.nytimes.com/2012/02/16/business/global/ for-london-youth-down-and-out-is-way-of-life.html?ref=landonjr-thomas.

It's not as if today's twentysomethings will wake up . . . to a revived economy: David Leonhardt, "The Depression: If Only Things Were That Good," *The New York Times* Sunday Review, Oct. 9, 2011, p. 1, www .nytimes.com/2011/10/09/sunday-review/the-depression-if-only -things-were-that-good.html.

"starting at the bottom is a recipe for being underpaid": Austan Goolsbee, "Hello, Young Workers: One Way to Reach the Top Is to Start There," *The New York Times* op-ed, May 25, 2006, www.nytimes.com/2006/05 /25/business/25scene.html?scp=1&sq=hello%20young%20workers& st=cse.

two-thirds of the wage growth . . . in the first ten years: Robert H. Topel and Michael P. Ward, "Job Mobility and the Careers of Young Men."

Katherine . . . began working for a catering company: Katherine Goldstein, "I'm Here to Serve: Why Catering Is the Best First New York Job You Can Have," *Slate*, Nov. 1, 2011, www.slate.com/articles/life/small _business/2011/11/what_s_the_best_first_job_out_of_college_try _catering_.html.

Take Scott Nicholson, twenty-four: Louis Uchitelle, "American Dream Is Elusive for New Generation," *The New York Times*, July 6, 2010, p. A1, www.nytimes.com/2010/07/07/business/economy/07generation .html?_r=1.

most of the 1,457 commenters . . . were outraged: The most interesting comments to the Uchitelle article (those that were most often "recommended" by other commenters) can be seen at community.nytimes .com/comments/www.nytimes.com/2010/07/07/business/economy /07generation.html?sort=recommended.

his own story seems to have ended happily: Scott Nicholson's LinkedIn profile, accessed in April 2012, is at www.linkedin.com/pub/scott -nicholson/22/634/a94.

how social media and smartphones affected their lives: "Cisco Connected World Technology Report for 2010," as well as the "Connected World Technology report for 2011," are described in a press release, newsroom.cisco.com/press-release-content?type=webcontent&articleId

=474852. The reports can be read in full at www.cisco.com/en/US/netsol/ns1120/index.html#~2010 and www.cisco.com/en/US/netsol/ns1120/index.html#~2011.

"bright and ambitious recruits": Dan Schawbel, "Reviving the Work Ethic in America," *Forbes*, Dec. 21, 2011, www.forbes.com/sites/danschawbel/2011/12/21/reviving-work-ethic-in-america/.

the average salary two years post-graduation: Amanda Fairbanks, "College's Value Added," *The New York Times* Education Life, Jan. 7 2011, www.nytimes.com/2011/01/09/education/edlife/09books-t.html, plus clarification from Arum email, Feb. 17, 2012.

G-chatting . . . is . . . how they get things done: Nona Willis Aronowitz, "Hustlin': For Millennials, Chat Rooms Are the New Conference Rooms," *Good*, Jan. 23, 2012, www.good.is/post/hustlin-for-millenials-chat-rooms-are-the-new-conference-rooms/.

"the behaviors . . . may actually enhance young people's productivity": Catherine Rampell, "A Generation of Slackers? Not So Much," *The New York Times* Week in Review, p. 3, May 29, 2011, www.nytimes.com/2011/05/29/weekinreview/29graduates.html?_r=1&scp=1&sq=a%20generation%20of%20slackers&st=cse.

"The younger generation is always right": The story about Mahler and Schoenberg was reported as an oft-told tale in Roger Sessions, "Questions About Music," Cambridge, MA: Harvard University Press, 1970, pp. 37–38.

"Do you ever wonder how everyone survives?": Ryan O'Connell, "Seven Things a Twentysomething Can't Do," *Thought Catalog*, Aug. 17, 2011, thoughtcatalog.com/2011/seven-things-a-twentysomething-cannot-do/.

maybe the cluelessness . . . really is something different: Annamaria Lusardi, Olivia S. Mitchell, and Vilsa Curto, "Financial Literacy Among the Young: Evidence and Implications for Consumer Policy," *Journal of Consumer Affairs* 44, no. 2 (2010): 358–80.

15 percent had made a financial decision . . . they regretted: Jones and Newport, "USA Today/National Endowment for Financial Education Young Adults' Finances Poll."

you'll need to invest more than *twice* that amount *every year*: Christina Vuleta, "Taking Stock of Your Finances in Your 20s," *40:20 Vision*, May 4, 2011, 4020vision.com/index.php/2011/05/taking-stock-of-your-finances-in-your-20s/.

made career decisions they wouldn't otherwise have: Jones and Newport, "USA Today/National Endowment for Financial Education Young Adults' Finances Poll."

young people with bachelor's degrees were so often considered "overqualified": Freeman, *The Overeducated American*, p. 21.

In decent economies, it's more like 4 or 5 percent: Don Peck, "How a New Jobless Era Will Transform America," *The Atlantic*, March 2010, www .theatlantic.com/magazine/archive/2010/03/how-a-new-jobless-era -will-transform-america/7919/.

the gap persisted for years: Lisa B. Kahn, "The Long-Term Labor Market Consequences of Graduating from College in a Bad Economy," *Labour Economics* 17, no. 2 (April 2010): 303–16. Kahn's figures indicated that for each percentage point rise at the time of college graduation, these young men were earning 4 to 5 percent less twelve years later, and 2 percent less eighteen years later.

the surest way to move up . . . is by changing jobs often: Robert H. Topel and Michael P. Ward, "Job Mobility and the Careers of Young Men."

the hard knocks of that early stretch . . . can haunt them: Krysia N. Mossa-kowski, "The Influence of Past Unemployment Duration on Symptoms of Depression Among Young Women and Men in the United States," *American Journal of Public Health* 99, no. 10 (2009): 1826–32.

the trend even then was to move around: "Number of Jobs Held, Labor Market Activity, and Earnings Growth Among the Youngest Baby Boomers: Results from a Longitudinal Survey," Bureau of Labor Statistics, released Sept. 10, 2010, www.bls.gov/news.release/nlsoy.nr0.htm. These results were also written up in Daniel Indiviglio, "Profiling Baby Boomers' Job Stability," *The Atlantic*, Sept. 12, 2010, www.theatlantic .com/business/archive/2010/09/profiling-baby-boomers-job-stability /62822/.

a significant subset who kept moving around even into their forties: "Number of Jobs Held, Labor Market Activity, and Earnings Growth Among the Youngest Baby Boomers: Results from a Longitudinal Survey," Bureau of Labor Statistics.

think of the QWERTY keyboard: Paul A David, "Understanding the Economics of Qwerty: The Necessity of History," *Economic History and the Modern Economist*, ed. William N. Parker, Oxford, UK: Basil Blackwell, 1986, pp. 30–49, www.mendeley.com/research/understanding -the-economics-of-qwerty-the-necessity-of-history/. Briefer descriptions of the QWERTY story are available at home.earthlink.net /~dcrehr/whyqwert.html and en.wikipedia.org/wiki/QWERTY.

Closing doors has always been part of growing up: Susan Littwin, *The Postponed Generation: Why American Youth Are Growing Up Later*, New York: William Morrow, 1986, p. 247.

the app calculates the trade-offs: Dan Ariely's app is called Oranges2Apples, danariely.com/apps-tools/. It's advertised as costing $1.99 at the iPhone app store, but we seemed to get it for free.

what 40 percent of new grads do even today: Jeffrey Jensen Arnett, "Why

Shouldn't They Take Their Time?" *The New York Times* Room for Debate blog on the question "Is Any Job Better Than No Job?" June 6, 2010, roomfordebate.blogs.nytimes.com/2010/06/06/is-any-job-better -than-no-job/?scp=17&sq=job%20search%20college&st=cse# jeffrey.

One recent study of young people on the job market: Sheena S. Iyengar, Rachael E. Wells, and Barry Schwartz, "Doing Better but Feeling Worse: Looking for the 'Best' Job Undermines Satisfaction," *Psychological Science* 17, no. 2 (2006): 143–50.

"I will get to where I want to be in life": Arnett, *Emerging Adulthood*, p. 16.

it was possible to compare expectations to reality: Krysia N. Mossakowski, "Unfulfilled Expectations and Symptoms of Depression Among Young Adults," *Social Science & Medicine* 73, no. 5 (2011): 729–36, www.sci encedirect.com/science/article/pii/S0277953611003777.

youthful dreams dashed or deferred is . . . an old story: Littwin, *The Postponed Generation*, p.16.

"Is the American Dream achievable?": "The State of Young America: Economic Barriers to the American Dream," Demos and Young Invincibles.

researchers from Notre Dame conducted in-depth interviews: Christian Smith, with Kari Christoffersen, Hilary Davidson, and Patricia Snell Herzog, *Lost in Transition: The Dark Side of Emerging Adulthood*, New York: Oxford University Press, 2011, p. 71.

"Have a nice house that belongs to me": Ibid., p. 93.

the Meaning of Life was expressed in terms of . . . material comfort: Ibid., pp. 105–7.

Chapter 4: Love and Marriage

the median age of first marriage has increased: D'Vera Cohn, Jeffrey Passel, Wendy Wang, and Gretchen Livingston, "Barely Half of US Adults Are Married: A Record Low," Pew Research Center, Dec. 14, 2011, www.pewsocialtrends.org/2011/12/14/barely-half-of-u-s-adults-are -married-a-record-low/.

The average age of first marriage . . . in Finland: "Marriages Are Entered into at Ever Later Age," *Statistics Finland* 6 (May 2011), www.stat.fi /til/ssaaty/2010/ssaaty_2010_2011-05-06_tie_001_en.html.

"at this stage in life, you want to have fun": Mark Regnerus and Jeremy Uecker, *Premarital Sex in America*, New York: Oxford University Press, 2011, p. 171.

a person "must be economically set" before marrying: Ibid., p. 183.

The couples who did best . . . married between ages twenty-two and twenty-five: Norval D. Glenn, Jeremy E. Uecker, and Robert W. B.

Love Jr., "Later First Marriage and Marital Success," *Social Science Research* 39, no. 5 (2010): 787–800.

"Cupid may have wings, but apparently . . . not adapted for long flights": Michael J. Rosenfeld, *The Age of Independence: Interracial Unions, Same-Sex Unions, and the Changing American Family*, Cambridge, MA: Harvard University Press, 2007, p. 39.

If a man gets off on having birthday cake smashed in his face: Mark Oppenheimer, "Married, with Infidelities," *The New York Times Magazine*, July 3, 2011, www.nytimes.com/2011/07/03/magazine/infidelity-will-keep-us-together.html?pagewanted=all.

online dating is now the third-most common way . . . to meet: Nick Paumgarten, "Looking for Someone," *The New Yorker*, July 4, 2011, www.newyorker.com/reporting/2011/07/04/110704fa_fact_paumgarten?currentPage=all.

Marina Adshade . . . calls it "beauty inflation": Marina Adshade, "Online Dating Sites Creating Beauty Inflation," *Big Think*, May 10, 2011, big-think.com/ideas/38356. Adshade recommends Craig Roberts, Emily Miner, and Todd Shackelford, "The Future of an Applied Evolutionary Psychology for Human Partnerships," *Review of General Psychology* 14, no. 4 (2010): 318–29.

the Internet has made it easier for people to cheat: Naomi Troni, "ERWW Study Reveals: Love is in the Air—And Online," *EuroRSCG Worldwide Social Life and Social Media*, Feb. 13, 2012, eurorscgsocial.com/2012/02/13/love-is-in-the-air%E2%80%94and-online.

In 2005 there were five million cohabiting couples: "Unmarried-Couple Households, by Presence of Children: 1960 to Present," U.S. Bureau of the Census, 2005, www.census.gov/population/socdemo/hh-fam/uc1.pdf.

proposals these days tend to be more mutual: Ellen Lamont, "Initiation During Courtship: Negotiating Gender Norms," Paper presented at the 2011 annual meeting of the American Sociological Association in Las Vegas.

two out of three first-time brides . . . are already living with the groom: S. Kennedy and L. Bumpass, "Cohabitation and Children's Living Arrangements: New Estimates from the United States," *Demographic Research* 19 (2008): 1663–92; also "Trends in Cohabitation: Twenty Years of Change, 1987-2008" National Center for Family and Marriage Research, 2010.

couples who lived together before marriage ended up less happy: Scott M. Stanley, Galena K. Rhoades, Paul R. Amato, Howard J. Markman, and Christine A. Johnson, "The Timing of Cohabitation and Engagement: Impact on First and Second Marriages," *Journal of Marriage and Family* 72, no. 4 (August 2010): 906–18.

intelligence . . . ranks high on men's lists of desirable qualities: Stephanie Coontz, "The M.R.S. and the Ph.D.," *The New York Times* Sunday Review, Feb. 11, 2012, www.nytimes.com/2012/02/12/opinion/sunday/ marriage-suits-educated-women.html?scp=1&sq=coontz&st=cse.

Oppenheimer . . . developed the "search theory" of marriage: Valerie Kincade Oppenheimer, "A Theory of Marriage Timing," *American Journal of Sociology* 94, no. 3 (Nov. 1988): 563–91.

that didn't sound like her own . . . experience: Monica Gaughan, "The Substitution Hypothesis: The Impact of Premarital Liaisons and Human Capital on Marital Timing," *Journal of Marriage and Family* 64 (May 2002): 407–19.

I know what Lori Gottlieb would say: Lori Gottlieb, "Marry Him!" *The Atlantic*, March 2008, www.theatlantic.com/magazine/archive/2008 /03/marry-him/6651/.

"every eight becomes a six over time": Ibid.

"What am I gaining by taking my time?": Jessie Rosen, "Dear NY Times: Here's Why I Haven't 'Grown Up.' Love, a 20-Something," *Lemondrop*, Aug. 19, 2010, www.lemondrop.com/2010/08/19/nyt-op-ed-what-is -it-about-20-somethings/.

the divorce rate . . . was at its lowest level since 1970: "National Marriage and Divorce Rate Trends," Centers for Disease Control and Prevention, National Vital Statistics System, Jan. 10, 2012, www.cdc.gov/nchs /nvss/marriage_divorce_tables.htm.

among married couples, there's been a decline: Betsey Stevenson and Justin Wolfers, "Marriage and Divorce: Changes and Their Driving Forces," Institute for the Study of Labor Discussion Paper No. 2602, February 2007.

young people hold on to some . . . romantic notions: David Popenoe and Barbara Dafoe Whitehead, "The State of Our Unions 2001: The Social Health of Marriage in America," The National Marriage Project, Rutgers University, June 2001.

about 20 percent of Americans were divorced: "Number, Timing, and Duration of Marriages and Divorces: 2001," U.S. Census Bureau, issued February 2005, www.census.gov/prod/2005pubs/p70-97.pdf.

kissing might be a good way to sample them: Jeffrey Kluger, "The Science of Romance: Why We Love," *Time*, Jan. 17, 2008, www.time.com /time/magazine/article/0,9171,1704672,00.html.

"Sustained sexual chemistry actually takes time": Regnerus and Uecker, *Premarital Sex in America*, p. 190.

A pithy summary of the findings: William Saletan, "Men Are from Cuddle, Women Are from Penis," *Slate*, July 11, 2011, www.slate.com/articles /health_and_science/human_nature/2011/07/men_are_from_cuddle _women_are_from_penis.html.

For men, it was major: "Couples Report Gender Differences in Relationship, Sexual Satisfaction over Time," The Kinsey Institute, July 5, 2011, newsinfo.iu.edu/news/page/normal/18996.html (accessed February 26, 2012). Full report available at www.kinseyinstitute.org/publications/ PDF/Heiman%20couples%20midlife%20and%20older%205% 20countries.pdf (accessed February 26, 2012).

"Don't you know what a hog is?": The line is from the Marx Brothers movie *Horse Feathers* from 1932, www.filmsite.org/hors3.html.

she wrote as much in a *New York Times* essay in 1991: The essay isn't available on *The New York Times* website (it was published back in the early days of the Internet, when authors could retain control of such things), but you can read it at www.nasw.org/users/robinhenig/family .htm.

"The more sex . . . the happier the person": David G. Blanchflower and Andrew J. Oswald, "Money, Sex and Happiness: An Empirical Study," July 27, 2004, for the Behavioral Economics special issue of the *Scandinavian Journal of Economics*.

"there is no way I will grow old alone": Bella DePaulo, *Singled Out: How Singles Are Stereotyped, Stigmatized, and Ignored, and Still Live Happily Ever After*, New York: St. Martin's, 2006, p. 3.

"mental blanketing aims to instill . . . the unshakeable belief": Ibid., p. 13.

Franklin Schneider isn't falling for that: Franklin Schneider, "Against Adulthood," *Washington City Paper*, Jan. 6, 2012, www.washingtoncitypaper .com/articles/42028/against-adulthood/.

Chapter 5: Baby Carriage

"The Marriage Crunch": The *Newsweek* cover was dated June 2, 1986. In March 2012 the issue was being sold on Amazon by the Indiana bookseller bookstar09 as a collector's item for $68, plus $3.99 shipping: see www.amazon.com/Newsweek-June-1986-MARRIAGE-CRUNCH /dp/B0054T9HLA.

the original calculations had been wrong: It took twenty years for *Newsweek* to publish a kind of retraction: Daniel McGinn, "It Turns Out That Getting Married After Age 40 Wasn't Quite as Difficult as We Once Believed," *Newsweek*, May 24, 2006. The article was reprinted on iVillage at forums.ivillage.com/t5/Discussions-Debates/Newsweek-retracts -spinster-scare/td-p/6520209.

a photograph of a naked, aging woman in profile: The *New York* cover was dated Oct. 3, 2011, with the cover line "Is She Just Too Old for This?"

It was less than five years after . . . the first American test tube baby: A chart of success rates for IVF from data compiled by CDC and Society for Assisted Reproductive Technology, 1985–2009, is reproduced at www.advancedfertility.com/ivfchanges.htm.

out-of-pocket cost of about $5,000 per cycle: Robin Marantz Henig, *Pandora's Baby: How the First Test Tube Babies Sparked the Reproductive Revolution*, Boston: Houghton Mifflin, 2004, p. 230.

600,000 babies were born . . . to women over thirty-five: Gretchen Livingston and D'Vera Cohn, "The New Demography of American Motherhood," The Pew Research Center, May 6, 2010, p. 6, executive summary at pewresearch.org/pubs/1586/changing-demographic-characteristics -american-mothers.

the success rate to as high as 70 percent: Beth A. Malizia, Michele R. Hacker, and Alan S. Penzias, "Cumulative Live-Birth Rates after In Vitro Fertilization," *New England Journal of Medicine* 36 (2009): 236–43.

an 80 percent increase to women in their early forties: Gretchen Livingston and D'Vera Cohn, "The New Demography of American Motherhood," p. 6.

"she has inadvertently squandered her fertility": Sylvia Ann Hewlett, *Creating a Life: Professional Women and the Quest for Children*, New York: Miramax, 2003, p. 199.

But 86 percent . . . had wanted to have kids someday: Ibid., p. 84.

careers had gotten in the way: Katha Pollitt, "Backlash Babies," *The Nation*, May 13, 2002, www.thenation.com/article/backlash-babies.

Classic cases . . . of creeping non-choice: Hewlett, "Executive Women and the Myth of Having It All," pp. 66–73.

"It's very hard to throttle back": Ibid.

"Go, doctors!": Hewlett, *Creating a Life*, p. 113.

a poll called Fertility IQ 2011: JoNel Aleccia, "Fertility Math? Most Women Flunk, Survey Finds," Today.com, Nov. 15, 2011, today.msnbc.msn .com/id/45262603#.T1ZflNFST81.

Women over thirty-five or forty have higher rates: John Mirowsky, "Age at First Birth, Health, and Mortality," *Journal of Health and Social Behavior* 46 (March 2005): 32–50.

these complications . . . are "not at prohibitive levels": Anne Z. Steiner and Richard J. Paulson, "Motherhood After Age 50: An Evaluation of Parenting Stress and Physical Functioning," *Fertility and Sterility* 87, no. 9 (June 2007): 1327–32.

Years later, the mothers over fifty did just as well: Ibid., pp. 1327–32.

older women and their partners may be unable: Ethics Committee of the American Society for Reproductive Medicine, "Oocyte Donation to Postmenopausal Women," *Fertility and Sterility* 82 suppl. 1 (2004): S251–55.

In some cities . . . they make 20 percent more: Belinda Luscombe, "Workplace Salaries: At Last, Women on Top *Time*, Sept. 1, 2010, www.time .com/time/business/article/0,8599,2015274,00.html.

those who waited until age thirty-five . . . had annual salaries $50,000 higher: Lisa Miller, "Parents of a Certain Age," *New York*, Oct. 3, 2011, nymag.com/news/features/mothers-over-50-2011-10/.

Miller made an "opportunity cost" evaluation: Amalia R. Miller, "The Effects of Motherhood Timing on Career Path," *Journal of Population Economics* 24 (2001): 1071–100.

It can be a "miserable bargain": Anna Fels, *Necessary Dreams: Ambition in Women's Changing Lives*, New York: Anchor Books, 2004, pp. 204–6.

there's a troubling disconnect in timing: Mirowsky, "Age at First Birth, Health, and Mortality," p. 34.

Even the early twenties seems too young: Michelle Horton, "Confession: I Lie About My Age," *Early Mama* blog, Nov. 25, 2009, www.early -mama.com/2009/11/25/confession-i-lie-about-my-age/.

A different study . . . pinned the "best age" even older, at thirty-two: Mirowsky, "Age at First Birth, Health, and Mortality," p. 36.

the optimum age . . . was thirty-one: Ibid., p. 37.

"optimal health outcomes from delaying motherhood into their thirties": Ibid., p. 48.

"14 years younger than a woman who gave birth at 18": Beth Hale, "Why 34 Is the Best Age to Have a Baby," *Daily Mail*, April 25, 2005, www .dailymail.co.uk/health/article-346163/Why-34-best-age-baby .html#.

even more fine is to have a *last* baby before age thirty-five: Angelo A. Alonzo, "Long-Term Health Consequences of Delayed Childbirth: NHANES III," *Women's Health Issues* 12, no. 1 (2002): 37–45.

couples have been spending their time trying to get pregnant: Hewlett, *Creating a Life*, pp. 214–15.

It's all about the ovaries: "Age and Fertility: A Guide for Patients," American Society for Reproductive Medicine, 2003, www.asrm.org/Fact -SheetsandBooklets/.

ovaries also contain stem cells: Yvonne A. R. White, Dori C. Woods, Yasushi Takai, Hiroyuki Seki, Jonathan L. Tilly, "Oocyte Formation by Mitotically Active Germ Cells Purified from Ovaries of Reproductive-Age Women," *Nature Medicine*, published online February 26, 2012, www.nature.com/nm/journal/vaop/ncurrent/full/nm.2669.html. The study was also written up in Nicholas Wade, "Scientists Use Stem Cells to Generate Human Eggs," *The New York Times*, Feb. 26, 2012, www .nytimes.com/2012/02/27/health/research/scientists-use-stem -cells-to-generate-human-eggs.html?_r=1.

about 70 percent after age forty: Victor Berman and Sallee Berman, "Who Runs a Higher Risk?: A Consultation About Childbearing After 30," in *The Pregnancy After 30 Workbook*, Gail Sforza Brewer, ed., Emmaus, PA: Rodale Press, 1978, p. 5.

age-associated changes in the reproductive system: C. Farquhar, "Endometriosis," *BMJ* 334 (2007): 249–53; "Fibroids," *The AMA Family Medical Guide*, Jeffrey R. Kunz, ed, New York: Random House, 1982, p. 583.

fathers over age forty increase their babies' risk: Lisa Miller, "Parents of a Certain Age," *New York*, Oct. 3, 2011, p. 47.

almost as hard . . . to *stay* pregnant as it . . . is to *get* pregnant: "Age and Fertility: A Guide for Patients," American Society for Reproductive Medicine, 2003, www.asrm.org/FactSheetsandBooklets/, p. 7; also Ruth C. Fretts, "Effect of Advanced Age on Fertility and Pregnancy in Women," *UpToDate*, Nov. 29, 2011, www.uptodate.com/contents/effect-of-advanced-age-on-fertility-and-pregnancy-in-women.

There was a clear age stratification for this success rate: Beth A. Malizia, Michele R. Hacker, and Alan S. Penzias, "Cumulative Live-Birth Rates after in Vitro Fertilization," *New England Journal of Medicine* 360 (2009): 236–43.

"We can't reverse the biological clock": Claudia Kalb, "Have Another 'Fertilitini,'" *Newsweek*, Jan. 26, 2009, www.thedailybeast.com/newsweek/2009/01/26/have-another-fertilitini.html.

"Manicures and Martinis": "Infertility Can Be Prevented: A New, Cutting-Edge Program Shows How," American Fertility Association, Oct. 23, 2009, www.theafa.org/article/infertility-can-be-prevented-a-new-cutting-edge-program-shows-how/.

Young women . . . "hear the ticking as loud as anybody else": Claudia Kalb, "Should You Have Your Baby Now?" *Newsweek*, Aug. 12, 2001, www.thedailybeast.com/newsweek/2001/08/12/should-you-have-your-baby-now.html.

"late-in-life childbearing is fraught with risk": Hewlett, "Executive Women and the Myth of Having It All."

"There's no room in Hewlett's view for modest regret": Pollitt, "Backlash Babies."

8,000 American women did in 2008: Lisa Miller, "Parents of a Certain Age," p. 46.

and the number keeps growing: T. J. Mathews and Brady E. Hamilton, "Delayed Childbearing: More Women Are Having Their First Child Later in Life," NCHS Data Brief No. 21, Aug. 2009, www.cdc.gov/nchs/data/databriefs/db21.pdf.

only a little older than . . . in 1980: "Median Age of Mother by Live-Birth Order, According to Race and Hispanic Origin: United States, Specified Years 1940–55 and Each Year 1959–94," Centers for Disease Control. Also, T. J. Mathews and Brady E. Hamilton, "Mean Age of Mother, 1970–2000," *National Vital Statistics Reports*, 51 no. 1 (Dec. 11, 2002), p. 12.

believed they'd be able to get pregnant into their forties: Hewlett, *Creating a Life*, p. 87.

egg freezing has been used on a few thousand women: Nancy Hass, "Time to Chill? Egg-Freezing Technology Offers Women a Chance to Extend

Their Fertility," *Vogue*, April 28, 2011, www.vogue.com/magazine
/article/time-to-chill-egg-freezing-technology-offers-a-chance-to
-extend-fertility/.

a baby born in 2010 will cost . . . $226,920: Jessica Dickler, "The Rising
Cost of Raising a Child," *CNN: Money*, Sept. 21, 2011, money.cnn
.com/2011/09/21/pf/cost_raising_child/index.htm.

they "buttressed" the pyramid "with a few architectural extensions": Douglas T. Kenrick, Vladas Griskevicius, Steven L. Neuberg, and Mark
Schaller, "Renovating the Pyramid of Needs: Contemporary Extensions Built Upon Ancient Foundations," *Perspectives on Psychological
Science* 5 (2010): 292.

parenting is . . . "the punch line of this developmental story": Tom Jacobs,
"Maslow's Pyramid Gets a Makeover," *Miller-McCune*, June 22, 2010,
www.miller-mccune.com/culture/maslows-pyramid-gets-a
-makeover-20682/.

"achieving maturity through having a child": Martha McMahon, *Engender-
ing Motherhood: Identity and Self-Transformation in Women's Lives*, New
York: Guilford, 1995, p. 91.

there's a line graph of the highs and lows: Daniel Gilbert, *Stumbling on
Happiness*, New York: Knopf, 2006, p. 243.

Chapter 6: Brain and Body

It's harder to put one over on a twentysomething: Ted Ruffman, Janice
Murray, Jamin Halberstadt, and Tina Vater, "Age-Related Differences
in Deception," *Psychology and Aging*, April 4, 2011, advance online
publication, doi: 10.1037/a0023380.

"continuous partial attention": The phrase is from cyber-theorist Linda
Stone, cited in Jamais Cascio, "Get Smarter," *The Atlantic*, July/Aug.
2009, www.theatlantic.com/magazine/archive/2009/07/get-smarter
/7548/.

84 percent get . . . interruptions at least once in any given hour: "Cisco
Connected World Technology Report for 2010," www.cisco.com/en
/US/netsol/ns1120/index.html#~2010.

incessant distractions don't bode well for the brain: Nicholas Carr, "Is Google
Making Us Stupid?" *The Atlantic*, July/Aug. 2008, www.the-atlantic
.com/magazine/archive/2008/07/is-google-making-us-stupid/6868/.

"toward what might be called a utilitarian intelligence": Nicholas Carr contribution to "Does Google Make Us Stupid?" an online forum hosted
by Janna Quitney Anderson, Elon University, and Lee Rainie, Pew
Internet and American Life Project, Feb. 19, 2010, pewresearch.org
/pubs/1499/google-does-it-make-us-stupid-experts-stakeholders
-mostly-say-no.

"no longer be a sign of intelligence, but a side-show act": Alex Halavais contribution to the online debate Does Google Make Us Stupid?" online debate.

a team of psychologists . . . gave sixty undergrads a bunch of trivia: Betsy Sparrow, Jenny Liu, and Daniel M. Wegner, "Google Effects on Memory: Cognitive Consequences of Having Information at Our Fingertips," *Science* 333, no. 6043 (Aug. 6, 2011): 776–78.

a tactile connection . . . that might be skipped by typing: Katie Zezima, "The Case for Cursive," *The New York Times*, April 27, 2011.

they are being replaced by "fluid intelligence": Cascio, "Get Smarter."

"searching the Web appears to enhance brain circuitry": Gary W. Small, Teena D. Moody, Prabha Siddarth, and Susan Y. Bookheimer, "Your Brain on Google: Patterns of Cerebral Activation During Internet Searching," *American Journal of Geriatric Psychiatry* 17 (2009): 116–26.

Urban Dictionary's Word of the Day: The quarterlife crisis, www.urban -dictionary.com/define.php?term=quarter%20life%20crisis.

a comprehensive map of the typical quarterlife crisis: Oliver C. Robinson and Jonathan A. Smith, "Investigating the Form and Dynamics of Crisis Episodes in Early Adulthood: The Application of a Composite Qualitative Method," *Qualitative Research in Psychology* 7 (2010): 170–91.

the psychosocial moratorium: Erik H. Erikson, *Identity: Youth, and Crisis*, New York: W. W. Norton, 1968, p. 156.

"a time for self-sacrifice or for pranks": Ibid., p. 157.

Darcy . . . pretty much fit his pattern: "Scientists Describe Five Phases of Quarterlife Crisis, Recommend the Experience," *Discover* Discoblog, May 5, 2011, blogs.discovermagazine.com/discoblog/2011/05/ 05/scientists-describe-five-phases-of-quarter-life-crisis-recommend -the-experience/.

86 percent of British twentysomethings . . . felt under pressure: Amelia Hill, "The Quarterlife Crisis: Young, Insecure and Depressed," *The Guardian*, May 5, 2011, describing a poll of 1,100 young people.

deep undertoad of disappointment: This isn't a typo; "undertoad" refers to the way a character in *The World According to Garp* (1970) by John Irving, Garp's son Walt, always managed to mishear the warning to "watch out for the undertow."

Every generation has its own defining drug: Margaret Talbot, "Brain Gain," *The New Yorker*, April 29, 2009.

Baby Boomers had their fun: Hamid Ghodse, "Uppers Keep Going Up," *British Journal of Psychiatry* 191 (2007): 279–81, 2007.

proportion of . . . college students who abused prescription drugs soared: "Wasting the Best and the Brightest: Substance Abuse at America's Colleges and Universities," The National Center on Addiction and Substance Abuse at Columbia University, March 2007.

similarities show up in couples who are just dating: Lauren M. Papp, "Prescription Drug Misuse Among Dating Partners: Within-Couple Associations and Implications for Intimate Relationship Quality," *Psychology of Addictive Behaviors*, 24, no. 3 (2010): 415–23. (In Papp's sample, 82 percent of the men and 85 percent of the women were white; 82 percent of the men and 90 percent of the women were in college or grad school.)

Baby Boomers, too, used illicit drugs: Kevin Chen and Denise B. Kandel, "The Natural History of Drug Use from Adolescence to the Mid-Thirties in a General Population Sample," *American Journal of Public Health* 85, no. 1 (1995): 41–47, based on a study of 1,160 young people who were in grades ten and eleven in New York State in 1971 (in other words, born around 1953–54), who were followed to age thirty-four to thirty-five. Almost no one began using drugs after age twenty-nine, and the use of illicit drugs had almost ceased by then.

Recreational drug users . . . tend to be those most at risk for depression: J. E. Lessenger and S. D. Feinberg, "Abuse of Prescription and Over-the-Counter Medication," *Journal of the American Board of Family Medicine* 21 (2008): 45–54.

young adults described themselves as "casual cooking enthusiasts": Caroll Phillips, "They're Willing to Spend More for High-Quality Ingredients: Who Knew? Millennials Are Foodies," *Millennial Marketing*, March 25, 2009, millennialmarketing.com/2009/03/who-knew-millennials-are-foodies/.

"a way to establish credibility among their peers": "A New Generation of Cooking Enthusiasts, Stirring It Up in the Kitchen," PR Newswire, Nov. 21, 2011, www.marketwatch.com/story/a-new-generation-of-cooking-enthusiasts-stirring-it-up-in-the-kitchen-2011-11-21.

I tend to "assemble" meals rather than "cook" them: Sam's tongue-in-cheek recipe for chickpea stew appeared in Juli Weiner, "Treats for the Disaffected 20—Something, Part IV: Special Guest Chefs!" *VF Daily*, Feb. 3, 2012, www.vanityfair.com/online/daily/2012/02/Treats-for-the-Disaffected-20-Something-Part-IV-Special-Guest-Chefs-Chickpeas-and-Hair-Straighter-Panino.

the highest prevalence of smoking was in young people: Roy Otten, Jonathan B. Bricker, Jingmin Liu, Bryan A. Comstock, and Arthur V. Peterson, "Adolescent Psychological and Social Predictors of Young Adult Smoking Acquisition and Cessation: A 10-Year Longitudinal Study," *Health Psychology* 30, no. 2 (2011): 163–70. Also "Cigarette Smoking Among Adults—United States 2007," *Morbidity and Mortality Weekly Report* 57 (2008): 1221–26, www.cdc.gov/mmwr/PDF/wk/mm5745.pdf.

fewer and fewer . . . were even *trying* to quit: "The Health Consequences of Smoking: A Report of the Surgeon General," Washington, DC: National

Center for Chronic Disease Prevention and Health Promotion, Office on Smoking and Health, 2008.

it interferes with fertility: "Women and Smoking: A Report of the Surgeon General," Washington, DC: U.S. Department of Health and Human Services. Public Health Service, Office of the Surgeon General, 2001, www.cdc.gov/tobacco/data_statistics/sgr/2001/index.htm.

"It's not OK to say I will smoke in my twenties": Emily Dunn, "Fertility in Your 20s, 30s, and 40s," *Sydney Morning Herald*, Nov. 23, 2011, www .stuff.co.nz/life-style/wellbeing/6019561/Fertility-in-your-20s-30s -and-40s.

Add Health began in 1994: Robert Bock, "The Adolescent Health Study," NIH Backgrounder, National Institute of Child Health and Human Development, Sept. 9, 1997, www.nih.gov/news/pr/sept97/chd -09.htm.

"What are the chances that you'll live to thirty-five?": Thomas W. McDade, Laura Chyu, Greg J. Duncan, Lindsay T. Hoyt, Leah D. Doane, and Emma K. Adama, "Adolescents' Expectations for the Future Predict Health Behaviors in Early Adulthood," *Social Science & Medicine* 73 (2011): 391–98.

the average life expectancy for their age cohort: "Life Expectancy by Age, 1850–2004," www.infoplease.com/ipa/A0005140.html.

The forecast . . . became a kind of risk factor: McDad, Chyu, Duncan, Hoyt, Doane, and Adama, "Adolescents' Expectations for the Future Predict Health Behaviors in Early Adulthood."

binge drinking on campus . . . was up 16 percent: "Wasting the Best and the Brightest: Substance Abuse at America's Colleges and Universities," National Center on Addiction and Substance Abuse at Columbia University.

"If most people are buzzed with two drinks": Barron Lerner, quoted in Adam K. Raymond, "A Brief History of Drunk Driving," *The Fix*, Nov. 23, 2011, www.thefix.com/content/brief-history-drunk-driving-dui -laws-thanksgiving7007.

J. L. Scott . . . soon watched her drinking spiral out of control: J. L. Scott, "Booze: My Final Farewell," *Drinking Diaries*, Aug. 22, 2011, www .drinkingdiaries.com/2011/08/22/booze-my-final-farewell/.

taking a quiz such as AUDIT: Thomas F. Babor, John C. Higgins-Biddle, John B. Saunders, and Maristela G. Monteiro, "The Alcohol Use Disorder Identification Test: Guideline for Use in Primary Care, Second Edition," World Health Organization, Department of Mental Health and Substance Dependence, 2001, whqlibdoc.who.int/hq/2001/who _msd_msb_01.6a.pdf.

Jay Giedd . . . started mapping children's brains: Jay N. Giedd, "The Teen Brain: Primed to Learn, Primed to Take Risks," *Cerebrum*, Feb. 26, 2009, www.dana.org/news/cerebrum/detail.aspx?id=19620.

"body and mind no longer exist": Joost A. M. Meerloo, *The Rape of the Mind: The Psychology of Thought Control, Menticide, and Brainwashing*, Palm Desert, CA: Progressive Press, 2009 (originally published in 1956 by the World Publishing Company), chap. 12. Meerloo also wrote, "The view from the screen doesn't allow for the freedom-arousing mutuality of communication and discussion. Conversation is the lost art."

young people "know when they have to focus": Don Tapscott, *Grown Up Digital: How the Net Generation Is Changing Your World*, New York: McGraw-Hill, 2009, p. 118.

Levinson called the twenties a time of great "biological vigor": Daniel Levinson, *The Seasons of a Man's Life*, New York: Knopf, 1978, p. 21.

nearly half of Millennials . . . had neglected some aspect of medical care: Sara Collins, Tracy Garber, and Ruth Robertson, "How the Affordable Care Act Is Helping Young Adults Stay Covered," The Commonwealth Fund, May 26, 2011, www.commonwealthfund.org/Publications /Issue-Briefs/2011/May/Helping-Young-Adults.aspx.

young adults . . . slipped on sixteen of the twenty standard indicators: Harris, Kathleen Mullan, Penny Gordon-Larsen, Kim Chantala, J. Richard Udry. "Longitudinal Trends in Race and Ethnic Dispanties in Leading Health Indicators from Adulthood." *Archives of Pediatrics and Adolescent Medicine* 160 (2006): 74–81.

American Stroke Association . . . confirmed and expanded: Cole Petrochko, "Young Adults' Health Behaviors a Confusing Mix," *MedPage Today*, May 3, 2011, www.medpagetoday.com/PublicHealthPolicy /PublicHealth/26264.

bad habits of the twenties will have some long-term consequences: Kathleen Mullan Harris, "An Integrative Approach to Health," *Demography* 47, no. 1 (2010): 1–22.

this can't bode well for middle age: Nguyen, Quynh C., Joyce N. Tabor, Pamela P. Entzel, et al., "Discordance in National Estimates of Hypertension Among Young Adult." *Epidemiology* 22, no. 4 (2011): 532–41.

Chapter 7: Friendship in Real Life

they'll probably mention some close, warm relationships: Harry T. Reis, Yi-Cheng Lin, M. Elizabeth Bennett, and John B. Nezlek, "Change in Social Participation in Early Adults," *Developmental Psychology* 29, no. 4 (1993): 633–45.

Neugarten . . . earned the world's first doctorate in human development: Elissa Rodkey, "Profile of Bernice Neugarten," *Psychology's Feminist Voices Multimedia Internet Archive*, A. Rutherford, ed., 2010, www .feministvoices.com/bernice-neugarten/.

people choose most of their adult relationships: Bernice Neugarten, "Continuities and Discontinuities of Psychological Issues of Adult Life," *Human Development* 12 (1969): 121–30.

Finding intimacy . . . is one of the five major life tasks: Robert Arnstein, "Young Adulthood: Stages of Maturity," in *Normality and the Life Cycle*, D. Offer and M. Sabshin, eds., New York: Basic Books, 1984, pp. 108–44.

lamenting the loss of "person as mystery": Zadie Smith, "Generation Why?" *The New York Review of Books*, Nov. 25, 2010.

"driven . . . by a desire to stay connected": S. Craig Watkins and H. Erin Lee, "Got Facebook? Investigating What's Social About Social Media," University of Texas at Austin, Department of Radio-Television-Film, Nov. 18, 2010, p. 2.

the length to which some people will go for those encounters: Wendy Donahue, "On the Road: One Woman's Quest to Meet All Her Facebook Friends," *Chicago Tribune*, Aug. 16, 2011, articles.chicagotribune.com/ 2011-08-16/features/ct-sun-fam-0814-facebook-friends-20110816_1 _facebook-friends-mafia-wars-online-friends. ArLynn Presser blogged about her own "quest" at arlynnpresser.wordpress.com.

"I'm not going to get to all 325 friends": Ibid.

About one third . . . used the site to organize what Facebook calls "events": Watkins and Lee, "Got Facebook?," p. 17.

"I see other 20somethings feeling pressured": Ariana Allensworth, *the twenty-somethings*, Feb. 9, 2011, http://thetwenty-somethings.com /2011/02/09/ariana-allensworth/.

narcissistic personalities . . . are more active on Facebook: Soraya Mehdizadeh, "Self-Presentation 2.0: Narcissism and Self-Esteem on Facebook," *Cyberpsychology, Behavior, and Social Networking* 13, no. 4 (2011), hfmyouth.com/wp-content/uploads/2010/08/FacebookNarcissism .pdf. Also Laura E. Buffardi and W. Keith Campbell, "Narcissism and Social Networking Web Sites," *Personal and Social Psychology Bulletin* 34 (2008): 1303, originally published online July 3, 2008, www .sakkyndig.com/psykologi/artvit/buffardi2008.pdf. Also Andrew L. Mendelson and Zizi Papacharissi, "Look at Us: Collective Narcissism in College Student Facebook Photo Galleries," in *The Networked Self: Identity, Community, and Culture on Social Network Sites*, Zizi Papacharissi, ed, New York: Routledge, 2011, tigger.uic.edu/~zizi/Site/Research _files/Look%20at%20meAMZP.pdf.

The proliferation . . . has turned digital age Millennials into "flakes": Leon Neyfakh, "So Sorry to Do This! Flakiness Epidemic Sweeps Digital New York," *The New York Observer*, Sept. 15, 2010, www.observer.com/2010/ 09/so-sorry-to-do-this-flakiness-epidemic-sweeps-digital-new-york/.

Urban Dictionary's Word of the Day: FOMO, www.urbandictionary.com /define.php?term=fomo.

leading Millennials to become smartphone-addled cybersluts: John Leland, "Out on the Town, Always Online," *The New York Times*, Nov. 19, 2011, www.nytimes.com/2011/11/20/nyregion/out-on-the-town-always -online.html?_r=1&scp=1&sq=always%20online&st=cse.

30 percent . . . use their smartphones to avoid interacting: Aaron Smith, "Americans and Their Cell Phones," Pew Internet and American Life Project, Aug. 15, 2011, pewinternet.org/Reports/2011/Cell-Phones /Key-Findings.aspx.

"I'm being social . . . just not social with you": Leland, "Out on the Town, Always Online."

"We met weekly for dinner at a neighborhood restaurant": Ethan Watters, "In My Tribe," *The New York Times Magazine*, October 14, 2001, www .nytimes.com/2001/10/14/magazine/the-way-we-live-now-10 -14-01-in-my-tribe.html?scp=1&sq=ethan%20watters%20urban% 20tribes&st=cse.

making friends is a crucial part of psychological health: Erikson, *Identity: Youth and Crisis.*

"It's a poignant thing to be a full-grown human and realize you're deficient": Ryan Blitstein, "Couple Seeking Couple for a Good Time," *Salon*, March 10, 2009, www.salon.com/2009/03/10/friend _blitstein/.

Harvard psychologists collected narratives from 40 young people: Robert J. Waldinger, Louis Diguer, Frank Guastella, Rachel Lefebvre, Joseph P. Allen, Lester Luborsky, and Stuart T. Hauser, "The Same Old Song?— Stability and Change in Relationship Schemas from Adolescence to Young Adulthood," *Journal of Youth and Adolescence* 31, no. 1 (February 2002): 17–29.

an experiment involving card-sorting: Laura L. Carstensen, "Evidence for a Life-Span Theory of Socioemotional Selectivity," *American Psychologist* 4, no. 5 (1995): 151–56.

Tim Smith . . . calls it a friendship disconnect: Tim Smith, *the twenty-Somethings*, March 24, 2011, thetwenty-somethings.com/2011/03/24 /tim-smith/.

More than half . . . have close friends of the opposite sex: Aurora M. Sherman, Jennifer E. Lansford, and Brenda L. Volling, "Sibling Relationships and Best Friendships in Young Adulthood: Warmth, Conflict, and Well-Being," *Personal Relationships* 13 (2006): 151–65. There were 102 undergrads in this study, aged seventeen to twenty-two.

"the need to discuss, and yet downplay, sexuality": Ibid., pp. 151–65.

flovers . . . people who were "simultaneously friends and lovers": James J. Bradac, "The Language of Lovers, Flovers, and Friends," *Journal of Language and Social Psychology* 2 (1983): 141.

That upper limit . . . has come to be known as Dunbar's number: "How Many Friends Does One Person Need?" video lecture by Robin Dunbar, viewed at fora.tv/2010/02/18/Robin_Dunbar_How_Many_ Friends_Does_One_Person_Need.

Dunbar's number . . . applies to social networks, too: Matt Ridley, "How Many Friends Can Your Brain Hold?" *Wall Street Journal*, Feb. 12, 2011, online.wsj.com/article/SB100014240527487044222204576130602460- 527550.html.

the desire for a less dauntingly large friend group: Jenna Wortham and Claire Cain Miller, "Social Networks Offer a Way to Narrow the Field of Friends," *The New York Times*, May 9, 2011, www.nytimes.com/2011/ 05/10/technology/10social.html?ref=mobileapplicationssocialnetwork ingandcommunications.

something Ingrid Connidis calls a "taken-for-grantedness": Ingrid Arnet Connidis, "Life Transitions and the Adult Sibling Tie: A Qualitative Study," *Journal of Marriage and Family* 54, no. 4 (1992): 972–82.

During childhood . . . siblings can do little to ease troubles with parents or friends: P. L. East and K. S. Rook, "Compensatory Patterns of Support Among Children's Peer Relationships: A Test Using School Friends, Nonschool Friends and Siblings," *Developmental Psychology* 28 (1992): 163–72; also R. Seginer, "Adolescents' Perception of Relationships with Older Siblings in the Context of Other Close Relationships," *Journal of Research on Adolescence* 8 (1998): 287–308.

for young adults, friends are higher-cost than relatives: Sam G. B. Roberts and Robin I. M. Dunbar, "The Costs of Family and Friends: An 18-Month Longitudinal Study of Relationship Maintenance and Decay," *Evolution and Human Behavior* 32 (2001): 186–97.

Others in Laura's position make similar adjustments: Robert M. Hodapp, Richard C. Urbano, and Meghan M. Burke, "Adult Female and Male Siblings of Persons with Disabilities: Findings from a National Survey," *Intellectual and Developmental Disabilities* 48, no. 1 (2010): 52–62.

Chapter 8: Parents as Co-Adults

"They can no longer be forced to accede to parental authority": Jane Isay, *Walking on Eggshells: Navigating the Delicate Relationship Between Adult Children and Parents*, New York: Broadway Books/Flying Dolphin Press, 2007, p. xi.

"Honey . . . you can ask me anything": *Postcards from Yo Momma*, one of the "Best Of" selections, posted April 14, 2009, http://www.postcards -fromyomomma.com/highest-rated/.

Four in ten speak daily to a parent: "Families Drawn Together by Communi- cation Revolution," Pew Social Trends, Feb. 21, 2006, pewsocialtrends

.org/2006/02/21/families-drawn-together-by-communication
-revolution/.

"I'm trying to create my own support system": Barbara K. Hofer and Abigail Sullivan Moore, *The iConnected Parent*, New York: Free Press, 2010, p. 16.

The researchers were dumbfounded by such an attitude: Ibid., p. 24.

Parents were always willing to drop everything and chat: Ibid., p. 23.

A lot of us think we're managing that balance pretty well: "Families Drawn Together by Communication Revolution," Pew Social Trends, Feb. 21, 2006, pewsocialtrends.org/2006/02/21/families-drawn-together-by -communication-revolution/.

This is how it's supposed to work: Lauren Rinelli McClain, "Cohabitation: Parents Following in Their Children's Footsteps?" *Sociological Inquiry* 81, no. 2 (May 2011): 260–71.

The refuge of home can be a lifeline: Motoko Rich, "A More Nuanced Look at Poverty Numbers," *The New York Times* Economix blog, Sept. 16, 2010, economix.blogs.nytimes.com/2010/09/16/a-more-nuanced-look -at-poverty-numbers/.

Parents are a safety net for twentysomethings: Karen Fingerman, Laura Miller, Kira Birditt, and Steven Zarit, "Giving to the Good and the Needy," *Journal of Marriage and Family* 71 (December 2009): 1220– 33; also Karen L. Fingerman, Yen-Pi Cheng, Lauren Tighe, Kira S. Birditt, and Steven Zarit, "Relationships Between Young Adults and Their Parents," in *Early Adulthood in a Family Context*, A. Booth, S. L. Brown, N. Landale, W. Manning and S. M. McHale, eds., New York: Springer Publishers, 2011.

46 percent who had offered advice in 1988: D. J. Eggebeen, "Family Structure and Intergenerational Exchanges," *Research on Aging* 14 (1992): 427–47.

the median age of home-leaving has crept upward: Myron P. Gutmann, Sara M. Pullum-Piñón, and Thomas W. Pullum, "Three Eras of Young Adult Home Leaving in Twentieth-Century America," *Journal of Social History* 35, no. 3 (2002): 533–76.

"a generation of coddled infants": Lisa Hammel, "Dr. Spock as a Father— No Mollycoddler," *The New York Times*, Nov. 8, 1968, www.nytimes.com /books/98/05/17/specials/spock-father.html.

Camille DeMere was twenty-two when her parents asked her for a loan: Mandi Woodruff, "Some Millennials Step Up to Support Cash -Strapped Moms and Dads Back Home," *Business Insider*, Nov. 18, 2011, www.businessinsider.com/some-millennials-step-up-to-support -cash-strapped-families-back-home-2011-11.

"We've all been placed at the mercy of her disease": Robin Romm, *The Mercy Papers: A Memoir of Three Weeks*, New York: Scribner, 2009, p. 11.

It's like that *Saturday Night Live* sketch: "Damn It, My Mom Is on Facebook," www.hulu.com/watch/184577/saturday-night-live-moms-on-facebook.

To explain this disconnect with their "developmental stake" hypothesis: Vern L. Bengston and J. A. Kuypers, "Generational Difference and the 'Developmental Stake.'" *Aging and Human Development* 2, no. 1 (1971): 249–60.

the same disparity . . . has been found: Roseann Giarrusso, Feng Du, and Vern L. Bengtson, "The Intergenerational-Stake Phenomenon Over 20 Years," *Annual Review of Gerontology & Geriatrics* 24, no. 1 (2004): 55–76.

Kids' complaints focused on relationship tensions: Kira S. Birditt, Laura M. Miller, Karen L. Fingerman, and Eva S. Lefkowitz, "Tensions in the Parent and Adult Child Relationship: Links to Solidarity and Ambivalence," *Psychology and Aging*, vol. 24, no. 2 (2009): 287–95.

one finding that was . . . a bit disconcerting: Carol D. Ryff, Young Hyun Lee, Marilyn J. Essex, and Pamela S. Schmutte, "My Children and Me: Midlife Evaluations of Grown Children and of Self," *Psychology and Aging* 9, no. 2 (1994): 195–205.

"often incomprehensibly inconvenient activities": Lionel Tiger, *Optimism: The Biology of Hope*, New York: Simon and Schuster, 1979.

"in a way I wish I was 25 starting all over": Mike Zwerin, "Loudon Wainwright 3d, the Clown Prince of Song," *The New York Times*, Aug. 12, 1999, www .nytimes.com/1999/08/12/style/12iht-loudon.t.html?scp=1&sq =loudon percent20wainwright percent20rufus percent20jealous& st=cse.

"digging one's own grave": Brad Sachs, "Parents and Young Adults Struggle with Leaving the Nest," *Transitions 2 Adulthood*, Sept. 30, 2010, transitions2adulthood.com/2010/09/30/parents-and-young-adults -struggle-with-leaving-the-nest/.

Index